Spiritual Passages

Benedict J. Groeschel

SPIRITUAL PASSAGES

THE PSYCHOLOGY OF
SPIRITUAL DEVELOPMENT

"for those who seek"

CROSSROAD · NEW YORK

1984

The Crossroad Publishing Company
370 Lexington Avenue
New York, N.Y. 10017

Printed in the United States of America

Library of Congress Cataloging in Publication Data

Groeschel, Benedict J.
Spiritual passages.

1. Perfection (Catholic)—Psychology.
2. Spirituality—Psychology. I. Title.
BX2350.5.G76   1982   248.2   82-17139
ISBN 0-8245-0497-6
ISBN 0-8245-0628-6 (pbk.)

Nihil obstat   James T. O'Connor, S.T.D.
Censor Librorum
Imprimatur   †Joseph T. O'Keefe
Vicar General, Archdiocese of New York

The book is gratefully dedicated to
Terence Cardinal Cooke
and to
the bishops, priests, deacons,
and
seminarians of the
Archdiocese of New York
in whose service it was written.

Contents

Preface

If you are a Christian trying to take your own spiritual development seriously and if in some way you hope to help others, this book is intended for you. However, this is not a "how-to" book. Such guides can be useful, but, like simplified road maps of superhighways, they don't help very much when you get off the track. Rather than provide another simplification, this book is intended to relate some of the sounder insights of contemporary psychology to the classical outline of the spiritual journey contained in the immense and fascinating literature of spirituality. The immediate goal is to assist you to find your place on the journey and to identify personal traits which, for a long time, may have been obstacles on the road to greater knowledge and service of God. The overall goal of this study is to help you prepare energetically to recognize and take the next good steps along the spiritual way.

We are considering an area of study which includes an unbroken line of profound spiritual writers, many of them saints, and a diverse company of scientific psychologists, some of them geniuses, and some members of both groups (such as Augustine and John of the Cross). Therefore, it strikes me as impertinent to strive for originality. Thus, there is no intention to be original in this book, except in a few, clearly defined places where I attempt to make a useful synthesis between the doctrines of Christian spiritual tradition and the more tested and realistic insights of that *potpourri* called "modern psychology." My real aim is to express a practical working relationship between ancient wisdom and the deeply felt spiritual needs of modern people who have become more self-conscious because of the popularity of psychology.

This book may be read in different ways and for different purposes. If you are reading for your own personal growth, you may find it preferable to pass over Chapter 5 on the application of psychology to spirituality and to read it last. You may also find it helpful to be guided during your reading by the meditation in Chapter 9. On the other hand, if you are interested in a more academic study of the psychology of religious development, you may find it challenging to examine your own present thinking on the uses and abuses of psychology by reading Chapter 5 early on. However, eventually you may find it helpful to apply the classical ideas synthesized by this book to your own journey even if you don't agree with my interpretation of them. Chesterton has observed that our relationship with God is the only subject really important enough to argue about.

FOR WHOM THIS BOOK IS WRITTEN

Friends have suggested that I write for believing Christians who are looking for some time-tested explanations of what they experience as they attempt to follow Christ. Although what follows comes out of my experience of almost half a century as a Catholic Christian, I write with a view to other Christians as well. I think in particular of a fervent young Baptist minister who attended a lecture on the spiritual life and afterwards told me that it was the first time anyone had been able to tell him "what was going on inside me all of my life." I have often found Evangelical Protestant Christians very receptive because they had little familiarity with the study of spirituality. The approach to spiritual development used in this study is more widely known to Roman Catholic and Eastern Orthodox Christians (as well as Episcopalians), although many of these have never heard of the doctrine of the three ways of the spiritual life. I am also mindful in these pages of many searching young adults with whom I have come into contact.

An increasing number of people, especially young adults, have been torn from the religious roots of their families. Their adolescent experience of religion was often not as compelling as the contradictory messages of their culture. At times young people's religious experience is initially repulsive to them. This book is written also for the young who have rediscovered the call of faith and who join those who are seeking God.

This is not a bedside book, nor is it one of those pleasant works we all love and find so nourishing. To profit from this study, one must work to understand some distinctions relating to behavioral types and stages of development. I hope that these distinctions, after careful explanation, will assist the individual toward growth in self-knowledge or help the spiritual director to understand others.

Although this book is not written in a devotional style, quotations from great mystical authors will run through it like the threads of a fabric. These quotations should be reread on one's knees and written in one's heart. The rest of the book should be read with a critical eye and, ideally, with a prayer, while sitting quietly in a comfortable chair and, if you like, enjoying a cup of coffee.

Acknowledgments

I must acknowledge my gratitude to a great number of teachers and writers who over the years stimulated my interest in the spiritual journey. I have been able to cite most of the principal writers, but the best teachers, those who have taken the journey with great singleness of purpose, must for the most part go unnamed.

I am deeply grateful to Charles Pendergast for his invaluable assistance in preparing the manuscript, and to Roger Sorrentino, as well as to Martin Olivieri and John Lynch for checking it over. I am grateful to Richard Payne for his constant encouragement and advice, and to Rabbi David Blumenthal and Father William Smith for their scholarly suggestions. And finally, I must thank my generous typists, Karin Samuel, Elaine Barone, and Charlotte Lowitt, for their patience and skill, and Kathryn Cousins for preparing the index.

Benedict J. Groeschel, OFM Cap.

Trinity Retreat
Larchmont, New York
Pentecost, 1982

Jesu, spes poenitentibus
Quam pius te petentibus
Quam bonus te quaerentibus
O quid invenientibus?

Jesus, hope of the penitent
How kind You are to those who ask
How good You are to those who seek
What must You be to those who find?

—*St. Bernard of Clairvaux*

PART I

THE PSYCHOLOGY
OF SPIRITUALITY

Chapter 1

The Call of God

A young man immersed in worldly pleasure-seeking finds himself crying in the back of a church. A college woman concerned with a career stares out a window and spends a profound hour looking into herself. Her sense of time collapses before eternity. A hard-nosed professor of science puts aside his instruments and is led to thoughts about those things that cannot be measured and yet are most real. A clergyman pauses between worship and the usual Sunday afternoon duties and is overcome with awe at the words he has just uttered at the Eucharist in the name of the Incomprehensible One. A housewife pauses over her baby's crib and muses on the stream of life she has passed on, its origins and its destiny. A prisoner in solitary confinement knows that he is not alone. An addict in his craving cries out in despair, wondering whether anyone can deliver him from addiction's iron grip.

These are not imaginary people; I have known each of them personally. They are a sampling of the immense number of people in our troubled times who experience the call of an inner force which is beyond either their rational speculations or emotional impulses. This interest in the "spiritual," for that is the term given to this cumulative experience, is evident in every nation and culture of our secularized age. The more simple and traditional adherence to religious beliefs and practices, passed on by the family, is eroded by technology and the psychology of self-seeking. Yet, the rootless and often faceless multitudes who inhabit modern cities have produced many young people who are looking for and often even claiming to have found meaning and reality that lie beyond the narrow confines of superficial sense perceptions. It is paradoxical that as cultural religion has declined, a sense of the mystical has increased. This phenomenon was observed as early as 1950 by the great psychologist Gordon W. Allport.[1]

If one has definite religious beliefs and is equipped by church and family to express religious impulses in conventional terms, religious expression comes more easily, as Jung has pointed out. But many must seek, often with difficulty, a more intense and meaningful religious expression. This book attempts to include the journey of those who have had both kinds of experience—the conventional and the startling.

WHAT IS THE SPIRITUAL LIFE?

What does "the spiritual life" mean? Does it mean formal religion? Not always. Does it mean a preoccupation with one's own inner thoughts, inspirations, and fantasies? It can, but according to the masters of the spiritual life, inner preoccupations are often an obstacle to the spiritual life. Does it mean intellectual speculation or even a comprehensive knowledge of the teaching of the great religious leaders? Not really. There are in the history of spirituality people of little or no intellectual acumen alongside mental giants. A valid definition must include such well recognized spiritual and intellectual lights as St. Bonaventure and Cardinal Newman on one side of the classroom desk, and St. Thérèse of Lisieux and General Booth on the other, with St. Francis and St. Bernadette looking distractedly out of the window and not keeping up with their lessons at all. As important as Sacred Scripture is in the life of Jewish, Islamic, or Christian seekers, one cannot identify spiritual development even with the knowledge of Revelation, since the first great spiritual seeker of revealed religion, Abraham, never saw a Bible and many of the saints never read one because they did not know how to read.

Perhaps the best description of the spiritual life is *the sum total of responses which one makes to what is perceived as the inner call of God.* However, the spiritual life is not locked up inside a person. It is a growing, coherent set of responses integrated into the complex behavior patterns of human life. To think of the spiritual life as something apart from the rest of one's individual life is to flirt with ancient and persistent errors. When the individual has decided to respond to the call of God experienced within, and strives to make this call the center of activity and choice, he or she may be called a truly spiritual person. The call then becomes the integrating factor for the one who has responded; the spiritual life becomes the work of a lifetime. The experience of travellers on this road is best described by St. Bernard in the words: "How good You are to those who seek!"

Unfortunately, most people who are drawn to the spiritual life pursue it half-heartedly or inconsistently. We organize life around the call of God but with an all-too-familiar pattern of distraction and conflicting goals. The drama—frequently sad—of the spiritual life concerns an individual who does not take completely to heart the parables of the treasure hidden in the field or of the pearl of great price. We tend to bargain for the field and haggle about the price of the pearl. We run out into the desert to find the Son of God when His coming is really like the sunrise which we almost ignore.

METHOD

The method of this study will be to pose certain questions. First, "What do I seek?" Then, "Am I seeking in a Christian way?" Later, we will ask: "What blocks my way?" and even, "Who am I as a person?" and finally, "Where am I on the way?"

It is important to take note of the many possible answers presented after the questions for the reader's meditation and insight. Categories defining possible answers will be drawn from classical, spiritual, and psychological sources. You should note that categories shade from one to another, so that you may find yourself in two of them (e.g., anxiety and depression) at the same time. Or you may discover that you are experiencing some effects of both the purgative and the illuminative way at the same time. The categories, including the one to be introduced as the "Four Voices of God," are not exact, but they are comprehensive. If you do not find yourself in one or two categories, either you are lacking in self-knowledge or you are very original.

WHAT DO I SEEK?

What do we, the spiritually motivated, seek? A study of people interested in the spiritual life, whether they are saints or still struggling to be holy, reveals that they are very different. Father Elmer O'Brien in his *Varieties of Mystical Experience* reached the conclusion that mystics are very different from one another.[2] When Christians who are engaged in a serious struggle reveal their experiences to others, it becomes obvious that there are profoundly subjective differences in the way they hear the call of God and in their response. This diversity reflects the divine immensity and is a rich source of meditation. It demonstrates, as William James pointed out, the uniqueness of the individual.[3]

We are created with a capacity to seek and find God, to be the living stones of His Church, to be the finite creature in direct relationship with the Infinite. In each instance the uniqueness of the individual in the spiritual life is preserved. As Von Hügel emphasizes in his monumental study of the mystical element in religion, "The mystery of the spiritual life is ultimately seen as unity in unimaginable diversity."[4]

Amid this vast diversity the individual finds a unique place, based on that act of the divine will that called each one into being, giving each an everlasting destiny. Characteristic types may be found in this individuality. Looking at individual experience, one can make certain generalizations. Just as we sort out elements, stars, or animals by classifying them according to size, shape, composition, or density, or by a great variety of standards, so in a more revealing way can we classify human beings as to what they expect when they journey toward God. These classifications are not discrete like animal species or tables of metals, but like all psychological classifications of human functioning, they are related to each other as colors of a rainbow. One shades into another. I have called these the "four voices of God" to simplify a profound and ancient philosophical teaching.[5]

The Four Voices of God

To respond to God in one way does not mean that we are responding to Him in all possible ways. The essential relationship of the Christian to the divine life in which the individual knows God, the triune life, is a result of the revelation of Christ, the Incarnate Word. Before we come to that key relationship originating with the Godhead itself, however, we must consider human beings according to their subjective response to God.

A general look at great spiritual persons reveals the variety of ways in which they have perceived God. The terminology used here to describe this perception of God is based on an analysis of divine being rooted in the scholastic tradition and going back to Greek philosophy. This philosophical tradition may be more useful in studying the types of response to God than one drawn from Sacred Scripture, for the Bible tends to evaluate persons simply in relationship to their positive, partial, or negative response to God, thus categorizing them as the saints, the lukewarm, or the lost. Western philosophy suggests that human beings know and seek God as the *One,* the *True,* the *Good,* and the *Beautiful.* If you analyze yourself or those you know well in terms of the spiritual life, you will notice that most people fit rather well into one or perhaps two categories. Some examples from the lives of great Christians may be helpful.

GOD AS ONE

God known as the One, the Supreme, and Living Unity will attract a person whose life is an intellectual and emotional pursuit of integration.

Usually such a person has always been aware of internal contradictory or opposing forces which threaten to tear the self apart. These forces threaten the very balance necessary for useful functioning as a human being. God will then be seen as bringing unity into experienced chaos.

St. Catherine of Genoa, the great lay mystic of the fifteenth century, is described by von Hügel as a person of such powerful and contradictory inclinations that she had but one choice: surrender to the call of God or fall apart.[6] She used her tremendous energy and talent to seek a spiritual life and at the same time to direct one of the largest charitable institutions in the world. She was responsible for beginning the effective reform of the Catholic Church. If you read her life, you come away with the impression of a continuous effort to focus all her personality in pursuit of divine love. Catherine could have led a life combining Renaissance-type indulgence with pious respectability. She simply found this depressing and impossible. After several years of chronic neurotic depression, she resolved to turn all her attention to the love of God and of neighbor. So powerful was her unity of purpose that she managed to reconcile her total dedication to God with a strong affection for her husband, family, and friends.

The contemporary French writer, Jean Genet, is a quite different example of a person in conflict. He made a mockery of all things spiritual and then complained that the prison chaplain did not speak of God. Genet attempted to find unity in a total commitment to evil. He tried to bring to this pursuit of evil the same purity of heart which characterizes the life of a mystic. He was even called the devil's saint. However, since evil can never totally satisfy, his life deteriorated into ever greater conflict. Genet represents those who have not been able to find that unity which would bring them peace because the pursuit of evil, of its nature, leads to disintegration of personality. My own experience with members of Alcoholics Anonymous has shown that it is not unusual for persons seeking psychological equilibrium to find that the scars of a difficult life bring them to their knees before the one God.

If you feel drawn to God as One, you should accept this aspect of your spiritual life rather than fight it. One of the anomalies of wounded human nature is that we do not accept the very answer we seek when it is given because we have become so accustomed to pain and confusion. Many such people seem to say: "I am my real self only if I am in conflict with myself." True, there is a finality in the total surrender to the One which leads to the integration described in the Sermon on the Mount. For those who are called and pay the price, there is a peace that the world can never give. One must not be afraid to find it.

God as True

Next in the spectrum are those who are called to God as the True. A passion for truth often subsumes other passions so that seekers of the truth are usually more calm, methodical, and curious than others. They love to question and delve. They delight in discussing their insights with others. Such people feel called by God as He is ultimate reality, Truth itself, unlimited Being, that which simply *is*. They are not so different from the seekers of the One as we might expect, but they tend to be more placid and less in conflict. However, they, too, are driven. Not finding truth, they may become disheartened, skeptical, or cynical.

St. Thomas Aquinas is certainly an example of one of those summoned by the truth. Not only does his personality fit the description of this type, but he succeeds in his search. He comes to the truth beyond rational speculation. In the magnificent crowning moment of his life, he accepts a personal revelation of truth before which he falls silent, the ultimate statement about Truth Itself. "Such things have been revealed to me that all I have taught and written seems quite trivial to me right now."[7] But there are sad examples of those who have come seeking an intuition of the truth and have turned away. Bertrand Russell, always a passionate seeker after subjective certitude, was apparently once touched by the divine truth.[8] Having turned away from it, he lived and died an equally passionate enemy of religion and faith. One hopes that such passion may at least have a redeeming element.

The great spiritual danger for those drawn to God as the True is not that they will turn aside. The danger is that they will tarry on the way, getting involved with this side road or that. Modern scholarship, with its great number of published theories, many of them of some interest and merit, offers a labyrinth of ideas wherein to hide from the Living Truth. Unfortunately, the institutional Church with its profound insight into the unity of philosophical, theological, and revealed truth, has accidentally provided the leisure not only for academic study but also for intellectualization which dulls the voice of Living Truth. The simple prayer of St. Francis, "I wish to know You so that I may come to love You," is a good antidote for the persistent temptations facing seekers of the truth.

God as Good

The other half of the spectrum is occupied by two other types, closely related to each other, but rather different from the first two. They are the seekers of God as the Good and as the Beautiful. Those who seek Him as the Good are at once the most beloved and affectionate of human beings. They appear to have very little of the defensiveness which marks the inner struggle of most men and women. Consequently, they are usually cheerful, compassionate, and gregarious. But they suffer much in a wounded world. They are often manipulated, deceived, and even betrayed. Others enjoy taking advantage of them, almost in spite of themselves. The sins of the good are unplanned and often the result of manipulation, weakness, or naïveté. Those drawn to the Good usually encounter disaster if they deviate from the unworldly pursuit of God as the Good. On the other hand, if they remain faithful to the pursuit of the Good, they become spontaneously involved in a life of generous service.

St. Francis was such a person. Bonaventure describes him as generous, cheerful, and compassionate even as a youth.[9] Few people would call his experience at San Damiano the conversion of a sinner, as he persisted in referring to himself. It was, rather, the logical development of a very good life. But Francis's life was a story of betrayal, manipulation, and sorrow. He had more of the simplicity of the dove than the wisdom of the serpent. The election of his worst enemy as general of his order during his lifetime is a sad commentary on how a fallen race may treat such people. But somehow, like Francis, the seekers of the Good look through their tears and find the Good God everywhere. At the same time they experience a constant penitential sense that they have not served Him as well as they might have.

A danger for such seekers of the good is a kind of stunned disillusionment. They may even be tempted, as the Curé of Ars was, to run away from it all. Or they may comfortably settle for less than the Absolute and hide from all that is ugly and damaged. With good reason did St. Francis keep his eyes on the horror of the Crucifixion. It taught him that goodness in this world will be rejected and vilified; therefore, one must glory only in the Cross.

GOD AS BEAUTIFUL

Finally, there are those who seek God under the aspect of Beauty. They are a complicated group, indeed, because beauty can be deceptive. As the Greeks knew and as Plato taught, we find unfailing and infinite beauty only if we pass fram transitory beauties to essential beauty.[10] Since beauty and pleasure, however, are two sides of the same experience, there is always the temptation for the seekers of Divine Beauty to settle for less.

The best example of the seeker of Divine Beauty is the young Augustine. Later, as a bishop, his complex personality extended to other directions, but for the Augustine of the *Confessions* God was "Beauty, ever ancient and ever new." The following passage illustrates the response of the call to beauty.

> But what is it that I love when I love you? Not the beauty of any bodily thing, nor the order of any seasons, not the brightness of light that rejoices the eye, nor the sweet melodies of all songs, nor the sweet fragrance of flowers and ointments and spices; not manna or honey, not the limbs that carnal love embraces. None of these things do I love in loving my God. Yet in a sense I do love light and melody and fragrance and food and embrace when I love my God—the light and the voice and the fragrance and the food and embrace of the soul. When that light shines upon my soul which no place can contain, that voice which no time can take from me, I breathe that fragrance which no wind scatters, I eat the food which is not lessened by eating, and I lie in the embrace which satiety never comes to sunder. This it is that I love, when I love my God.
>   Late have I loved Thee, O Beauty so ancient and so new; late have I loved Thee! For behold Thou wert within me, and I outside; and I sought Thee outside and in my unloveliness fell upon those lovely things that Thou hast made. Thou wert with me and I was not with Thee. I was kept from Thee by those things, yet had they not been in Thee, they would not have been at all. Thou didst call and cry to me and break open my deafness; and Thou didst send forth Thy beams and shine upon me and chase away my blindness; Thou didst breathe fragrance upon me, and I drew in my breath and do now pant for Thee; I tasted Thee and now hunger and thirst for Thee. Thou didst touch me, and I have burned for Thy peace.[11]

There are great dangers for the seekers of beauty. From Michelangelo, who said his prayers regularly, to Oscar Wilde, who said them only when in trouble, there are all sorts of seekers of the Divine Beauty who get stuck along the way. Almost every fiber of the human being cries out for some pleasure or beauty. The lover of divine beauty has to be constantly vigilant. He or she also has to be prepared to fall and rise again. Therefore, along with the seeker of the Good, he or she will be intuitively aware of the need for penance and a divine reassurance of pardon. If these are taken away, he or she escapes into a mindless religiosity or unreligious hedonism, becoming a sad clown whose smile is a mask for the tears within.

Understanding Your Call

The first step toward understanding one's spiritual life is to recognize what beckons us: the One, the True, the Good, or the Beautiful. Our Savior assures us that "He who seeks finds, and to him who knocks, it shall be opened" (Mt. 7:7). The Hindus wisely say, "What you desire, that you become." We are all led by the divine and by one, or perhaps two, of the four voices of God, although the others are never entirely absent. The danger always is settling for less. We seek Heaven, but we play with things which will ultimately lead us either downward and away from our eternal destiny, or at best leave us suspended between Heaven and Hell. This is, after all, the description of Purgatory. "For where your treasure is, there will your heart be also" (Mt.6:21). When the heart is divided, progress is slow and painful; life is purgatorial. It should be clear that psychologically divided loyalties, such as the serving of two masters, are a kind of neurosis. The goal of the study of spiritual development is to identify, understand, and overcome by grace the neurotic tendency to settle for what is less than God when He has called us.

Chapter 2

How Christian Is My Spirituality?

In answering the question posed by this chapter, it is too simple to say, "completely" or "not enough." The purpose of this chapter is to identify the spiritualities of other religions and to contrast your personal Christian spirituality with them. We will go on to identify specific aspects of Christian spirituality which are unknowingly overlooked, or perhaps contradicted by trends in contemporary religious practice. You should be rather specific in identifying just how and where an authentic Christian world vision fits into your own spiritual life.

The Spirituality of Other Religions

Today a great many Christians, especially young adults, are fascinated and sometimes helped by ideas and writings originating outside the Judeo-Christian tradition. Perhaps this interest comes only after one has "given up Christianity" without ever really knowing anything about the Christian spiritual tradition.

A few years ago a woman author who had left the church of her childhood wrote me a very concerned letter about the large number of Christian young adults who had become intrigued with Eastern religions. She herself had only just become aware of the Christian spiritual tradition despite the fact that she had gone to school and college under religious auspices. She was pleasantly surprised to learn that a priest knew anything about spiritual writers and even more surprised that I had read some of the non-Christian spiritual classics and found them helpful.

In confronting you with the question, "Are you seeking the God of Christianity?", I am not belittling the other world religions. But I agree with the Dalai Lama who pointed out when he spoke at New York's St. Patrick's Cathedral that while honoring each other's traditions, we must recognize that they are very different. "Buddhism is Buddhism, and not Christianity."

With the possible exception of child-rearing, the study of a person's relationship with God is the oldest and most integrated of all human endeavors. Almost every great culture has given rise not only to popular religiosity but also to a spirituality arising from popular attempts to court the divine powers by prayer, or to understand them through the study of signs. Besides the religions which grew out of God's revelation to Abraham, several important spiritual movements have flourished including Buddhism, Hinduism, and the Graeco-Roman philosophical religion, which found its greatest expression in Plato. These movements are generally characterized by presenting a pattern of spiritual progress. This is the most important element shared with Christian spirituality. Because the movements differ greatly in their expression, I will attempt to summarize their common spiritual elements with apologies for many oversimplifications. The Christian reader may be helped toward an understanding and appreciation of these movements through a summary of their notions of spiritual progress in the following way. I hope this summary will be an honest synthesis of the experience of many truly spiritual people outside the Judeo-Christian tradition.[1]

Like the spiritually awakened Christian, the individual is increasingly aware of a spiritual craving within. He or she is drawn by one of the aspects of being (sometimes intellectually conceived as nonbeing) which leads to a profound personal conviction that one possesses a spark of the Divine. The world of the senses and the inner world of emotion, thought, and intuition respond together to this inner spark. The seeker finds others—perhaps a teacher or guru—with similar experiences and desires. The person tries more and more to change his behavior, overcome less spiritual impulses, and lead a godlike life. Relying on divine help, he may come to know more about the spiritual mysteries which are unknown to most others. When he goes through the doors of death, he hopes to enter the stream of divine life; his constant growth in purity of life and desire is his exact preparation for this divine state whether he conceives it as being or nonbeing.

Since most human beings, especially the spiritually involved, realize the fragile quality of their virtue, those drawn toward intangible reality generally conclude that the journey to perfection requires several lifetimes. Hence, reincarnation is often seen as a plausible theory.[2] Since spiritual progress is based on what one comes to know (or not know in a rational way), the word "*gnosis*" (knowledge) has been applied to several of these spiritual movements. Unfortunately, the term "gnostic" has also been applied to many pseudomystical movements which are as varied as popular forms of religion. Some of them are touchingly spiritual, some silly, and some hideous. The beautiful thanksgiving prayer of Lucius illustrates how a gnostic search may approximate the experience of a Christian:

> Thou holy and eternal savior of mankind, always generous to the weak, thou sendest sweet mother-love to the forlorn who are in distress. But I am of too small a spirit to thank thee as thou dost deserve, and I am too poor to bring thee the right sacrifice. . . . So I will gratefully perform what a pious poor man can. I will conceal in the most secret depth of my breast the divine countenance and thy most holy form, and I will ever preserve it there and keep it before my soul.[3]

We shall return to these spiritual movements and their authenticity after we have shown how they differ from Christianity. As we have seen, many young Christians today are drawn to these movements; thus it is important to relate them carefully to the experience of Christianity and at the same time point out their differences.

The Spirituality of Biblical Religions

Again, we must oversimplify, much like an artist using watercolor strokes, which we hope will not distort but outline in general ways a vast and intricate structure. There are three religions informed by direct biblical revelation of God: Judaism, Christianity, and Islam. These three are based on a covenant made with the personal God, the mysterious Infinite Being, who is even more mysteriously interested in and capable of some contact with his human creatures.

Moslems know God through the books of the Hebrew Scriptures, as well as through an immense spiritual literature describing experiences of God, who is known as Allah. It is not difficult to trace many gnostic trends in Islamic spirituality, which has been in constant contact with both Eastern and Western traditions.

The Jews, the chosen people of God, know the very personal but unspeakable and awesome Lord through their vast, rich Scriptures representing many periods and styles of writing which are all accepted as the Word of God.

The Christian religion, now unfortunately divided among many churches, has as its revelation the Gospel of Christ, the Living Word. Writings about His revelation were collected and published by the only authority able to do so, the ecumenical councils and then by the bishop of Rome. This was accomplished only four centuries after Christ's death and resurrection.

Because revelation is an accepted fact, the maturing schools of spirituality in these biblically based religions all have a firm (if variously expressed) conviction of the need for the obedience of faith. For the ancient Oriental or Platonist, it was a matter of personal choice whether one wished to swim easily in the river of life as it returned to its source. The river itself was unconcerned with your choice, but terrible was your fate if you tried to swim against the river of life, as did, for example, the tyrants. For the believer in the God of Abraham, the choice was different. God called *you*. He made you a promise and gave you a command. "Do My Will! Follow My Law!" And however you conceived salvation, you would receive it from His loving mercy.

The biblical believers were deeply convinced also of the reality of a fallen world. They stood with the first parents pitifully trying to reenter paradise. They needed to be saved, delivered, and healed. This notion of salvation is not generally part of the nonbiblical religions. In many of these nonbiblical religions it is believed that one can come to know the divine and it is this knowledge that saves. The good who have become divinelike survive death, because everlasting life is part of the nature of things for the spiritual person. But the God of biblical revelation comes and saves those who would be lost if left to their own efforts.

With all their beauty and riches expressed in popular religion, their spirituality, public worship, good works, and prophetic teaching, both Islam and Judaism leave, as they must, many unanswered questions. These unanswered questions, especially as to the nature of salvation and its attainment, have been woven by holy Jews and Moslems into the mysticism of their tradition. A few examples may be helpful in appreciating this "mysticism of the unfinished and unanswered."

Islam has emphatically proclaimed the holiness and sovereignty of God. Its central shine, the Ka'abah in Mecca, is a completely empty room, symbolizing the otherness or transcendence of God. It was cleansed by Mohammed of pagan images which had been kept there. Rabi'a of Bosra (752–801?), the only Moslem "nun," epitomizes the spirituality of the mysterious God in her prayer:

> O God, whatsoever thou has apportioned to me of worldly things, do thou give that to my enemies; and whatsoever thou has apportioned to me in the world to come, give that to thy friends; for thou sufficest me. O God, if I worship thee for fear of Hell, burn me in Hell, and if I worship thee in hope of Paradise, exclude me from Paradise; but if I worship thee for thy own sake, grudge me not thy everlasting beauty.[4]

While we cannot review even the basic insights of the Islamic mystical tradition, it is important for the reader to know that this religion has a profound sense of the presence of the Almighty, who is seen as the caring and loving creator of His people. Islam expresses this presence very much in its revelation, the Koran, which is accepted in a sacramental way and which is committed to memory by the devout believer. The essential work of Islam is to make known this revelation which is seen as the central part of human existence.

Having grown up on the edges of the largest Jewish community in the world, I have always been fascinated by the unique qualities of Jewish spirituality. To illustrate this fascination, I recount a very touching incident as an example of the "mysticism of the unanswered question" which is much like the Florentine Pieta—beautiful in its misty, unfinished lines. One day I met a dear friend, a rabbi, on the street and together we went to offer some comfort to a young Jewish couple whose son had died in a tragic accident. The devout, spiritual rabbi whose own life had been scarred by the Holocaust gently took my arm as we rang the doorbell and said, "Don't try to answer the question, 'Why?' Just be there and listen." The incident highlighted a profound quality of Jewish spirituality, so well enunciated by Rabbi Abraham Isaac Kook:

> So long as the world moves along accustomed paths, so long as there are no wild catastrophes, man can find sufficient substance for his life by contemplating surface events, theories and movements of society. He can acquire his inner richness from this external kind of "property." But this is not the case when life encounters fiery forces of evil and chaos. Then the "revealed" world begins to totter. Then the man who tries to sustain himself only from the surface aspects of existence will suffer terrible impoverishment, begin to stagger . . . then he will feel welling up within himself a burning thirst for that inner substance and vision which transcends the obvious surfaces of existence and remains unaffected by the world's catastrophes. From such inner sources he will seek the waters of joy which can quicken the dry outer skeleton of existence.[5]

The central focus of the Jewish mystical experience is the desire for the reestablishment of the intimate covenant relationship between the chosen people of God which existed when the Lord was present to and led the children of Israel by visible theophanies. Although Jewish spirituality has never lost the sense of the presence of the Lord in the Torah and in the living community of the people of Israel, it longs for the day when the presence will be as palpable and complete as it was when the glory of the Lord rested over the Ark and on the Tabernacle. This is the heart of the Messianic hope. A story from another dear friend and rabbi who recounted to me a very special moment: One morning, very early, when the birds were singing the praises of their Creator, his eldest son, age six, crept into his room and whispered, "Papa, I think I heard the shofar of the Messiah." For the Jew, this hope and prayer, too, are part of the "mysticism of the unanswered question."

While Jewish spirituality would not usually speak of "union with God" as the ultimate term of the journey, the actual processes of repentance and purification, and of divine instruction or enlightenment, are recognized as leading to the most intimate and loving relationship attainable by humans here, in this world. These mystical moments are a foretaste of the Messianic age and of the world-to-come.[6]

The Christian may never disparage the spirituality of expectation which is at the heart of the Jewish mystical experience. For many holy people, the road to God is the road of expectation. This is precisely the experience which the Church tries to live in the season of Advent.

Christian Spirituality

After a cursory look at the depths of the spiritual quest as conceived in nonbiblical religions, and a brief look at the special beauty of Islam and the unique mystery of Israel, all of which form a background to our discussion, we move on to Christian spirituality. Libraries have been written on the subject so there is no question here of reviewing this vast topic, still less of engaging in the fool's enterprise of trying to say something "new" about it. We will try instead to highlight the most significant features of the great structure of Christian spirituality in the context of the study of spiritual development. The basis of our discussion is the question, "How Christian is my spirituality?"

The center of Christian spirituality is the Incarnate Word of God. He is the center, not as a point of gravity, but as a single source of light in an utterly dark and lifeless universe. Just as He is the source of light and life to the material creation ("Through Him all things came to be," Jn. 1:3), so is He the source of salvation and spiritual life. "To all who did accept Him, He gave power to become children of God" (Jn. 1:12). These words from the great Christological hymn at the beginning of St. John's Gospel give the key to the entire doctrine of spirituality in Christianity.

The following text from Philippians 3:8–16 is one of many that highlights the Christological foundation of the spiritual teaching of the Church:

> Not only that but I believe nothing can happen that will outweigh the supreme advantage of knowing Christ Jesus my Lord. For him I have accepted the loss of everything and I look on everything as so much rubbish if only I can have Christ and be given a place in Him. I am no longer trying for perfection by my own efforts, the perfection

that comes from the Law, but I want only the perfection that comes through faith in Christ, and is from God and based on faith. All I want is to know Christ and the power of His resurrection and to share His sufferings by reproducing the pattern of His death. That is why I can hope to take my place in the resurrection of the dead. Not that I have become perfect yet: I have not yet won, but I am still running, trying to capture the prize for which Christ Jesus captured me. I can assure you, my brothers, I am far from thinking that I have already won. All I can say is that I forget the past and I strain ahead for what is still to come. I am racing for the finish, for the prize to which God calls us upward to receive in Christ Jesus. We who are called "perfect" must all think this way. If there is some point on which you see things differently, God will make it clear to you.

The followers of nonbiblical religions sought to know God by means of a perfect imitation of the divine image in themselves and the devout followers of the Scriptures of Israel entered into the covenant with God who alone was able to save them and make them holy by His covenant. The Christian does not see salvation in this way. The Christian is saved and made holy by the revelation of Christ within him, a saving knowledge that goes beyond intellectual understanding to become that mysterious psychological reality called "living faith." So profound and so integrated into life is this faith that when we understand its saving power, the great theological debate over faith and works seems a semantic problem. For when the faith of which St. Paul speaks in Philippians takes hold of a person, life itself becomes a series of good works performed by Christ living within the person and increasingly operating through his or her acts. The essential personal good work is to consent with all one's being to the knowledge of Christ within.

The affirmation that Christ by His redemption and grace is the foundation and center of Christian spirituality has been repeated so often as to seem almost a cliché. Like a piece of music that has been heard too often, the startling meaning of this doctrine is often lost. Perhaps this explains why so many Christians of all traditions are unaware of the unique qualities of their spirituality. Rather than appreciating other spiritual traditions as we have suggested, many searching Christians who are alienated from the Church tend to get absorbed by them. It is a worthwhile enterprise to ask yourself now, "How Christian is my spirituality? Have I been thinking—accidentally at least—in a way that is less in line with New Testament spirituality?"

One way of looking at this question is to see how the Christian spiritual tradition has maintained its purity against tendencies within historical Christianity which have tried to pull it in one direction or another. Most of these attempts were made by devout believers who were trying to make the spiritual doctrine contained in the New Testament, and especially in the Johannine and Pauline writings, relevant to the thinking of their own times. Rather than reviewing all Christian doctrines relating to spirituality, let us look at a few which are being challenged at the present time and view them in light of this study to see what elements in Christian spirituality are particularly important for contemporary Christians to recognize.

UNITY OF HUMAN NATURE

You are perhaps saying to yourself: "Well, of course I believe in the unity of human nature. I'm not a dualist." Let's take a look.

One of the first challenges to Christian spirituality came, understandably enough, from early members of the Church who had come to Christ by way of the Greek philosophical religion. It is not unrealistic to interpret the First Epistle to the Corinthians (who were, in fact, just such converts) as Paul's effort to correct a mistake so often made today by spiritually oriented Christians, namely, the tendency to treat the individual as a soul who only temporarily uses a body, not unlike Descartes' famous angel in the machine. Strangely enough, this is a common error even in secular society. Daniel Yankelovich has pointed out that this odd view of human nature separating *what I think* from the rest of the reality of life, is at the heart of the popular myth of selfism which has dominated American culture for fifteen years. All sorts of disciples of the self-actualization theories are really dualists who separate their own personal satisfaction from responsibility to the rest of the human race, even to their own families.[7]

The mysterious dogma of the resurrection of the dead, and the spiritual unity of the human being, has been continually called into question by esoteric spiritual writers from the Manicheans to the proponents of modern Christian Science. Just as it is a denial of Christianity to think of the human being only as a body with attendant functions, however psychologically complex, it is equally an aberration to think of the human being only as a soul. A balanced spirituality is both humanistic and eschatological. It sees the radical importance of this earthly life and one's deeds on earth because this life determines one's fate in an everlasting life where the person will be restored in all its essential functions at the eschaton. It should be pointed out that Christianity, together with the best in Islamic and Jewish spirituality, holds the view of a dynamic tension between the temporal and the everlasting, between body and soul. The dogma of the Incarnation, however, is the supreme expression of this dynamic tension.[8] The resurrection of the dead in Christ, as St. Paul explained to the Corinthian converts from Neoplatonism, is the final term and resolution of this tension.

A believer who struggles with unusual behavioral problems such as sexual compulsions, or with physical addiction such as alcohol, may well look within himself or herself for any of these dualistic tendencies. The implicit denial of the unity of the person is to be found both in puritanical strains of thought and in the opposite error which sees physical acts as having little or no spiritual significance. We should examine our attitudes to see whether they reflect the unity of the Gospel vision rather than the historical distortions of the vision.

TRANSCENDENCE OF CHRIST

A second challenge for Christian spirituality is our tendency to identify Christ with the divine image we perceive in ourselves. We all tend to have our own "Christ." A flick of the radio dial on Sunday morning will demonstrate how many "Christs" there are among sincere Christians. As we have seen, the spiritually awakened of all religions are aware in some way of this inner image. No doubt this is a reflection of the universal creative and salvific will of God. But it is too easy to say that this image is Christ. Surely it is related to Christ and to our status as children of God which He came to establish and share. But identifying Christ with our own human experience is an oversimplification that omits essential areas of the spirituality of redemption. For example, it leaves out the historical Jesus of Nazareth and all that His life in this world was meant to teach. One aspect of this common error (oversimplification) is that it allows one to choose only those elements of Christ's life which catch one's fancy. Many abhor a certain pious image of Christ or dislike a nineteenth-century saccharine painting of the Good Shepherd; yet they cherish within themselves an image of Christ which is just as invalid and subjective.

The tendency to identify completely this inner personal image with Christ also militates against the recognition of the need for the Church, which, as the existential Christian community, is the mystical presence of Christ in the world. Augustine identified this tendency when he wrote, "How shall you love and kiss the head and trample on the members?" Christian spirituality has consistently identified all the baptized as members of Christ, and all the unbaptized as potential members. The person who accepts his or her own inner image of Christ as the ultimate one will be a spiritual elitist. It has long been an insight of the saints that Christ does not fit into human estimations. He constantly took his contemporaries off guard—whether friend or foe. In this regard, you should ask yourself two questions: How much of my image of Christ is merely a projection of what I would like? Second, is my conception of Christ consistently growing and is it fed by the Scriptures and sacred tradition?

The most dangerous and deviant of all tendencies arising from the inner awareness of Christ is to make the historical Christ simply the best of teachers and the most godlike of men; taking it a step further, to see Christ as one who became the adopted Son of God in a spiritual way, thus providing the prime analogue of our own adoption. The Jesus Christ presented by the Church is not the guru of gurus. If one accepts the only historical Christ we can know, the one portrayed in the Gospels, it cannot honestly be said that He made any such claim. Unlike Buddha or Ramakrishna, He did not claim to have discovered the way to beatitude or even to have been taught it by a special enlightenment. He claimed to be and was proclaimed by His disciples to be the Son of God who had come down from the Father and was equal to the Father. No one can read John and Paul and avoid the fact that this unparalleled claim was made by the followers of Christ even in the earliest Pauline writings. This was and is the Christ of the Church. Von Balthasar sums up this point very well in his excellent classic, *Prayer* (which ought to be read by anyone wishing to pursue this subject at length):

> Natural mysticism and religion, which starts from man and is directed towards God, is an *eros* whose impulse is to take flight from and transcend utterly the things of the world—necessarily, indeed, and inculpably so. But in its desire to reach beyond the things that point the way to God, only seeing them as that which is not God, it is in constant danger of losing the two, both the world and God as well—the world, because it is not God, and God because He is not the world, who without the aid of the things of the world which mirror Him, can only be experienced as absolute void, *nirvana*. Christ, however, returns from the world accesible to our senses and mind to the Father, and for the first time, opens the true way to contemplation. He does not abrogate the images and concepts which tell of the Father, which He first devised when a man living among men. On the contrary—and this is the great theme of Pauline theology—He transposes them from the earthly, literal level to the heavenly, spiritual level, from the sphere of prophecy to that of fulfillment; and we who die, rise again and are carried to heaven with Him, are empowered by His movement from the world to the Father to accomplish with Him the transformation of the old world into a new, spiritual and divine one.[9]

One of the most important spiritual contributions of Vatican II was to proclaim that Christ is uniquely the Savior of mankind and of the individual. In *Lumen Gentium,* the Fathers of the Council providentially reiterated this dogma, thereby correcting tendencies to water down

Christian spirituality and to deny the importance of the temporal life of humanity. At the time of the Council it seemed far-fetched that a new Pope would have to reiterate the dogma contained in *Redemptor Hominis* as forcefully as Pope John Paul II did less than two decades later.[10] Those interested in the authentic spiritual tradition of the Church might well meditate on the place of the Christ of history, of the Church, and of the Redemption in their own lives and concepts. One of the pathetically silly phenomena of the post-Vatican II period has been to minimize the uniqueness of Christ in Christian spirituality and, indeed, in religious education. We should ask ourselves whether a touch of this pseudounitarianism has influenced us. It came as a shock to some Christians when the Dalai Lama reminded us that Buddhism and Christianity have essential differences. For the Christian, the essential difference is Christ.

Good and Evil

The most significant, persistent, and troublesome challenge to Christian spirituality has always come from the problem of evil. A number of psychologists of religion have identified the search for an answer to the problem of evil as the most powerful of religious motives.[11] If this is the case, it is not surprising that those with a spiritual interest have so frequently sought to cope with or even overcome the mysteries of evil, sin, and suffering in the course of their spiritual journey.

Evil is mysterious in its existence, in its relation to human nature, and in the possibility of its destruction. Each of these questions about evil and especially about moral evil, or sin, will have a profound effect on your spiritual attitudes. Each affects your approach to spiritual development since this development goes on in the face of intrinsic or extrinsic evil. In the great prayer of Christ we are taught to pray to be delivered or liberated from evil.

The existence of evil has always been a problem of those who believe in God. The conflict between God and evil opens and closes the Bible. There is always a tendency for spiritually oriented people either to make evil a thing, an existing reality, or to deny it any existence at all and consider it merely an erroneous evaluation of the mind. Evil is not a being, but it is a reality. Even the Prince of Darkness is good, inasmuch as he is a creature of God and has being from God (ontological goodness). His total moral evil comes from his complete rejection of God's authority and will. Thus, the Fathers and Doctors of the Church have seen evil as a real lack of some good thing or quality that should be present; a darkness, an absence of light where light is supposed to be. It is important for us as believers to struggle with this negative quality of evil if we are to grow spiritually. St. Augustine's great prayer in the *Soliloquies* is concerned with his answer to the mystery of evil:

> God, through whom all things are, which of themselves could have no being!
> God, who does not permit that to perish, whose tendency it is to destroy itself!
> God, who has created out of nothing this world, which the eyes of all perceive to be most beautiful!
> God, who does not cause evil, but does cause that it shall not become the worst!
> God, who reveals to those few fleeing for refuge to that which truly is, that evil is nothing!
> God, through whom the universe, even with its perverse part, is perfect!
> God, to whom dissonance is nothing, since in the end the worst resolves into harmony with the better!
> God, whom every creature capable of loving, loves, whether consciously or unconsciously!
> God, in whom all things are, yet whom the shame of no creature in the universe disgraces, nor his malice harms, nor his error misleads.[12]

As St. Augustine sees it, the worst of physical evils can result in some good. Without earthquakes and volcanoes, there would be no atmosphere, no life. Most importantly, moral evil is not a thing but a lack of moral good, an absence of a right ordering of the human will and, consequently, of the whole of human action to the divine will. Such physical evils as starvation and famine are often the result of generations of moral evil in the form of exploitation and social irresponsibility.

Relative evil, or evil which occurs as a result of a failure in development, is the most important concept for us to consider here. "When I was a child, I used to talk like a child, and think like a child and argue like a child, but now I am a man, all childish ways are put behind me" (I Cor. 13:11). Evil in the spiritual life or in any form of psychological development is often relative: A person may have failed to develop as far as he or she should or could have done. Although the presence and degree of real individual moral responsibility is impossible for any other human being to assess accurately, it is safe to say that inclinations or deeds in the life of a spiritual person are seldom the result of pure malevolence. Sinful acts often represent a regression, or a fixation at a level of development which one should have passed. Dag Hammarskjold in his *Markings* cites the touching example of the little girl with the spring frock who was innocently proud of it although it was a hand-me-down. Her behavior is healthy, and may even be morally virtuous, since she is not pouting because the frock is not brand-new. In an adult, however, pride in one's clothes is certainly unspiritual; it is related to vanity and relative moral evil because it expresses and reinforces values inconsistent with spiritual maturity.

QUIETISM AND THE DEVIL

Perhaps the most persistent error of the spiritually interested is to deny that evil exists at all. This indeed is the answer among many Oriental religions. Christians have been drawn into it by what is called "Quietism," a kind of laissez-faire attitude toward moral and physical evil; as a result, many have failed to see Christ hungry and naked around them. The opposite attitude is to see evil as a being, or beings, and constitutes the subtle error of Zoroastrianism. For the Christian, even the Prince of Darkness is not to be seen as existential evil. This mysterious being shared with us an eternal destiny of love which it has voluntarily thwarted in the everlasting now of eternity. The saints suggest that at times we all make subtle pacts with this hideous force. Since all voluntary sin is a contribution to what Dostoyevski calls "the mystical body of evil," which is the tidal wave of unlove that runs through history, it is good to keep in mind that Satan is not another god. Evil when personalized is neither ubiquitous, omniscient, nor omnipotent. Perhaps the terrible quality of evil is its banality, its tapering off into nothingness. To know someone who has surrendered to evil and who lives entirely by and for self, is to witness how utterly evil is *not,* to what dreadful nonbeing it leads. We all face choices of good and evil. When they suddenly come before us, it is wise to stop and look where the road of evil leads. It leads to disappointment, to nothingness.

In the Incarnate Word, we see being and goodness so personal that the worst that relative evil could do was to inflict death on an innocent man. But ultimately evil had no power at all. Christ did not engage in combat with those who had sold out to evil. "Do you think I cannot appeal to my Father who would promptly send more than twelve legions of angels to my defense?" (Mt. 26:53). His absolute qualities of spirit, His obedience to the Father, and His love overcame the nonbeing, or rather antibeing, of this most evil human deed.

While it is not in vogue to speak or write of evil, personalized or otherwise, we who are involved in the spiritual quest ought to take stock of our ideas of the mystery of evil. The orthodox mystics have consistently seen themselves in a kind of spiritual combat. This view is certainly in keeping with the Gospel and utterly contrary to Quietism. We should scrutinize ourselves in regard to evil. It is a responsibility necessary for a valid view of Christian spirituality.

ORIGINAL SIN

If the words "original sin" make you wince, you should ask yourself whether you are a disciple of Pelagius. Here I can afford to be somewhat judgmental for I live in New York where everyone, even atheists, are personally, if only implicitly, convinced of original sin. In any large metropolitan area, plagued with social and human problems of all kinds, the question is, "Have we really been saved?" It is only in the comfort of placid and affluent neighborhoods far removed from social ills that people ask, "Have we been lost?" "Is there a problem?"

This consideration brings us to the larger and more persistent question of moral evil and its origin. Different answers to this question have been given at various times. An extremely powerful response was provided by the Celtic monk, Pelagius, in the fourth century. He taught that moral evil is the result of bad example and poor teaching; this, he held, constituted original sin in its essence. After all, Pelgius pointed out, children are born innocent. If raised properly, they retain that innocence and exhibit a high degree of moral responsibility. If raised in morally poor environments, they will be sinful and irresponsible. Christ is our Savior because He taught the way to a life of virtue and moral responsibility. This is not so different from the old Greek idea of the divine image nor from what a great many Christians think today. This view has many ramifications, some of which you may recognize in your own philosophy of life. We should ponder this question carefully because incipient Pelagianism is a very popular heresy, which is implicitly shared by many Christians who are spiritual minded but poorly informed.

Pelagianism is dangerous because it divides the saved and the lost by circumstances of birth and family origin. It reinforces distinctions of social class. While it seems to be a more enlightened and positive view of human nature, denying any intrinsic disorder in the newly born, it places an ever-growing need for external moral perfection on its adherents. For if one is born into a devout home and given proper education, there is no excuse for any sin. One is totally responsible! Unruly tendencies (once called "concupiscence") really offer no excuse. With Pelagius, a form of rigid puritanism descended on the Celtic nations, which characterizes them even today. One should notice the paradox: Celts are often Pelagian in regard to moral severity, while they are Calvinistic in their view of human nature. Since Pelagius ultimately denies one of the most obvious facts of human existence, namely, that something is wrong with this fascinating and contradictory human creature, his disciples become increasingly unrealistic in their moral expectations of human beings.

The great theological adversary of Pelagius was St. Augustine. He had been raised not in the chilly monastic isles, where little boys had better behave, but, as he said, in the boiling cauldron of the declining pagan Roman empire. He was deeply aware of the Pauline teaching that Christ had come to save us from evil forces that reigned within and without. Even when the divine law failed to save us (see Romans 6 and 7), Christ had saved us. Augustine never believed evil to be some existential reality. But he did teach that even the best of human beings could not save themselves. He had a vital, existential view of the goodness of wounded human nature. The *Confessions,* although presenting a much less rosy view of human beings than Pelagius did, represent a view that has formed Christian theological teaching and has had an immense appeal for Western minds, whether Catholic or Protestant, believer or unbeliever.[13] The third view of original sin saw it as totally triumphant, rotting human nature to the core. In fairness to those who espoused this view, it was motivated not by a masochistic desire to negate or despise human nature, but by a desire to glorify God and Christ, at a time when the Renaissance humanists were glorifying the human being. Calvin did not set out to be mean; he wanted to be realistic in an artificial age. His *Soli Deo Gloria* (To God Alone Be the Glory) was a saying that many Catholic reformers could accept.

Nevertheless, the position that human nature is totally depraved effectively ended the possibility of a Calvinist spirituality. Spiritual development becomes an absurd notion if one accepts the view that justification and salvation could come entirely from without, superimposed by Christ on the depraved human spirit, as Luther had said, like snow over a pile of dung. Because external propriety and decent behavior were, as we have seen, taken as signs of predestination to beatitude, Calvinism as a religious movement paradoxically looked like applied Pelagianism. Although the two theories were diametrically opposed, the incipiently Pelagian Catholic and the Calvinist came to expect the same external behavior and often vied with each other in being unrealistic about child rearing. Ultimately they both ignored the possibility of spiritual growth as it had been outlined by the great mystical writers for 1500 years.

At this point it would be a good idea for you to see where your prejudices lie. The Fathers and Doctors of the Church have consistently taught that human nature, though wounded, is good. The human being can be saved only by Christ who comes as the sower seeking good ground and as the bridegroom of the parables demanding some response of acceptance. Although divine assistance or actual grace is required at all stages of the way, the response and cooperation of the individual are also necessary. Salvation and personal holiness are possible only because of a growing bond of sonship with the Father through the adoption won by Christ in His perfect obedience as a human being. We must follow His example in order to live according to the law of the spirit of life in Christ Jesus (Ro. 8:1–2).

Augustine has often been interpreted as overly pessimistic; in his view, it is said, man does not contribute to his own spiritual growth. This assessment, however, does not do justice to the man known as the "Doctor of Grace." The following quotation clearly describes the conflict, the victor, and the outcome of the spiritual struggle:

> Since, therefore, it is necessary that we be first brought down from the vanity of pride to humility of spirit, that rising thence we may attain to real exaltation, it was not possible for this spirit to be produced in us by any manner at once more glorious and more gentle, subduing our haughtiness by persuasion instead of violence, than that Word, through whom God the Father reveals Himself to the angels, and who is His power and wisdom; who could not be discerned by the human heart so long as it was blinded by desire for visible things, should condescend so to reveal and to exercise His personality in human form as to make men more afraid of being elated by the pride of man than of being brought low after the example of God. Therefore the Christ who is preached throughout the world is not Christ adorned with an earthly crown, nor Christ rich in earthly treasures, but Christ crucified. This was ridiculed at first by multitudes of proud men, and is still ridiculed by a remnant. It was the object of faith at first to the few but now to multitudes; for when at first, notwithstanding the ridicule of the multitude, Christ crucified was preached to the few who believed, the lame received power to walk, the dumb to speak, the deaf to hear, the blind to see, and the dead were restored to life. Thus, at length, the pride of this world was convinced that, even among the things of this world, there is nothing more powerful than the humility of God.[14]

Anselm, Thomas, Bonaventure, John of the Cross, and Newman all accepted the Augustinian interpretation of the Pauline theology to which they added their own insights. Most modern Catholic theologians appear to do the same. Eastern spirituality developed its own set of images and interpreted the role of Christ as Savior in its own mystical and iconic ways; yet when one steps back from the theological controversy over words, the Eastern and Western positions are closer to each other than they are to Pelagianism or to Calvinism. The proximity between East and West, despite some different points of view, may stem from the fact that Catholicism and Eastern Orthodox theology are clearly supportive of spirituality. They both defend a vision requiring the individual to develop his or her response to the grace of adoption in Christ through the Holy Spirit.

AND YOU?

And so, good reader, where are you? Don't throw up your hands and say, "I accept all that my Church teaches," or, "I follow Vatican I or II, or both." If you model your spiritual life and attitude on what you believe to be the teaching of Scripture and Tradition (as you should to be a Christian), this review of some popular misconceptions should be worthwhile. Are you a Catholic Pelagian? It really can't be done. Some of your best friends may be pseudo-Hindus or Pelagians; some of mine are. But if you want to build your life on Christian spirituality, it has to be intellectually authentic, that is, it must flow from Scripture and Tradition.

There is, however, one last question. Do you pray with Christ?

CHRISTIAN HOLINESS AND THE SACRED LITURGY

Since Christ is the center and source of the spiritual life of the Christian, it is essential to have vital contact with Him through the liturgical life of the Church. The word "liturgical" is used here in that rich, comprehensive sense which takes into account the whole presentation of the Living Word of God through Scripture, Tradition, and the Sacraments, coming to a center of radiance in the Holy Eucharist as Presence, Sacrament, and Mystical Sacrifice. As early as the time of the desert fathers, there were devout believers, even saints, who appear to have lived on the periphery of the Church's liturgical life. Careful inspection of their lives will show that the Christ of the Church was indeed the center of their existence, but their rather anticommunitarian ways kept them from frequent liturgical participation. However, it has been demonstrated by Bishop K. E. Kirk that the anchorite of old (and, I might add, the anchorites of the present) tended to be on the fringe of the Church.[15]

Saints and great spiritual writers, each one a citizen of his or her time, lived in the light of Christ, who teaches, saves, and sanctifies in the Church as He did in His earthly life. Such spiritual writers of our century as Marmion, Guardini, Bouyer, and von Balthasar have brought their intense awareness of Christian spirituality into sharp focus. Union with Christ in the liturgical life of the Church is operative and available in parish life for all, including children. Each aspect of liturgical life—the social, educational, cultural, sacramental, and mystical—can be brought into the life of every active member of the Church. Those drawn to the spiritual life, especially those for whom it is the focus of their lives, will find the highest expression of their being in the mystical depths of the Paschal mystery, of which the liturgy is a living presentation. The Fathers of the Church recognized that although the individual is known and loved by Christ, we come to Him in the unity of His

Mystical Body. This phrase is not a pious abstraction; it denotes the ultimate spiritual reality for the spiritually sensitive person.

Do you appreciate the Paschal Mystery as the center of your spiritual life? To develop spiritually as a Christian means to grow as a child of God according to the example of Christ and His grace. The Johannine writings, especially John 14–17, make clear the depth of this union with Christ. The Pauline writings even create new ideas, "to live with Him," "to die with Him," in order to express a concept which is unique in the literature of world religions.

Growth in Christ, according to the words of Jesus, implies a dying to a certain aspect of self so as to live with Him. This dying to self is usually called the doctrine of the Cross because of Christ's words in Matthew 16:24–26: "If anyone wants to be a follower of mine, let him renounce himself and take up his cross and follow me."

In the liturgy the Christian is plunged into the mystery of death and life. The Eucharist simultaneously celebrates Christ's dying and resurrection in obedience to the Father, and manifests on earth in our *now* the ultimate reality of human existence, the eternal life of the saints in union with Christ. At the center of the Eucharist there must be a contemplation, as von Balthasar points out so well.[16] It must be more than a simple reflective contemplation, such as the highest forms of nonbiblical religions suggest; it must be a dynamic reaching up and surrendering to God with Christ. It is not a symbol, myth, or even memory, but a participation, through the Holy Spirit, in the center of reality, the Trinitarian life of God.

There is always a tendency among the devout to look for something more because they have not looked deeply enough into what they already have. St. John of the Cross gives the following advice to those who have not looked deeply enough into the mystery of Christ:

> God, in giving us, as He hath done, His Son, Who is His only Word, has spoken to us once for all by His own and only Word, and has nothing further to reveal. . . . God has now so spoken that nothing remains unspoken; for that which He partially revealed to the Prophets, He hath now wholly revealed in Him, giving unto us all, that is, His Son. And therefore, he who should now inquire of God in the ancient way, seeking visions and revelations, would offend Him; because he does not fix his eye upon Christ alone, disregarding all besides. To such a one the answer of God is: "This is My beloved Son, in whom I am well pleased; hear ye Him. I have spoken all by my Word, my Son: fix thine eyes upon Him, for in Him I have spoken and revealed all, and thou wilt find in Him more than thou desirest or askest. He is my whole voice and answer, my whole vision and revelation, which I spoke, answered, made and revealed when I gave Him to

be thy brother, master, companion, ransom and reward. I descended upon Him with My Spirit on Mount Tabor and said: 'This is My beloved Son, in whom I am well pleased; hear ye Him.' . . . While thou hast Christ, thou hast nothing to ask of Me. . . . Look well unto Him, and thou wilt find that I have given all in Christ. If thou desirest a word of consolation from My mouth, behold My Son obedient to Me and afflicted for My love, and thou wilt see how great is the answer I give thee. If thou desirest to learn of God secret things, fix thine eyes upon Christ, and thou wilt find the profoundest mysteries, the wisdom and marvels of God hidden in Him; 'in Whom,' saith the Apostle, 'are hid all the treasures of wisdom and knowledge.' These treasures will be sweeter and more profitable to thee than all those things thou desirest to know."[17]

Do I Have a Dynamic Christian Spiritual Life?

There are many paintings of the Agony in the Garden depicting our Savior in various positions of desperation, exhaustion, and pain. Each work of art portrays a human suffering which admittedly fits the Scriptural account of that deeply moving event, which is filled with the tension of the Incarnation, of the divine and the human. Yet these paintings seem to me to convey a neurotic passivity unworthy of One who could say, "Not my will, but Your will be done." One painting of this event, however, depicts something else—dynamic tension. William Blake's regrettably unfamiliar rendition of the Agony shows Christ in total darkness, with both arms reaching up to the sky where the gloom is broken by the bright figure of an angel reaching toward Him with the same emphatic gesture. Blake's image may not be the most valid representation of the Gospel incident, but anyone who has tried seriously to follow the Christian way will know the urgency and desperation involved at times in seeking union with Christ. He becomes the Angel of our agony as we take His place in the lonely watch of the night.

The Christian who wishes to grow in an authentic spirituality according to the teaching and tradition of the Church will realize that such growth is possible despite the wounds of original sin; it will be effected, moreover, only in union with a community of believers and, through them, with all human beings. Karl Rahner points out that the wound of sin permeates the whole of life, society, and relationships, becoming part of the human reality in which the individual is immersed.[18] Sin is within and without. Christ speaks His saving word of grace which gives us the Spirit to shout, "Abba! Father!" Our human nature, good in essence yet damaged, good even in its operations, can now use its own potential to "put on Christ." This is made possible not as the result of a mystery play or symbolic rebirth, like that of Apollo. It is due to a historical human being, the Son of God, who died in agony, rose in glory, and is now seated at the right hand of God. Christian spirituality is therefore deeply human and utterly divine. It is profoundly related to earth and to heaven, denying neither and embracing both. It is based on a single Person, yet demands the conscious, free, and continuous participation of each individual as he or she grows in humanity and adopted divinity.

To this we have been called. To affirm the truth of a unique Christian spirituality is not to belittle in any way the spiritual roads discovered by the mystics of nonbiblical religions; nor is it to denigrate the ways of religious philosophies, still less to disparage the insights of Islamic and Jewish spirituality. It is not difficult for the believing Christian to see everywhere in these movements the operation of grace, which has as its single source the grace won by the Son of God in His life and death. But the Christian, through Revelation and the teaching of the Church, is aware of the source of this grace and of its mode of operation. We who call ourselves believing Christians and have embarked on the spiritual road marked out by Jesus of Nazareth, the immortal Son of God, must think, feel, and act in a way that is consistent with our identity.

Chapter 3

Understanding
Human Development

Understanding Father John, Sister Marie, and Jerry:
Those Who Are Called

The following personal histories are drawn from the lives of people who have consented to my using their journeys to illustrate religious development. I have changed a number of details. We will refer to these cases in the next chapter (4) on religious and spiritual development and add others to elucidate certain important points.

FATHER JOHN'S STORY

Father John grew up in an Irish Catholic neighborhood where most people were devout, practicing Catholics. The rest were devout Jews or Protestants. Worship of God was an unquestioned given in his life. John did moderately well in parochial school. He was an altar boy and a Boy Scout and went to a large Catholic prep school. Without giving it a great deal of thought and with practically no pain he joined several of his classmates and went to the diocesan seminary. The rules were strict, but there was much camaraderie among the seminarians that made up for any discomfort. The seminarians studied for eight years and learned to live with a system that was rather impersonal, because of its formality and because of the large number of seminarians in each class. One soon learned that the diocese did not need priests and that especially they did not need *you*. Thus if you wanted to be ordained, you had better fit into the system. Academic ability was recognized by preferential treatment. Since John was no scholar and wanted to be a parish priest, he avoided this preference himself but often resented its being given to more academically capable students.

Naturally John's closest friends were all seminarians, although he kept up some contact with a few fellows from his own neighborhood. He had dated a bit in high school, but dating was forbidden after entering the seminary. He did not resent this nor did his friends. Those who dated quietly during the summer vacation usually stayed home in the fall.

Finally, John was ordained. Equipped with much theology and few pastoral skills, he never, in those pre-Vatican II days, studied applied psychology or counseling or even much about being a pastoral person. His first Mass was a glorious occasion for his parents and family and a bit of a triumph for himself.

He was assigned to a large parish with four other priests where he enthusiastically took on work with "the kids." Although some of his colleagues in the rectory appeared to consider youth activities a frill for the parish and something of a nuisance, John worked hard and was rewarded with a part-time appointment from the diocesan Youth Office. At the age of thirty, he started to lose interest in things. He went through the motions. Subtly, the youngsters recognized it. The old people at the 6:45 daily Mass no longer were delighted when he showed up on the schedule. He was losing contact with his peers from the seminary. One day one of his closest friends called John to say "goodbye." He was leaving the priesthood and, even then, knew whom he hoped to marry. John was shaken. Gnawing doubts began to plague him and he fell into a moderately severe depression. He bothered and was bothered in return by his pastor. He stopped going to events with other priests. The young people of the parish, sensing his indifference, kept their distance.

John signed up for a retreat and left in the middle of it. He could not pray; Mass was a real burden. Did he believe at all? Was he being a hypocrite?

A young woman in the parish waited after a meeting, told him he did not look well, and offered her sympathy. What was wrong? At first John was annoyed, but he sat down to talk. She said he needed a little social life. She was having friends over on the following Sunday for a picnic. Her parents would be there and the rest would be people of her own age group, business people who were single. John said he would come. It was great. He had not laughed in a long time. The singles kidded him about his black suit. They promised to buy him a sport shirt. He assured them that he had sports clothes and the next time they met, he came dressed to kill. Actually, he had bought new sports clothes for the occasion.

It was a great evening. He felt better, prayed better, and the old people at the 6:45 Mass thought that he was back to his old self. Soon, at another of the singles parties, John met an attractive girl who was different. Liz was an odd blend of the really religious and the moderately irreverent. She practiced meditation and told mildly off-color jokes. She was involved in social action. She told John that he was "out of it," behind the times, hopeless. When he looked depressed at her estimation, she laughed. But when everyone kissed good night, she whispered in his ear, "Phone me."

The relationship grew. It was good. It got expressive. John started to feel that he was falling through space. It was wrong, but it didn't seem wrong. It was a sin, but was it a sin to God? It didn't seem to be a sin. John told his priest confessor who counseled caution and prayer. John tried both half-heartedly, but it was beyond him. Liz and John were both believers. They both loved the Church, each in their own way. Liz was frightened too, but she never told John. "Men think, women feel," she told a friend who was shocked by what was happening. Most of the singles supported them. One girl, the one who had invited John in the first place, confronted Liz. John will lose his priesthood; she would be excommunicated. Liz replied: "What does the Pope know?" She even surprised herself when she said it.

John took a leave of absence. His parents were stunned, but his brothers and sisters were supportive. "It is his life," they said. John looked for a job for quite a while; Liz helped him with money. They were married in City Hall and John prepared the papers for dispensation. John told me that after the marriage, when he woke up in the morning, he still didn't believe what had happened.

John and Liz lived through their dream and through its disappearance. They held on together by love for each other. Liz admits she found John disappointing. He was delighted when his dispensation finally arrived. She was annoyed that they had to go through a religious service to exchange marriage vows again, but she did it for John.

John has found himself gradually drawn to the parish where he lives. He notices himself doing critiques of the Sunday sermon. The local priests, some of them old friends of his, have given him a job or two around the parish. He is delighted. Liz told me, "He is still a priest; I suppose he always will be."

John actually had been involved in a developmental crisis. At the same time, the Church was going through profound institutional changes. He had become alienated from his vocation and from priest friends who had previously supported him. John is a classic disciple of God as the One. Religious things have always held him together. Belief in God is the integrating force of his life. When external religious supports disappeared, his ability to function was severely impaired.

John failed to confront himself either spiritually or psychologically when his vocation to the priesthood was crumbling. If he had not met a potential spouse, he might have grown more and more alienated and gone into severe depression. If he had had more insight and a greater sense of prayer, he could have reaffirmed and revived his commitment to the priesthood. The children of the parish and the old folks were waiting for him. But given his resources, his emotionally inadequate preparation for life, and lack of real insight, it was almost determined that he follow the path that he took. If it had not been Liz, it would have been someone else.

To understand John's problem simply from a psychological perspective is to miss the point. John was and is a believing Catholic. He respected the priesthood and tried to pray and remain in it. The forces at work in his life are spiritual and psychological, as are the questions. Life's questions will remain spiritual as well as psychological for him and his wife for the rest of their lices. If you wish to understand John, you must take the time to study both aspects of development, the psychological and the spiritual. If John is to make a happy adjustment as a believing, religious Christian, he must also take the same two elements into account.

Sister Marie's Story

Like John, Marie went to Catholic school in the postwar period. Her family were upper middle class, Irish and German, but they had a strong American identity. Only her great grandparents had come from Europe. Marie's parents wanted to provide the best they could for their children; thus education held a high priority in her family. Marie went to a girl's academy conducted by sisters. She enjoyed herself, but found the school restricting. After seriously considering entering the community at eighteen, she opted to go to a nonreligious college and take premed courses. Marie was already interested in what was then called "mental prayer." She learned this technique of meditation and has seriously pursued it all her life. Although never a rebel, she did not like restrictions that cramped her style. Indeed, left on her own, she often subjected herself to a discipline far more real than what others could have imposed by external restraint. During her third year in college, Marie began to think more seriously about a religious vocation. She recalls all this in very personal terms. "I believed that Christ was calling me to do something for others. I knew Him, and I prayer to Him, and He answered me." With a little laugh, she added, "What else could I do?" Marie decided that being a physician and a sister could be complicated so she switched to nursing, hoping eventually to be in nursing education. She found a community of sisters at some distance from her home where she could make a new start. She enjoyed novitiate and her early years. She obtained an advanced degree in nursing education and at the age of thirty-six was an accomplished teacher in the college of her order. It looked like smooth sailing for Marie.

But great changes were overtaking the Church. The complex transformation sparked by Vatican II and by the new "self-actualization psychology" swept through her community, as it did through the whole Church in America. Things thought certain suddenly became different. The sister who had been her novice mistress left and married shortly after. People even questioned whether the community should be committed to nursing and hospital administration. Their new recruits all but disappeared and there was a general feeling of malaise. Marie, the optimist, thought that it would all work itself out. She was convinced that just over the hill there would be some answer. The answer never came.

Gradually, Marie grew depressed. At first she could not put her finger on the causes. She discussed all this with her spiritual director, a wise man of the old school. One day he said to her in so many words: "Marie, you are angry with God. Why don't you face the fact that you feel that He let you down?" She recalls that she went home and had a good cry. She even got angry and read some of the angry psalms to God. "Where are you, Lord; why are you asleep?" She also asked the question: "Should I leave my community? Who would even care?" But Marie had spiritual resources that John never developed. She suffered a lot of pain for several weeks and then came to a decision. She would remain in the community, do her job, even if everybody else left, but she was not going to be a pollyanna anymore. Marie decided that the big old motherhouse had become too painful a place to be home. The old sisters were her real standbys, but she could not move into the infirmary at forty. She found a few other sisters, some from other communities, and, with permission, they rented a modest house. For the first time in years she began to experience community again. She kept her job teaching, but she got involved in other aspects of life in the small city where she worked. She still faithfully visits her friends, the old sisters, and goes to all community functions when possible, though at times she finds them trying.

Marie states that she finds her identity and meaning in prayer. Life did not turn out to be what she expected, but, unexpectedly, she has found some peace which she tries to share with others. What does the future hold, as far fewer young sisters remain to care for the old? Ever the optimist, Marie leaves it up to God and talks about the real courage she observes in the very few young women now joining the order. "They have courage and faith," she will tell you. As I listened, it was obvious that Marie and others like her probably have a great deal of faith too.

Marie's life can be seen as a fairly straight line of development. Like many other followers of God as the Good, she felt betrayed, but she kept giving and growing. Her strength is founded on several things. Her optimism is a continuation of parental attitudes and a fairly tranquil childhood. Her religious faith has been consistently fed by her thoughts, studies, prayer, and behavior. Her independence, often won by conscious effort despite strong dependency needs, has psychologically kept her going. As we trace psychological and spiritual development, Marie will provide us with an interesting example of a person who is not just a survivor but who has actually grown through disruptive times.

JERRY'S STORY

Our third and last case history is in some ways the most interesting and also the most difficult to describe because it may sound overly dramatic, almost made-up. Psychologically, it makes the least sense to the superficial student of human behavior. But Jerry represents a great many people. Like many persons in early adult life at this time of our history, he is a disciple of God as the Beautiful.

Jerry grew up in affluent suburbia. His parents were trying to do many things at once. They were paying off a large mortgage and tried hard to cover up (even to each other) the fact that their lifestyle was beyond their income. Although they had two cars and belonged to a beach club (a junior country club), they were living from paycheck to paycheck to keep it all going.

Jerry's parents had a successful mixed marriage. His father was a chemical engineer with a tenuous affiliation to the Congregational Church, which he attended a few times each year. Jerry's mother, an Italian American, had a large extended family which she loved and rejected at the same time. She seldom mentioned her family origins, but when with her family she thoroughly enjoyed the warmth and noisy good humor. She compensated for her alienation by studying and producing Florentine ceramics as a hobby. She took pride in the fact that her parents had educated themselves far beyond many other immigrants and sent all their children to Catholic school and college.

Jerry has two sisters, one elder and one younger, both intent as teenagers on marrying and staying married to successful men. He admits that he finds his sisters and their husbands a bit tedious. One of his sisters is now on the threshold of divorce. In high school, Jerry, a young man of superior intelligence, enthusiastically embraced everything and tried everything. A fairly good athlete, he was also interested in art, music, drama, and girls. He did not take religion very seriously, but liked its aesthetic qualities. The strong faith of his maternal grandparents intrigued him because it gave them so much solace in their old age.

Drugs terrified Jerry. Some of his friends, to use his own expression, had "gone completely down the tubes." Yet, he enjoyed smoking marijuana and thinking he was another Coleridge. He is embarrassed by this now, but still thinks it made his mind more open to new sensations.

In college Jerry enjoyed freedom and beauty. Being away from home, he decided to experiment with every form of beauty and pleasure, especially sexuality. Although he always intended to marry and have a family, he became promiscuous, but was careful not to involve a girl who did not know what she was doing. A few times Jerry even tried homosexual encounters when he had been drinking, but found these very unsatisfying and frightening.

Then, like Dante whom he admired, he met his Beatrice. He fell completely in love with Patty, a devout evangelical Protestant. He was uneasy with her religious convictions, but found her qualities of kindness, determination, and faith "unbelievably attractive." To please her, he went to church, sometimes to her church, sometimes to his own. Her commitment to chastity before marriage bothered him. It seemed superstitious, old-fashioned, and inhuman. Love was love, and God had made it to be enjoyed. Eventually he persuaded Patty that he was right and they had a short painful affair for a few weeks. Patty went along although she had had no previous sexual experiences. Then suddenly, "she fell apart." She went into a deep depression and told Jerry that she was deeply hurt and angry. He offered then and there to marry her and "she looked at me with a look of outrage and pain that I will never forget." This was the end of their friendship. Patty eventually got some help from a counselor in her church and went on to marry someone else.

Jerry was desolate. He didn't know where to turn. Even when speaking about it years later, tears come to his eyes. "I never intended to hurt anyone; I just wanted to be happy and have fun." Jerry began to pray. He went to confession after years away from the sacraments. Looking back on it, he realizes that this event brought him to a great spiritual awakening, although he still feels guilty about Patty. Jerry changed his entire life. For a while he joined a prayer group and even received the "Baptism of the Spirit." He is no longer active in the Charismatic Renewal, but maintains that this period of community prayer and invitation to experience God was one of the most valuable and cherished times of his life.

At Christmas of the following year he returned from college for the holidays and absolutely startled his family with the news of his religious involvement and plans to investigate becoming a priest or brother. His mother said: "I didn't know whether to laugh or cry, so I did both." After some counseling with the priest at college, who was also in the Charismatic movement, Jerry determined to work for a year or two as a lay missionary in Latin America. He had to study for six months because he really knew very little about his faith. The Bible had been his constant companion and he developed a sincere interest in the literature of spirituality. The year in the missions provided maturity and a strong growth in faith. Jerry is now convinced that faith and service to the poor will be the focus of the rest of his life. At twenty-nine he has found the beauty he sought, but he has found it in people. He is now unsure whether his vocation is to the priesthood, to marriage, or to a life of single service. His spiritual director has advised him to wait. Like Sister Marie, he is very much at peace. He is deeply convinced that he is being led and that God will open the next door for him. In the meantime, he works in a creative social service project and lives with two other young men interested in entering the seminary or religious life. They pray together and have informal community life. Jerry knows that this will not last forever and he is willing to wait for God and have Him show the way.

Jerry is not as unusual as you may think. The degree of his religious interest is more profound than most, but is familiar to most spiritual directors. His journey is far from complete. He has yet to resolve all his guilt, but he is aware of it. He is not frightened at the possibility that some of his zeal may be psychologically founded. Laughing, he will tell you that he enjoys his work with the poor so much that it can't really be a penance. His real penance, which he performs cheerfully, is to be part of the parish where he lives. This parish is not equipped to deal with so incandescent a spirit. Warned about neurotic forms of penance, he assures me that if I hear he is running the parish bingo, I will know that he has succeeded in finding the most neurotic penance. Jerry represents a group of young people who simply must take life seriously. They are the people who will keep the Church going.

As we continue our discussion of psychological and spiritual maturity, we will return to John, Marie, and Jerry and introduce a few new people along the way. They will help us fit into the abstract categories of spiritual development other people whom we know—perhaps even ourselves.

The Mold and the Garden—Two Models of Development

Until very recently, many genuinely religious young people, especially those who entered the seminary or religious life, were fitted into a mold, a static and basically uncreative psychological frame of reference. Indeed, this static view also pervaded secular education. Often, a person

was expected to practice mature virtues by reason of a liturgical cere-
mony or act of public commitment. A high level of maturity was expected as soon as a habit was put on or marriage vows exchanged. Such a
view did not consider the individual's past or future potential. Young
people were expected to conform at once to a precise model of behavior
and were thought ill-intentioned if they did not. The case history of
Father John illustrates that many developments in post-Vatican II religious life can be understood as a reaction to this view and to the "mold."
Yet to dismiss the static view which is based on external norms is to risk
religious anarchy. Perhaps the good features of the static approach can
be salvaged if they are enriched and vitalized, and integrated with a
developmental understanding.

The more creative, developmental approach to human growth began
to appear in secular psychology with the publication of *Childhood and
Society* by Erik Erikson.[1] In attempting to synthesize many psycho-
dynamic theories, Erikson identified eight stages of human growth and
the critical conflicts of each of these stages. Borrowing principles from
the theories of Freud, Erikson described the development of human
potentials far beyond Freud's original insight. He seems at times to
contradict Freud's pessimism and antispiritual bias. Some of the potentials identified by Erikson must be called "spiritual values," such as personal altruism and wisdom. Throughout his work he recognizes the basic
insight of developmental psychology, namely, that human beings are in
a constant process of becoming. When we are moving or becoming in an
appropriate way, we are growing. When we cease to grow or to be
involved in a dynamic process of becoming more creative and more
productive, we are in a negative process of becoming, or a decline.

Another view of development, emphasizing more intangible and interior human events, had been developed over a lifetime by Carl Jung.[2]
While using such powerful images as the "shadow" and the "archetypical
ideas" to indicate the components of the inner struggle for maturity,
Jung's constant theme is that of becoming. In fact it may be said that
Jung, and not Erikson, was the trailblazer; the former's theories are so
complex, however, that the single element of development does not
stand out as clearly as it does in Erikson.

Taking a different point of view, Gordon Allport saw personality not
as a static unity but as a dynamic complexity of traits, again in the process
of becoming.[3] In fact, Allport used the word "becoming" as the title of
one of his studies on personality.

Many other significant writers have been intrigued by the idea of
becoming in human development. Piaget has examined this idea exten-
sively in the growth of children, and more recent studies, like those of

Levinson, have focused on midlife.[4] A valuable synthesis of these studies and their relation to religious growth has been prepared by Evelyn and James Whitehead.[5]

In order to understand the idea of spiritual development, it is of paramount importance for us to grasp the nature of the development of a living thing. Ask yourself this question: "When does an acorn become an oak tree?" Answering in an Aristotelian and static manner, you might say that at some discreet, if unknowable, moment, the acorn (an oak tree in potency) ceases to be and the oak tree comes into being. However, you should consider that the life of the acorn never ceases to exist until the oak tree dies, perhaps hundreds of years later. During all this time the same life continues, always in the process of becoming. If you ponder this new and less obvious way of looking at living things, you begin to see "being-in-time."

Let's turn our attention now to the human being. The unborn child is growing old from the first moment of existence. The old person is constantly becoming while the child never completely ceases to be, even in very old age. In fact, in periods of regression (or falling backwards) as a result of pressure or trauma, the child of long ago may reappear and dominate the entire personality and behavior of the individual for some time.[6]

When living things are looked at in such a way (what we call the "developmental point of view"), what happens to the present, to the *now*? At first sight it appears almost to collapse between past and future. However, when this developmental view is considered in depth, the present takes on a new significance, heretofore unrecognized. The present moment becomes the totality of the entire past. At the same time, the present, in varying degrees, determines the future through the creative exercise of the human will. The reflecting free person is able, in the present moment, to become not only all that his past has made him, but what he determines to become within the potential of his present situation. Thus, he also determines to become what he shall be.

Perhaps no more dramatic and revealing description of this process may be found than in the Gospels, which along with presenting the significant life events of the Messiah, also describe His formation and teaching of His disciples. Throughout the Gospels, the theme of the development of these ordinary folk into spiritually mature men can be traced. But you may object that they really did not develop. They failed the first test miserably. It was an insight of St. Catherine of Siena that the darkness of this failure was a necessary part of the development of St. Peter and the apostles.[7] For to develop means always to attempt what is a bit beyond one's capacity. This is obvious when one watches an infant try to walk. It is the reason why great artists are always perfecting their technique. It is why St. Francis—and in this he was like many other great mystics—said to the friars at the end of his earthly life, "Let us begin now for thus far we have done nothing."

We come now to a new idea that is puzzling and abstract. You may be wondering: "What difference does it make whether I am in some way at all stages in the spiritual life at one time? I am where I am right now." That is true. Yet, every person who has begun to grow in a personal knowledge of the divine life within, who experiences the vital force of the Incarnate Word in his or her own life, will become aware of being at some particular stage of the journey. The next chapter will describe the three stages rather fully. Here we will simply call to mind the three ways or stages of *purification, illumination,* and *union.*[8]

If you are still wondering whether this complex consideration is helpful, you will be startled to realize that by placing the abstract principle of development in such a context, you have experienced in a small way the life of the great contemplatives and even a taste of heavenly life. It may be a new idea, but this is the case. The Fathers of the Church refer to the heightened experience of the beginner as "sparks" of the divine light. The surprising realization that a small share in contemplation comes even to children or adults when they are first spiritually awakened leads to several conclusions. First, all such experiences should be taken seriously even though they are predominantly grounded in psychological and emotional need. As the history of spirituality demonstrates repeatedly, the most instantaneous experiences, such as the conversion of St. Francis or of St. Catherine of Genoa, although they are obviously rich in psychological significance, must be considered manifestations of divine action and grace by reason of their far-reaching good effects on history. We shall return to this intriguing subject in the next chapter.[9]

Another conclusion derived from the developmental point of view is that even a person who has made some progress is quite capable of regression, or falling backward. This happened to Father John, although he was able to recover. A more adequate conception of this experience is that the earlier, less mature configuration of personal dynamics was never really passed, but surfaced again when the present personality organization was inadequate to cope with the existing pressures. Again, the individual may have decided to regress and take the opportunity for an easier way out. Thus sin or moral failure is possible throughout the entire journey; since the pressures and challenges increase with spiritual progress, there is always the possibility of regression. The old Irish adage, "The higher we climb, the higher the devil climbs," is a rather simple but pointed expression of this phenomenon.

Marie could have regressed, but she had the good sense to use inner resources she had never thought of.

The third and most important conclusion of the developmental analysis is that we must constantly strive for the next level of adjustment. Put simply, we must strive to take the next good step. Only a decade or two ago, the notion of striving for perfection was often badly applied because perfection was seen as a static reality, a "land of milk and honey" to be arrived at. The appalling picture of what this concept led to was revealed in dramatic form in *The Nun's Story* by Katherine Hulme.[10] Very good people, spiritually well advanced, some of them like Hulme's Mother General, were constricted by an artificial ideal of perfection. If we take the analogy which the Greek Fathers borrowed from athletics to describe the striving for perfection, it must be seen at least as a developmental, dynamic ideal of daily growth, rather than as something arrived at in short order and preserved artificially at all costs by repressive discipline.

Stages of Human Development

As we indicated above, a number of excellent studies in recent decades have concentrated on the stages of development. Jung and Erikson have looked into the whole range of life from infancy to old age, while particular studies have been done on certain ages and the development of certain human functions. Levinson's *Seasons of a Man's Life* has already been mentioned in terms of the concept of becoming. Neugarten,[11] Vaillant,[12] and others have all done research on various phases of the midlife of middle class people. Oscar Lewis[13] and Franklin Frazer[14] among others have studied the lives of those held down by poverty and injustice. Fowler[15] and his associates have related much of the research to the development of the religious person. As has been mentioned, perhaps the best summary of major theories in relation to the development of religiously active Christians has been done with great thoroughness by Evelyn and James Whitehead.[16]

It goes beyond the scope of this book to review all these theories or even any one. However, as in Chapter 2, we will attempt to place some of the principal insights of these theories into a perspective that relates to this discussion of spiritual development. It should be noted that none of these theoretical systems attempts to analyze spiritual development as it has been studied by the mystics and great spiritual writers. Even the Whiteheads' study of the patterns of Christian life really concerns human development within the community of the Church. They carefully avoid discussing the psychology of spirituality as presented by St. Augustine or St. John of the Cross. Their study of the human development of the Christian as a socially religious person not only is legitimate, but will throw greater light on our discussion of spiritual development when we come to it.

UNDERSTANDING YOUR OWN DEVELOPMENT: WHO AM I AS A PERSON?

You should use the following brief summary of developmental theory to identify significant events or trends in your own life. No one has had a perfect development, for we were all born into a fallen and wounded world; we will find defects and deficiencies all the way through. The following questions should be kept in mind as this review unfolds:

What were the strengths and deficiencies in my environment as I was growing up—in my family, school, job, neighborhood, church?

What habits or traits did I develop to capitalize on strengths or to cope with shortcomings?

What inner resources did I rely on in order to cope?

In what ways did I withdraw, hide, or pretend in order to avoid realities I was afraid of?

What effect do these experiences have on my life today?

It is also helpful to identify crossroads or crises in life. These are very special times of decision, often punctuated by times of trial and depression. A religious conversion may occur at such times, or an unnoticed but damaging decision to sell out in life. To decide not to make a decision may be the most disastrous decision of a lifetime. Because it is so important to appraise the spiritual life from the viewpoint of development, the following summary of developmental psychological theory may be helpful to the reader. As you read this summary, try to examine the successes and failures, the opportunities and deficiencies in your own development. This understanding will assist you greatly in recognizing what tasks from the past remain incomplete.

EARLY YEARS OF LIFE (UP TO SIX YEARS OF AGE)

No individual can have control over the early years of life, though they are the most significant. During this period, the outlines of personality are shaped. Although one is later free to build on these foundations, both genetic endowment and early environment will trace the broad outlines of what is to come. Despite the importance of the early years, we should avoid determinism, i.e., the notion that all genuine psychological change is impossible after childhood. An analogy may help to avoid this error. Early life provides a foundation; for some it is large and broad, for others, small and narrow. The individual whom circumstances have blest with a solid psychological foundation may not necessarily achieve a healthy life adjustment. On the other hand, a person whose early life has been marred by adversity may overcome obstacles and lead a well adjusted life. The one with a large foundation and great potential may build a mansion or a hovel, whereas the one with more modest potential may construct a charming cottage.

According to Erikson, the great foundation stones of childhood are learning to trust, to function with some autonomy, and to develop initiative. Insofar as the child fails to develop these critical values, he or she is prey to mistrust of others, a crippling sense of shame and self-doubt, and neurotic guilt. Failure to develop in these areas may not necessarily be the result of a neglectful home environment. It may be caused by parents' inability to let a child develop independently of their expectations, or it may stem from trauma caused by misfortune or illness. In fact, failure may come from many circumstances which may not at the time be recognized. Strangely enough, within the same family one child may suffer a serious failure to develop, while another may not. Ordinarily, failure to develop is called a "fixation" (or in popular terms a "hangup"), which causes some part of the psychological life to remain fixed at the childhood level.

A serious failure in developing the ability to trust causes in later life a tendency toward psychosis, that is, a permanent set of traits which grossly distort reality and force the individual either into withdrawal or into chaotic emotional instability. Failure in this early stage may also result in the development of a criminal personality, a person without any active moral sense in regard to his or her own behavior. This condition goes by various names, but the most consistently used have been "antisocial" or "psychopathic" personality.

Persons in both categories of serious personality underdevelopment may be quite religious. However, their religious development is so idiosyncratic as to be almost unrelated to the outline provided by the great spiritual writers. Nevertheless, it is my opinion that some canonized saints, such as Benedict Joseph Labré, showed a substantial tendency toward psychosis. Criminal personalities have their own patron in the strange figure whom Tradition has called the "Good Thief." Anyone familiar with his kind of personality can easily identify it in his manipulative dialogue with Christ at Calvary.

At the next stage, we can recognize that failure in developing an independent personality, coupled with a pathological sense of shame and doubt, is characteristic of many people. They struggle all their lives with a nagging sense of worthlessness and fear. Often they are responsible and caring people, capable and even accomplished, but life is a dark forest and they remain alone. The spiritual development of these people is frequently a painful struggle, but as they grow spiritually, they often overcome some of their excessive fears. The timid sister in the opera *Dialogues of the Carmelites,* who overcame her fear and returned to the condemned community, is an example of how grace may help such a person.

Those who become permanently fixated at the third stage (age three to six) fail to develop real initiative or, more frequently, achieve it only with conflict. They always feel guilty. Here a wide variety of personality difficulties appear, ranging from the typical neurotic conflicts to self-destructiveness. They often experience difficulty in sexual orientation; they may be excessively preoccupied with sexuality, afraid of it, or drawn to arrested forms of sexual development which appear as deviations.

Many spiritually advanced people have emerged from this group. The literature of spirituality is filled with those who overcame scruples and fear, driven needs, and great depression. Among those of the recent past who identified with this set of modern problems, we may number St. John Neumann who struggled with guilt all his life, as well as Simone Weil and Charles de Foucauld whose difficulties in childhood gave rise to a need to take on themselves all the sins of the world. None of the people whose case histories we have examined belongs to these groups because they are all too healthy. We should keep in mind that there are great souls who show at least some traits of fixation at this level.

Childhood and Early Adolescence

Following early childhood, Erikson believes that the healthy child develops a creativity and individuality which in adult life will grow into generosity and an altruistic care for the next generation. Young children are far from a totally altruistic life, but they are capable of an industrious and ordered self-assertion which respects the rights and needs of others. Many children, however, become victims of a strong sense of inferiority, perhaps because of tragic mistakes made in the first years of childhood. Competition, lack of sensitivity to the gifts and needs of each child, and excessive conformity often cause children to experience a growing sense of inferiority. It is not farfetched to see John with strong traits which partially identify him with this group. These negative traits did not appear until he began to regress in the face of pressure from his assignment. Many children compensate for a sense of inferiority by over-achievement in sports or academic studies and as a result become rather lopsided in their development. Others become bitter, negative, or even sadistic. Still others accept inferiority and seek pleasures which soon fade in early adult life. Regrettably, contemporary Western society is filled with people who developed as far as adolescence and then were corrupted by a hedonistic anticulture. They were not successful in meeting the challenges of adult life.

On the other hand, from the group who have arrived at a level of true industriousness come many saints of the Church who are universally recognized as great men and women. Prodigious workers, prolific writers, and builders of institutions, they are found in all forms of human endeavor, with many representatives in religion. It is also quite possible to do good and effective work as a Christian and not arrive at sanctity. Effective Christians in many areas who did not attain great spiritual heights may be found in this category. (The Whiteheads give a very good description of such persons.) Sister Marie is perhaps a good representative of this type. She does not see herself approaching great heights and would reject any obviously heroic behavior as pretentious. Although going against the tide, she is not inclined to give the impression of taking a stand; yet she has laid the foundations of heroism in her quiet fidelity.

LATE ADOLESCENCE AND THE BEGINNING OF MATURITY

In complex civilizations, an understanding of adolescence is of major importance in comprehending spiritual development, for the adolescent is the child becoming an adult. In agrarian societies, adolescence may last only a few months, followed by a rapid transition to adulthood according to well-defined cultural lines and ritualized rites of passage. In affluent, highly developed societies such as our own, adolescence is artificially extended into the twenties. Adolescence realistically ends when the individual is able to be an independent, self-supporting, self-directed member of society.

Adolescence, especially when protracted, may bring many problems: aimlessness, boredom, indulgence in pleasure and resultant self-hate or guilt, self-destructive tendencies and several other psychological mishaps, especially for those who have suffered scars in childhood. For those who have been severely fixated as described above, the crises of adolescence will bring into sharp, and often tragic, focus the deficiencies which childhood may have hidden. Even for those who arrive at adolescence with a sense of industry and self-expression, it can be a difficult time. Most adults would not relish the idea of passing through adolescence again.

Erikson identifies the critical conflict of adolescence as one between identity and role confusion. This conflict pertains to things as varied as the trial selection of a career or vocation, clarification of gender role and the establishment of sexual identity, and problems concerning faith and the acceptance or rejection of the religious denomination of one's family. It also involves experiments with intimate personal relationships of many kinds including peer relationships, the choice of a potential spouse, and relating to supervisors and employers. Unfortunately, teenagers often become involved in manipulative relationships where they learn to use others as objects rather than respecting others as individuals.

The beginning and the end of adolescence are of particular importance to those interested in religious development. Both periods are likely to be times of strong positive and negative feelings about religion. Both the early and late teenage years may be marked by profound religious conversions which open up vistas of thought beyond the strength of the individual and require years of readjustment. Anyone who has worked with religiously oriented people in their late teens or early twenties knows that they can appear to be wildly inconsistent, moving from zealous virtue to irresponsible and even antireligious behavior. This often suggests insincerity to adults who forget that such inconsistency is really a reflection of conflict between behavior and ideals. As a result of the static view of religious commitment, much of this inconsistency was repressed, thus causing occasional regression or even cynicism. This was true especially when the individual had been prematurely recruited into a religious vocation; it is obvious in the case of Father John. A developmental approach, while much wiser and more human, requires more patience and individualization. As stated above, this approach must also be guided by solid moral and cultural norms, so that the individual does not lack direction in his or her growth.

Later we shall see that adolescence may be accompanied by a genuine spiritual awakening which places a very young person squarely on the purgative way. The calendar of saints is dotted with people who were well into this stage as they approached their twenties. Unfortunately, as biography is a limited tool and hagiography (the biography of saints) is even more limited, we have little information about the struggles of the spiritually awakened teenager. Some genuine insights have been provided by Thérèse of Lisieux, but she was unusually advanced—to say the least. It is rare, for example, to find any discussion from a psychological point of view of the sexual conflicts of the young who are seeking to be good Christians. Much work needs to be done in this area.[17]

Jerry is typical of the serious adolescent who lost his way and later experienced an obvious conversion. As often happens in conversions, the very occasion of the call is a time of doubt and confusion. Pure psychology is unable to deal with the operation of grace in such a conversion which is the experience of the call of the Lord to forgiveness and healing. This forgiveness and healing are so powerful and integral to the experience that I question whether anyone can seriously study conversion without taking these possibilities into account. Jerry, an articulate young man with a high sense of objective self-awareness, is an excellent example of the phenomenon of spiritual and psychological conversion at the end of adolescence.

Adolescence passes very gradually and its ending is marked by the task of beginning a life of stable, mutually supportive relationships. Success in this enterprise, according to Erikson, is "intimacy"; failure to achieve such relationships is known as "isolation." It is important to understand that only a few people become totally isolated in what must be called "psychotic adjustments." Many with inadequate and basically unsatisfactory patterns of relationship may, even in marriage, remain more or less isolated. In the following passage, the Whiteheads give a very good description of successful intimacy in the life of the religious person:

> Intimacy often appears as a synonym for sexual expression or romantic sharing. We use this word in a broader psychological sense to refer to those strengths which enable a person to share deeply with another. These strengths come into play across a range of relationships—friendship, work collaboration, community living. Whenever there is personal disclosure and mutuality, intimacy is involved. A well-developed ability to be intimate enables me to be with different persons in a rich variety of different ways, ways that are appropriate to my own personality and to the demands of different situations. It is upon these intimacy resources that I draw in my attempts to live closely with others, to share my talents and ambitions, to merge my life and hopes with those of some one, some few others.[18]

From the above description, it is obvious that religious affiliation and active membership in a church may be a tremendous help in establishing a wide variety of relationships which, if not altruistic, are at least directed toward common concerns. In many countries, the only real meeting place after one leaves school is either the church or the pub-club-type activity which is often self-serving. Unless they have the opportunity to share in a service-oriented volunteer activity with uplifting ideals, many people sink into a life of enclosed self-seeking. We have all seen couples who, often in isolation, become totally preoccupied with a house, which then becomes both castle and prison.

On the other hand, religious values may threaten a person's ability to relate in an intimate way. An unbalanced preoccupation with the "spiritual" may actually represent a kind of withdrawal from life into a spirituality that is largely based on fantasy and sublimation.

Yankelovich has identified the ethic of affluence as the one that has most influenced Americans in the past fifteen years. This influence is so strong that it has caused many Americans to seek, at least partially, their own fulfillment without regard to the needs of others. It has minimized the sense of commitment to others.[19] This ethic has also been obvious in recent spiritual movements. Many good Christians have turned in on themselves and become, unfortunately, "their own little self with God." This can be a god of their own making. It is imperative for those interested in the spiritual life, even if they are frightened or have been hurt, to move out and belong to the whole Christ by compassion and love. St. Augustine insisted on a spirituality related to the whole community of Christ's members, as a pertinent teaching for his own rather self-centered age.[20]

When we have been genuinely awakened to the spiritual life, we are often concerned lest we be drawn into relationships which are exploitative and inappropriate. In this area spiritually sensitive adults can provide leadership for newcomers. Young people need to be drawn into opportunities for sharing, mutual support, and charitable activities. Neither adult mentors nor the struggling young adult must be deterred if these relationships lead to emotional experiences of sublimation even though the individual realizes that much of his or her "love" for others is based on psychological need. Doing good works and sharing the lot of the unfortunate, involvement with people of totally different values (or none at all) are all antidotes to false intimacy and emotionalism which can impede spiritual growth. St. Vincent de Paul is quoted as saying, "Love the poor and your life will be filled with sunlight." One supposes that this holy man had learned the value of helping others in terms of his own development.

One other subtle form of isolation must be mentioned in this context. There is often a tendency for the religiously motivated to hide from intimacy in some great cause or work. Older adults who favor one cause or another may lose sight of the fact that much of the energy expended in the cause may be an avoidance of real relationships. The cause may be religious, social, political, or all three. It may be liberal, conservative, or radical, pro- or anti-establishment. Whatever the cause, it is better to be involved than to be hidden at home or in a disco serving self. But it is wise to keep in mind that despite the legitimacy of the cause, some of the zeal may be a flight from real relationships and growth.

Sexual Maturity

Sexual intimacy is an important part of the lives of most adults. Some time ago I made a resolution to keep my mouth shut concerning things I know nothing about; thus the best I can do is to suggest a reading of many religiously enlightened books on the subject, especially if they are written by happily married people. It appears to me that advice on these matters is often given by those who have not been very successful in establishing a permanent marital relationship. Celibates often mistake sexual intimacy for geniune relationship because of their own naïveté. Sexual interchange may occur regularly where genuine intimacy is lacking. This represents a flight from intimacy and leads to a situation in which other human beings are regarded as "sexual objects."

Romantic ideas of erotic human relationships often give rise to unrealistic attitudes toward marriage. As anyone knows who grew up with the movies of the 1940s and 1950s, romance can be pleasant and intriguing. It can also lead to spiritual escapism for the religiously motivated, often marked by bitter disappointment. The reader might well ponder a few things about romance.

As we understand it, romantic infatuation is essentially a phenomenon of early adult life. A person who remains fixated at this stage of sexual development will be either romantic or disappointed for the rest of life. This explains, for instance, why committed celibates such as priests are often either pleasantly romantic about married life or sadly disappointed with other people's marriages. The world today is immersed in sexual exploitation and banality and could certainly use a dose of romance. This may explain the anomaly that the Marriage Encounter movement, which has helped literally hundreds of thousands of couples rediscover some romance in their marriages, was founded by members of the only identifiable group of committed celibate males in the Western world, namely, Catholic clergy.

Much heat has been generated in religious psychological circles in recent years over the issue of whether a practicing, committed celibate can lead a well-balanced life. Some, in their attempt to justify a celibate lifestyle, have given away the keys to the castle so that the finished product may be a person who is celibate (i.e., unmarried) without being chaste. This is hardly a Gospel value. I might as well add further confusion to the interminable discussion of celibacy by saying that in my view a person committed early in life to chaste celibacy is likely to remain at an early adult level of sexual development. This means that the well-balanced celibate who has not hidden in various kinds of isolation may bring to pastoral work a special tenderness and a much-needed, if naïve, belief in the possibility of continuing romance in marriage. How many graduates of Catholic schools have not found a special kind of understanding from a particular sister, brother, or priest, even though some other clergy or religious might have appeared uncomprehending?

Immature attitudes concerning human sexual relationships are not restricted to believers or celibates. Such immaturity is frequently present to an astonishing degree among those who admit wide sexual experience. Familiarity does not always result in understanding or maturity because overall human maturity, specifically maturity of outlook about sexuality, is rooted in many functions and dynamics of the personality rather than in some biological experience. I once had the delightful opportunity of having coffee and a conversation with the well known psychologist Erich Fromm, author of *The Art of Loving*. Those familiar with Dr. Fromm knew him as a gentle and somewhat utopian man. Toward the end of our conversation, I summoned the courage to ask a pointed question. I explained that after reading *The Art of Loving* I had concluded that St. Teresa of Avila and St. John of the Cross seemed to be the only two people to achieve a degree of self-giving and personal altruism capable of so idealized a relationship as had been defined in the book. With a twinkle in his eye the old gentleman confessed, "Ah, yes. It is true. And they weren't really interested."

Arrested Sexual Development—A Partial Failure at Intimacy

No honest discussion of early adult life can fail to mention the problem of arrested sexual development. This is something quite different from the stabilization of development at early adult life, described above, which is likely to happen in the case of the celibate who had chosen to remain so for religious reasons. Many persons, married or single, show signs of a partial sexual fixation which leaves them at a level of development much before early adult life. They exhibit such symptoms as excessive sexual preoccupation or, the opposite symptom, puritanical denial of sexuality (sometimes called "extreme modesty"), or sexual identity confusion (also wrongly termed "bisexuality" or "homosexuality"). The sexually arrested person who is profoundly afflicted by obsessive thoughts and fantasies, or by compulsive behavior which is totally at odds with moral convictions, may apply a certain label to himself, thereby placing himself in this or that category. The label will be some substantive word indicating that constituitively one is fixed in this or that identity. Often it is claimed that this is the work of God. Frequently such words as "homosexual" or "bisexual" are used. Unfortunately some moralists, attempting to be understanding, will seek reasons to agree with a basic rationalization of a pathology or psychological malfunction, for that is what an arrested sexual development is. Many persons with such problems feel strongly that they should not be stigmatized with a word like "pathology." All human beings, however, have some pathology. "Sexual pathology" is indeed a frightening term, but it applies to any kind of malfunction in a person's sexual development. A person who stutters or chain-smokes or worries excessively about his or her health or eats too much has a pathology too. One hopes that all these people, including those with sexual pathologies, would strive to improve these maladjustments.

Arrested sexual development has many forms of expression, especially those called "deviations," such as promiscuity, homosexuality, sadomasochistic traits, and compulsive masturbation. Deviant acts and willful desires have long been recognized as contrary to the moral law by Christians in general and they have usually been considered contrary to social mores as well. Consequently, society has tended to ignore their existence or at least to see those so compelled as wicked or diabolical. As more enlightened attitudes continue to prevail, as they have done in the areas of mental illness and alcoholism, it is to be hoped that these sexual problems will be recognized for what they are, that is, pathological tendencies which result from arrested sexual development or, at times, from bad example coupled with a self-destructive and negative self-image. The best way to present the moral aspect of these problems in practice is to assist a person to see the possibility of a better life adjustment in keeping with the moral law (founded on Scripture and Tradition and recently reiterated by the Church's highest pastoral authority). We must also help the individual to accept the possibility for spiritual growth offered by the Gospel imperative to change. Years of psychological and pastoral experience have convinced me that this is the only realistic point of view, if one is willing to consider the person's entire life and destiny rather than to be preoccupied with this or that painful circumstance.

Intimacy and Spirituality

Intimacy, then, is the great task of early adult life. Whatever the individual's life, one must grow with others if one is to grow spiritually. It was Harry Stack Sullivan's insight that we learn to be and remain functioning individuals only in relation to others; this is an important concept in the spiritual life.[21] During a recent visit to a monastery dedicated to the austere eremitical traditions of St. Bruno, I was surprised by the

possibilities there for genuine and deep relationships. The religious related well to each other as they followed what the world must regard as a
solitary life. It is true that such a life poses certain dangers; intimacy can
be avoided and one may even be fleeing from intimacy by entering such
a life. Wise leaders, however, would not let this occur, lest the very basis
of the spirituality of the Gospel be thwarted.

A few hours of serious conversation in broken French with a previously unknown solitary monk effected a special bond of intimacy between us. How disagreeable it was, therefore, to sit in the train later that
afternoon next to a nice, well-meaning woman who talked for two solid
hours about absolutely nothing. She revealed a life of harmless superfici-
ality which made her oblivious to any real depth within herself. The
interior life was unknown to her because she had never learned that
solitude is the other side of intimacy.

The customs of religious life in the immediate past were used to dis-
courage intimacy. Neither mutual sharing nor vulnerability was encouraged and these are the two essential components of intimacy. This led to
a crisis of intimacy which has been painful to all in the Catholic world.
The varied possibilities for intimacy in relationships where there is no
sexual component (that is to say, in most relationships) were ignored by
those who had been taught to use complete repression as a form of
sexual control. Some clergy and religious who had been so restricted
suddenly saw intimate relationships with sexual expression, which are
proper only in marriage, as the only mode of authentic relationship.
This is precisely the problem faced by Father John who had had only
limited relationships with other priests and was naïve about other relationships.

A certain moral relativism precipitated this flight into sexual intimacy
which startled even those outside the Church who had a regard for
Catholic beliefs and convictions. A degenerative form of clerical privilege, which places above the law those set apart to uphold the law, made
its first public appearance since it had been violently burned away in the
fires of nineteenth-century anticlericalism. But those who are in a position to understand the rationalization behind this shabby privilege knew
that most often it related to a failure in training young clerics and religious in the use of healthy, nonsexual relationships. These relationships
are more subtle and at times more demanding; yet they are perfectly
acceptable since they have little to do with sexual attraction or expression.

Father John never thought he had a privilege to go beyond the law
and would have been hurt if anyone suggested that he had. But finding
himself carried along by forces which gradually grew beyond his control,

John had to rationalize. So did Liz, who was more concerned about all this than she appeared. In other decades this rationalization would not have been permissible and John would probably have been able to resist the pressure. Many priests and religious who did resist the pressure had more inner independence and a more active spiritual life.

Jerry got caught in the rationalization of the times because of a lack of religious conviction and limited religious experience. Patty, his girl friend, had strong views that enabled her, with a lot of personal pain, to resolve the conflict. Sister Marie, who has always been a well-related person, would not have been swamped in the first place. Though disappointed with her life situation, she was able to preserve her values without any need for rationalization.

Intimacy is not charity. It is not love of God or of our fellow human beings. It is, however, a way to prepare the individual to receive divine love. The question posed in Sacred Scripture as to how we shall love God whom we have not seen when we do not love our neighbor whom we see, has been repeated by every important spiritual writer since New Testament times. Spirituality and prayer, however much they invite us to solitude and silence, can only grow and develop toward divine love in the one who is open, giving, and vulnerable. These qualities often lead to pain. Christ's last discourse to His disciples makes clear that in a divine way He thought it better to love and lose than not to love at all.

MIDLIFE

Generativity or stagnation were the crucial alternatives offered to those in midlife, according to Erik Erikson. He implies wisely that even those who had some developmental failures in the past could adjust, make up, and become productive in some real way. He also clearly affirmed that religious celibacy could be just as creative as the more typical form of generativity which is begetting and propagating the next generation to take over as one passes on in life.[22]

As we have already mentioned, several recent works, such as Levinson's, have focused attention on midlife. Rather than reviewing this study, which we strongly recommend to those interested in midlife, we shall try to summarize the insights of *Season's of a Man's Life* which are pertinent to an understanding of spiritual development.

Time to Choose

Levinson's study indicates that the task of early midlife is to make choices which are related to the rest of one's life. These choices are made tentatively at first in the midtwenties; after gathering new information and developing a more mature judgment, the individual reiterates or perhaps changes the choices in the early thirties. Levinson found that the men whom he studied had developed a dream or idealized conception of life in late adolescence and early adult life. Unreal expectations had to be resolved in the transitional stage of their thirties. Without such a resolution, the individual would live a half-life of unreality and disappointment leading to many negative personality traits, including unproductive habits, stagnation and selling out to life, or even erratic behavior, like addiction or sexual deviations. Although Erikson and Levinson were approaching the same subject with a different methodology, both affirmed the need for the individual to choose for oneself in order to achieve a healthy adjustment.

Choice is of utmost importance for spiritual growth. Only when religion becomes fanaticism or sublimation to a dangerous degree is it so compelling that one does not need to make a choice. Apart from fanatical religion, external religious behavior and inner spiritual endeavors are matters of deliberation and choice. It is useless to attempt to understand genuine religion and spirituality from the myopic viewpoint of a pure psychodynamics of need and drive. Such an approach ignores the great army of saints, mystics, and religious leaders who march through human history. They were men and women of choice. They chose to believe what they could not see and to pursue an ideal which had nothing to do with unresolved childhood needs. Often they did this at the cost of their own lives.

No modern writer in the field of psychology and religion has expressed the need for choice and decision more effectively than Viktor Frankl. His early work, *Man's Search for Meaning*,[23] is written with the passion of one who had survived torture, imprisonment, and the constant threat of arbitrary murder. The experience of life had literally become a nightmare for him. He simply had to choose what attitudes to adopt in the face of a terrible injustice perpetrated by the Nazis. The believer seldom faces such a dramatic challenge. However, the fading dream of adolescence may challenge every possible fiber of choice for the individual. How dramatically is this challenge of choice seen in the Gospels where Christ gradually unveils to His followers the true dimensions of the Kingdom, as well as the awesome dimensions of their inability to live up to the challenge. They must go on, choosing Him, knowing that they will fail and that He will go to death. "Follow Me" gives place to "You will all leave me alone." "Satan has sifted you like wheat" is followed by "I have prayed for you that you shall confirm your brethren." The choice of the Christian literally goes beyond one's own personal strength.

When the choices of life are not faced or made deliberately, the familiar picture of a lukewarm believer begins to emerge in midlife. Faith, while not destroyed, becomes perfunctory in its expression. Perceptible spiritual growth slows down or disappears. However nice the person is, the challenge of Jesus, "I have come to cast fire on the earth," seems unrelated to life.

Time to Settle Down

Levinson calls the next period of life "Settling Down." I think he might have used a better expression, one less suggestive of lethargy, but his description of this stage of life is more encouraging. For the maturing person, it is a time characterized by such qualities as stability, sincerity, nobility of purpose, opportunity to express ambition, and even willingness to take risks.

Before looking further into this period, we should consider two other cases which will illustrate the dynamics of this time of life. We will stop to meet Father Carl and Helene whose lives exemplify the difficulties and triumphs of those who try to settle down in turbulent times.

FATHER CARL'S STORY

Father Carl came from a strong, well-ordered, German-American home in the plains of the Midwest. His parents were farmers who raised a large family with the absolute conviction of those who have no time for questions amid the struggle to survive. Early in life he went to the seminary of an active religious community and was ordained almost without incident. He obtained a master's degree in music from a secular university and enjoyed the opportunity to see a bit of the world outside the Church. Carl was pleased to return to the college of his order and enjoyed teaching. In fact he enjoyed everything in life. He was soon a very young superior and was recognized as a friendly, efficient man who never asked questions. He followed with interest the liturgical movement during the 1950s; the closest he came to ruffling a few feathers was to turn the altar round before it was officially sanctioned.

In the late 1960s while Carl was superior of a large community in the seminary, things began to change. People called him a dictator; conversations stopped when he went by. He saw things moving in a direction of which he did not approve and this led him to do something he had never done before: He bucked the community and was eventually taken out of office. Carl, who had never failed in his life, failed miserably.

He decided to fight back. He objected to every change he could. He was made pastor of a small parish where, thank God, the people loved him. He grew to love them, but it still made him sick to go near his confreres. Carl enjoyed the parish because he could spend a bit more time in prayer and reading. Then one day, some of the young people asked to have a prayer group. At first he was annoyed: "More nonsense. What is the matter with the Mass? Isn't that enough?" Finally he consented and they asked him to come and join the group one evening, explaining that there would be older people present, too. He took that as a challenge.

Carl was pleased being with the young people even though he disliked their music. It was like old times in the seminary, being surrounded by the young. One evening they asked if they might pray over him. It wouldn't hurt to go along. Secretly, Carl was afraid to refuse the request because he liked the group and he needed to be liked. He knelt down and they prayed for a long time over him. Suddenly, he felt his arms go up in the air; he lost control. He started to sing, to speak a kind of song without words. They called it "the gift of speaking in tongues." All the people in the group were overjoyed. Carl had become a charismatic. It was unreal.

He survived that night. The next morning he was embarrassed. He thought it over carefully: Maybe he should not go back . . . what would they think at "headquarters"? "Carl had lost his buttons." But Father Carl went back; he had changed. He didn't become the world's greatest charismatic, but after all the excitement died down, he found that he fitted in very well. He joined a priest's charismatic group. It was great; he was alive again. He took as his motto: "This my son, who was dead, has come back to life" (Lk. 15:24). Carl is now sixty and hopes to stay at his parish and get a compatible assistant who will eventually become pastor. He has softened about things and has been greatly encouraged by the writings of Pope John Paul II. "He speaks my language," Carl says. Sometimes Carl realizes that he has changed. His confreres for the most part don't believe it and still treat him as if he were the old dictator. "So what?" His real community is his parish, his prayer group, and all the friends he has made through this group. Secretly he chuckles to himself and says, "I was dead and have come back to life."

HELENE'S STORY

Helene, now fifty-seven years of age, is the mother of three grown children, all of them married. She is Polish-American and proud of her ancestry. Her father was a moderately successful musician and music teacher, and her mother, who had taught in Poland, tutored when she and her husband came to America after the First World War. Helene married a young man of eastern European background who was study-ing law. He was never admitted to the bar. When their oldest child was ten, he announced to Helene that he was leaving her. She loved her husband and was devastated. He paid child support sporadically until his youngest child was eighteen. Helene was horrified to learn that while he was still living with her, he had been carrying on an affair.

Since the day her husband left, Helene has clung to her family and to God. Always a deeply religious person, she took up the practice of spirit-ual reading, especially St. Teresa of Avila. Her mother looked after the children and Helene became an executive secretary.

She felt very lonely at first, but gradually expanded her horizons by reading and occasional short trips with her children, and deepened her spiritual life. Although one or two very fine men were interested in her, Helene resolved never to remarry because of her religious conviction against divorce. She also admits that one marriage was enough.

She found it hard to let her children go, even though she was deter-mined to do so. It is a great burden to her now that only one of the three children is a practicing Catholic. About four years ago, Helene became involved in an organization called Separated and Divorced Catholics which tries to help people with issues and problems they face. She was initially reluctant to join the group because she had long since settled these issues for herself. She does not see her life as a tragedy but as a struggle in which God has helped her. She has tried to forgive her husband who has led a miserable and unhappy life and at times even come to her for help. Separated and Divorced Catholics opened a new vista for Helene. While not active in the social aspects of the organiza-tion, she has helped a steady stream of recently divorced men and women in their adjustment and in keeping their faith alive in times of trial. As Helene has worked with these people, her spiritual life has grown more and more. This gives her a great deal of peace and joy.

The Whiteheads, relating Levinson's view with some basic religious values, identify three areas of challenge in midlife. Again, their observa-tions are perceptive enough to merit extensive quotation:

> Psychologically the mid-years are marked by the dominance of three interwoven themes: personal power, care, and interiority.
> *Personal Power.* The middle-aged person wants to be, needs to be, effective in the tasks that define her or his work. Competence and experience combine to place the middle-aged in positions of authority. The desire for responsibility, willingness to assume leadership, an ability to take control are important motivating factors in middle age.

They create channels through which one's personal power is both manifested and put in the service of a larger social world.

Care. The middle-aged person wants to be, needs to be, responsible for others. The mature person "needs to be needed." Much of the competence and power of the middle-aged is focused in nurturance—of one's children, of younger colleagues, of clients, of an institution or project or plan. The commitments of the middle-aged often make altruism, the unselfish service of the welfare of others, a necessity. Their psychological resources make such generous concern a real possibility.

Interiority. The outward movement of expanding responsibility in the mid-years is accompanied by a movement within. There is a heightened sensitivity to the self and an increasing focus on inner needs. For some this new introversion is frightening. It is experienced as "middle-aged depression," and attempts are made to avoid it. Others welcome it as a new, or reawakened, experience of their interior life.[24]

It will be noted that with the introduction of the concept of interiority, the Whiteheads see the growth of the symbolic and the interior as an integral part of Christian existence by midlife. Indeed, this growth in interiority may represent for many their first effective spiritual awakening. For some it may be a renaissance, which is not all that rare an occurrence. Others, for whom interiority has been a goal for some time, may suddenly find this new growth easier and more spontaneous, but it may upset the equilibrium of their lives which had previously been given over to good works. This is true in the case of Helene. It might seem at first that she has merely come on some fortune; that is, as the saying goes, "God gave her a break." But in reality, her perseverance in her own commitment and the operation of grace have brought her to a new and more peaceful level of development.

For others growth in interiority may be a disturbing experience, a time of darkness. Certain people will consider it the Dark Night of the Senses, that period of purification which occurs between the end of the first or purgative way and the beginning of illumination. "Yet was I sore adread/ Lest, having Him, I must have naught beside," writes Francis Thompson in "The Hound of Heaven," summing up the experience of most persons who, in middle age, reach a point where they are beyond what Ernest Becker has termed "the denial of death."[25]

Father Carl is an example of this type of person. Looking back on his experience at the end of his seminary career, he realizes that his anger covered up a great deal of hurt and darkness. He realizes that the darkness stripped him of complacency and ambition and an overly institutionalized spirituality. He sees his entrance into the charismatic renewal as a direct gift of God. He had never before thought about things in that perspective.

Sister Marie also went through a similar darkness, but she did not have so much to lose. Carl, the disciple of God as True, experienced more pain and suffering than Marie, who is a disciple of the Good.

We should also note that Father John went through a period of real darkness as his marriage lost its dreamlike quality. He is beginning to recover his balance and his faith and it is hoped that he will find meaning in the difficult role of the dispensed priest who wishes to be active in parish life. Such a role has real spiritual possibilities. It may, however, generate some conflicts with Liz, his wife, who may not be prepared to enter into this kind of relationship with the Church.

From midlife on, existence takes on a greater sense of purpose. The realization that life is a journey becomes more vivid and at a certain point we understand that we could not possibly live to twice our present age. Mentors and teachers of the older generation begin to die or become incapacitated. Others, often the most revered, pass into a state of interiority; for them many of the concerns of worldly life lose their urgency and, like Henoch, they are not seen again among people.

If interiority is not accepted as a component of middle life—and it must be accepted even though the invitation arrives spontaneously—there appears the calamity of the aging adolescent. At times such a person seems to be mildly laughable, but a smile often hides a profound discomfort: those of us in our late forties know that we have like tendencies. The aging adolescent who runs away from midlife is not someone who necessarily relates well to the young. In fact the young often intuitively suspect such people of being competitve with them. Rather, the aging adolescent rejects interiority and denies the coming of old age by pathetic subterfuge. Such persons frequently are plagued with desperate sexual obsessions which represent symbolically the struggle not to grow old. They try to incorporate some of the vitality of the young and attempt to live again or for the first time what Kierkegaard calls the "dream of youth." Youth, as he points out, is a time of blossoming for the young, but its expression is to be abhorred in the grown man or woman.[26]

Late Midlife and Old Age

As midlife moves into the fifties, a real sense of bodily decline begins, as others begin to take one's place, first in physical and later in mental activities, the great question of life is raised: "Do I accept myself as I truly am?" Levinson, writing from a secular perspective, affirms that the new life situation must be established with a kind of secular wisdom parallel to what St. Ignatius calls "spiritual indifference." If the person clings to an idealized youth, the result will be bitterness, negativism, and overdependency on others. Erikson does not hesitate to call the critical conflict at the end of life "Ego integrity vs. despair." Both Levinson and Erikson suggest that as the first obvious signs of old age become manifest, the individual has need of "meditation" to resolve the basic conflicts of life and prepare for death. Those who fail to do this may hasten their own deaths and may actually come to die of life. We all know people in situations similar to those of Carl and Helene who have not been able to make the adjustment that they have made.

The person who has been leading a spiritual life, or who at least begins to follow such a path in midlife, that is, the way of interiority and meditation, will spontaneously develop new and alternate activities to replace those which are no longer appropriate. The jogger, for example, may learn to stroll; the avid television viewer may learn to enjoy the art of reading once again. Many may learn to slow the pace of life so as to derive more meaning from few events. Sometimes the person capable of genuine spiritual growth is not religious in the conventional sense. God works in mysterious ways and He is not limited even by His own objective order of salvation described in the first chapter. Like the son in the parable who said that he would not serve and did anyway, there are many who are disciples of the Incarnate Word without such an acknowledgement. On the other hand, some who have been conventional Catholics, even conventional disciples (one of those temporary accommodations which is ultimately a contradiction), begin to retreat at this dark juncture in life. They withdraw into smallness of mind and are filled with concern about their physical health or comfort; they lose the harvest of years of service because they simply stopped giving long ago. "Fear not to die, fear not to have lived," is Newman's warning to these people.

We can soften the dichotomy between the wise and the despairing by mentioning those in the middle; surely that is where most sincere people end up. They grudgingly surrender the controls, sadly accept their physical handicaps, and reluctantly pass the baton to the next runner who may scarcely look back over his shoulder as he accepts it. This state between wisdom and despair is like the eschatological state between Heaven and Hell which, as you will remember, is called Purgatory. This mysterious word applies not only to a period of transition after death, but also to earthly existence where growth is still possible. Many Christians have trouble with the concept of Purgatory because they fail to understand its meaning in terms of spiritual growth. The very people who recognize the need for healing in their own spiritual lives have unfortunately never been taught that that is what Purgatory is.

In the last years of a long and active life, Frank Sheed found the doctrine of Purgatory meaningful and necessary. He wrote: "I can't conceive a future life without a possibility of cleansing (which is what the word Purgatory means)—not because I deserve it but because I need it. The thought of entering the presence of the all-pure God as the spotted object that I am revolts me. . . . My will needs straightening; and that cannot be done without pain—not penal pain, pain in the sheer forcing of the will from habits grown into second nature. Here or hereafter, with God's aid I must will my own will straight. He will help me to do it. But He won't do it for me."[27]

St. Catherine of Genoa had the great insight that Purgatory begins in this life and continues into the next only if it is necessary for the final preparation of the individual. As a way of purification, she suggests a total acceptance of the divine will in all its manifestations—physical, psychological, and spiritual. She teaches that this is the road out of the conflict of life and refers to it as the doctrine of Pure Love. Insofar as one succeeds in the total acceptance of life, a beautiful last phase of life may emerge. It may continue for several decades. Contemplative prayer (if not contemplation, strictly speaking) may begin to flow through the individual's mind and being "like shining from shook foil . . . like the ooze of oil crushed," to borrow Hopkins's evocative phrasing. The poet concludes "God's Grandeur" with a description of the Spirit's presence: ". . . the Holy Ghost over the bent/World broods with warm breast and with ah! bright wings."

Instead of competing with the young, one supports them, equally content whether this support is appreciated, taken for granted, or ignored. The experience of futility and failure which comes to almost all older people is now transformed into the humble prayer of St. Francis, "Let us begin now." One learns to accept one's shortcomings. How deeply moving it was for me once to confess to an old sister in the missions my feelings of hypocrisy (a guilt shared by all whose vocation is to preach holiness beyond their own ability). Her reply was, "O come on, Father, I've been a fraud for years." This type of spiritual realism characterized one who had grown old, yet remained genuinely young at heart. This sister was in fact just beginning a new career—her fourth—at the age of seventy-six.

STAGES OF LIFE AND INDIVIDUAL DIFFERENCES

We should reemphasize at this point the danger of losing sight of the individual when employing any set of classifications, be they static or developmental. There are unique things in every life and personality. Though called by the same Master to the same earthly fate and heavenly destiny, Sts. Peter and Paul lived lives and had traits and abilities which were totally different. They clashed on weighty matters and no doubt caused each other pain. Every life is different; as the richness and fullness of life varies according to individual capacity, so will its harvest be correspondingly bitter or sweet. At the end of life, hidden things will be revealed, decisions made in the darkness of the soul will be seen in the light of day, and things said in the secret places of the inner person will be preached from the housetops. St. Teresa of Avila once said that the road to Heaven is heavenly. One might add that the road to Hell is infernal, and the road to Purgatory, conflicted and painful. Perhaps what makes differences so profound among human beings and so minimal among animals is the human capacity to evaluate and shape events and experiences. Decision, freedom, choice—call it what you will—is what directs our travels on the journey of life. Some examples from recent history may prove helpful.

The same conflict precipitated by changes and pressures outside the control of any single individual or nation altered the lives and brought about the early deaths of St. Maximilian Kolbe and his tormentor, Heinrich Himmler. For one it brought eternal life and canonization, and for the other death and condemnation. The same conflagration immolated Edith Stein and Adolf Hitler. As far as the human mind can judge these things, for one it was Heaven, for the other it was Hell..For many who survived, captives and captors, victims and their criminal persecutors, life is still a purgatory. And where will it end now that time has blurred the memories, healed the wounds but not the scars, and hidden the crimes away? As it is in all human things, the question is: What did the survivors choose at any given moment? Yet, it was a series of choices made throughout a whole lifetime, a series of *now* moments that shaped the lives of each of these people. Every one of them had an opportunity to reverse the course of action and reshape their lives. It was possible for St. Maximilian Kolbe or for Hitler to take another road at one of the many crossroads on their journey of life.

Two examples from their lives will illustrate the power of decision very directly. Albert Speer, Hitler's architect, mentions that only once before the collapse of the Third Reich had he seen Hitler deeply disturbed. In 1935 the Führer had what was supposed to have been a perfunctory meeting with the intransigent anti-Nazi Archbishop of Munich, Cardinal Faulhaber. The half-hour meeting lasted several hours and Hitler was badly shaken at the end of the interview.[28] Considering the future career of the Cardinal, who was one of Hitler's most outspoken critics in Germany and a staunch defender of the Jews to the end, it is reasonable to assume that Faulhaber pointed out to Hitler the spiritual implications of the road he was on. Hitler never arrested Faulhaber for going so far as to have the Star of David with the yellow armband placed on the statues of Christ and Mary in the churches of his diocese. But he did reject the call to conversion. There was still a choice for Hitler in 1935. On the other hand, Maximilian Kolbe, like every other Polish priest in the concentration camp, had freedom and a quisling job awaiting him in occupied Poland for nothing more than his signature on a document denouncing the Catholic Church. The possibility of a different choice was present even as he starved to death in the hunger bunker. But like every other Polish priest in the camps, he chose to refuse compromise. Both Hitler and Kolbe were free in the *now* moment. Both men were drawn on by the series of life decisions they had made in the past. Both continued to be what they had seen. But, as Viktor Frankl points out (having seen life from the same camp as Kolbe), one was free to make of the existential moment whatever one willed.

Chapter 4

Development:
Religious and Spiritual

Having sketched with large strokes the stages of human development as it occurs in industrialized cultures (there will be some differences in agrarian societies), we can now apply the ideas of spiritual development to this framework. A human being can grow spiritually in any culture, but as the shape of an armature determines the proportions of a clay statue, so do cultural factors affect the opportunities for spiritual growth as well as the expression of that growth.

Religious Development

There are at least two ways we can look at spiritual growth. The first is from the viewpoint of the individual, his or her needs and responses; the second way is to examine the effect of grace on his or her life and functioning. Using a somewhat arbitrary designation, we shall call the first way "religious development," and the second "spiritual development."

RELIGION OF CHILDHOOD

Religious development, which has been considered by many students of human behavior, is simply the study of the responses of individuals to what they believe represents the Divine Being. Although his scheme for understanding religious development is not the most precisely articulated, von Hügel's outline of religious development[1] is brilliant, concise, and best suited to our present purposes. In presenting this scheme, I should point out that I have borrowed ideas from Allport, Clarke, Babin, and others, in order to flesh out von Hügel's structure.[2] It should also be noted that we are not specifically tracing the development of moral and ethical concepts here; they will be alluded to at a later time.

The religion of childhood, according to von Hügel, is emotional since the child thinks with his or her emotions. The child's psychic life is vital, pragmatic, and summed up by emotions which, although varied, are unitary throughout childhood. The term "unitary" indicates that only one emotion fills the child's consciousness at a time. As Freud observes, the salient underlying emotion of human beings is anxiety, or a deep fear of meaninglessness and oblivion which reaches into the depths of one's being. This is not how things were meant to be, but how they are. No doubt it is this fear which occasions the first great conflict Erikson describes, viz., trust versus mistrust. A powerful image of this fear is our first parents standing in terror before the gates of their lost paradise, longing for a forgotten peace and fearing what life might bring in the uncertain future.

Religion as we know it is born psychologically in the life of the child as he or she learns that there are forces at work in life which are simply beyond the individual's control. Jung perceived that the child who is not equipped to deal in a religious way with this elemental fear and with the hopes and aspirations it elicits, will suffer neurotic conflicts. They will arise from the inability to express and cope with religious aspirations. Not until the end of his life, apparently, did Jung come to believe that there was an objective reality corresponding to these needs, but even before that time he had realized the individual's profound need to learn ways of religious expression.[3]

Religion as it is practiced by children (and by many adults whose religion remains at a child's level of development) is a matter of attempting to control or manipulate the Divine Being by prayer, supplication, and good works. Religious education can and should form the image of God with positive, theologically well-informed emotions and ideas. The child's own image of God, however, will be most profoundly affected by general experience of life, parents, home, siblings, teachers, and church, if he or she belongs to one. For this reason, the most valuable work on behalf of children is to give them a positive and well defined set of images of all the persons included in their perception of the divine world—Christ, the Virgin Mother, the saints, etc. But no matter how positively the images are presented, the religious experience, like an interpersonal relationship, will still be one of *quid pro quo*, i.e., of doing nice things in order to receive nice things in return. In this way the doer of good works is born: the builder of temples, hospitals, and schools. The entire external fabric of religion is founded upon this impulse; it reaches from St. Peter's Basilica to the Taj Mahal, from Boys' Town to Care packages. It may or may not be uplifted by the deeper spiritual images of adult development. St. Edmund of Canterbury and Brother Elias of Assisi both built beautiful churches. The former built out of his holiness and love of God, whereas the latter built out of a desire to buy God off. One died a saint and the other an apostate.

RELIGION OF ADOLESCENCE

At the end of childhood the child develops an ability for abstract reasoning. Before this time, God is an old man with a white beard to most children of the Western world. But suddenly God can be conceptualized as a spirit, a being who cannot be seen and who is everywhere. Religious adolescence has begun. This ability to think of God in abstract terms corresponds to theological speculation at the age of eleven or twelve. It may plunge the teenager into doubt or even total unbelief. The adolescent who is beset by behavioral problems or psychological conflicts may exhibit an almost violent rejection of God and of many socially connected attitudes. Devout people tend to see this conflict as the work of the devil and as the sinister omen of an evil end; in the Providence of God, however, this conflict may set the stage for a deep-felt adolescent conversion later on. There is no more powerful example of such a conflict than the incident in the fourth book of the *Confessions,* where the teenage Augustine almost deprives his dying friend of the grace of Baptism and salvation. For the remainder of his life, the man who later became the Doctor of Grace frequently pondered this incident of his adolescence as a motive for further repentance and gratitude to God.

The religion of adolescence is intellectual and speculative, as is the entire mental life of the adolescent who has been encouraged to develop and is not thwarted by infantilizing attitudes at home or by a hedonistic culture. Although the emotions are still very strong, the growing youngster increasingly uses the mind rather than the emotions to make sense out of life.

Religious questions may enhance faith in certain individuals so that the teenager will become intensely involved in Scriptural studies and things ecclesiastical. Or he or she may become very philosophical and question everything. Is there a God and what is He like? Is Jesus Christ God? If so, how? And thus comes into being a theologian or a philosopher or, at least, one who may eventually become a follower of these two great adult pursuits. Yet there are often very good students of philosophy and theology who never get any further emotionally. The questions of youth and its intense commitments have filled obvious personal needs in the teenage years and early twenties. Unless the religions of young people mature and move on, they become stale, pedantic, and petulant in later life.

RELIGION OF MATURITY

Only an adult commitment to faith, which implies the death of self, can deliver the thinker so that he or she can become a lover of truth. Plato observed long ago that one can become a true philosopher (a lover of truth, not just a student of ideas) only if one dies to oneself. An example may illustrate this.

Cardinal Newman and George Tyrrell grew up in much the same circumstances, had magnificent educations which honed their brilliant adolescent minds into instruments of great power and agility. Both suffered from associates who did not and at times could not understand them. Both were very sensitive and were bruised by life. Both were eminently sincere. One died a great apologist, leaving behind a legacy which bears more fruit as the years go on. As his friend von Hügel points out, Tyrrell died a bitter man, a tragic example of the perennial conflict of the adult adolescent who cannot make the leap to believe and love; thus he lived a life of unresolved conflict and rage.[4] Let Newman explain the difference between the two attitudes:

> Faith is, in its very nature, the acceptance of what our reason cannot reach, simply and absolutely upon testimony.
> There is, of course, a multitude of cases in which we allowably and rightly accept statements as true, partly on reason, and partly on testimony. We supplement the information of others by our own knowledge, by our own judgment of probabilities; and, if it be very strange and extravagant, we suspend our assent. This is undeniable; still, after all, there are truths which are incapable of reaching us except on testimony, and there is testimony which, by and in itself, has an imperative claim on our acceptance.
> As regards Revealed Truth, it is not Rationalism to set about to ascertain, by the exercise of reason, what things are attainable by reason, and what are not; nor, in the absence of an express Revelation, to inquire into the truths of Religion, as they come to us by nature; nor to determine what proofs are necessary for the acceptance of a Revelation, if it be given; nor to reject a Revelation on the plea of insufficient proof; nor, after recognizing it as divine, to investigate the meaning of its declarations, and to interpret its language; nor to use its doctrines, as far as they can be fairly used, in inquiring into its divinity; nor to compare and connect them with our previous knowledge, with a view of making them parts of a whole; nor to bring them into dependence on each other, to trace their mutual relations, and to pursue them to their legitimate issues. This is not Rationalism; but it is Rationalism to accept the Revelation, and then to explain it away; to speak of it as the

Word of God, and to treat it as the word of man; to refuse to let it speak for itself; to claim to be told the why and the how of God's dealings with us, as therein described, and to assign to Him a motive and a scope of our own; to stumble at the partial knowledge which He may give us of them; to put aside what is obscure, as if it had not been said at all; to accept one half of what has been told us, and not the other half; to assume that the contents of Revelation are also its proof; to frame some gratuitous hypothesis about them, and then to garble, gloss and colour them, to trim, clip, and pare away, and twist them, in order to bring them into conformity with the idea to which we have subjected them.

The Rationalist makes himself his own centre, not his Maker; he does not go to God, but he implies that God must come to him.[5]

The difference between Newman and Tyrrell is presumably the giant step to mature religion, the transcendence of self or, if one prefers, the death of self. The latter phrase frightens many and it is not currently in vogue, but it comes from the words of Christ Himself. The childish impulse to control God by prayer and works and the attempt of the adolescent mind to control Him by speculation and understanding must come to an end. The fundamental anxiety expressed by these two attitudes must be rooted out. The energy expended in the emotional need to control God must now be transformed into trust; the intellectual obsession with reducing God to one's categories of thought must now give way to the act of faith. These two changes constitute a real *metanoia,* i.e., a basic change of attitude made possible by grace. The *metanoia* takes place on two levels: that of the heart and that of the head. Neither faith nor trust destroys the mental process nor the emotional dynamism, but each directs these primary human powers away from their impulse to dominate God. The individual surrenders to grace, an act which is impossible without direct divine assistance because it goes completely contrary to the human personality. "No one can say that Jesus is Lord except in the Holy Spirit" (1 Cor. 12:3). Faith and hope are theological virtues; they are not self-given. They do not originate from the being of the individual. They are gifts and like all gifts must be received. They prepare the way for an even greater gift of charity or love. They make an effective termination of self-centered aspects of childhood or adolescent religion, and prepare the way for contemplation, or listening to God.

Faith and hope do require an inner act of the will. This is a choice on the part of the individual to step beyond the narrow confines of personal security. In their mature form, faith and trust (which is ultimate hope) imply a death of the child and adolescent self. The impulse to do good works or to speculate about the divine does not come to an end. It is transformed so that the builder of temples and the writer of books may say with St. Thomas, "Nothing but Thee," or with St. Teresa, "God Alone!" Everyone from Plato to Maslow has recognized the necessity to transcend the self. Perhaps no one has pointed out the next step better than Francis Thompson in whom child and adolescent struggled so hard to stay alive. The poet thus describes the transformation of self:

> *Pierce thy heart to find the key;*
> *With Thee take*
> *Only what none else would keep;*
> *Learn to dream when thou dost wake,*
> *Learn to wake when thou dost sleep;*
> *Learn to water joy with tears,*
> *Learn from fears to vanquish fears,*
> *To hope, for thou dar'st not despair,*
> *Exult, for that thou dar'st not grieve;*
> *Plough thou the rock until it bear;*
> *Know, for thou else couldst not believe;*
> *Lost, that the lost thou may'st receive;*
> *Die, for none other way canst live*
> *When earth and heaven lay down their veil,*
> *And that apocalypse turns thee pale;*
> *When thy seeing blindeth thee*
> *To what thy fellow-mortals see;*
> *When their sight to thee is sightless;*
> *Their living, death; their light, most lightless;*
> *Search no more. . . .*[6]

Spiritual Development

Having acknowledged the definition of spiritual development which takes into account the action of grace and the theological virtues of faith, hope, and love, we may properly move on to consider this development. The great leap of faith and trust which normally cannot take place before the end of adolescence (and may occur much later in life) ushers in mature spiritual life. One may be spiritually awakened before this time, but, if so, care should be taken that the young person not make apparently final choices prematurely. Fears and speculations may be driven underground only to resurface in much more dangerous forms later in life. The profound alienation felt by many Christians (including clergy and religious) in the post-Vatican II era may be traced partly to this premature choice and to an artificial, although sincere, commitment at too young an age to a life of faith. Premature vocational recruitment and unqualified commitment to a static view of spiritual progress produced at least one entire generation of people who died too early to themselves. Afterward they were left to cope with adolescent religious conflicts and doubts. When this state of affairs is coupled with unrealistic attitudes toward sexuality, a good deal of the religious alienation of the 1970s begins to make sense.

The spiritual life strictly so-called substantively begins for the Christian with a series of decisions to accept the grace of Christ, specifically the theological virtues. The effective acceptance of charity is still in the future, but mature faith is taking hold. The precise Christian dimensions of this faith, from the point of view of Scripture and theology, may be found in Rudolf Schnackenburg's illuminating little book, *Belief in the New Testament.*[7] The spiritual life, however, has often begun in its adoptive phase, or advent, much earlier in life. Theologically, the radical beginning for the Christian is the reception of Baptism and incorporation into Christ. The spiritual life, as von Balthasar points out so well, is essentially the life of Christ in the adopted children of God and it begins when one becomes a member of Christ.[8] We have already discussed the interesting experience of those who are touched by Christ's grace and grow in holiness outside the visible Church and the sacramental system. At some time in childhood or adolescence, or occasionally much later, the reality of grace begins to break through to the conscious mind of the individual in a religious experience. This event, known psychologically as an *awakening,* marks the beginning of the conscious spiritual life. The new rite of the adult reception of Baptism is an effective liturgical effort to bring together these two events: sacramental incorporation into Christ and the growing psychological commitment to the practice of the theological and moral virtues.

The Three Ways

The following description of the teaching on the three ways (purgation, illumination, and union) highlights experiential aspects of the theory; the psychological explanation will be considered in Part II. The reader will not find all these details in any particular summary, but they are reflected in various presentations of this common experience over the centuries. It should be emphasized that the focus of our attention is on the psychological aspects of this experience. We present the phenomenological description first, stressing events rather than causes. Many young readers are unfamiliar with the three ways; older readers may be helped by a summary of what is said to happen on a typical journey.

Awakening

Except for those who have always lived a devout life in highly religious circumstances, most people undergo an *awakening,* i.e., one or a series of memorable experiences of the reality of the intangible. The experience may be consoling or threatening, or both. It often occurs in circumstances which appear commonplace: a meeting with a stranger, a wedding, a funeral, a visit to a church or hospital, or to the sea. Aspects of reality which have not been seen previously now leap into prominence. It may be a very intimate awareness of the Father or the Son or the Holy Spirit as a personal presence, or it may be a sudden, frightening encounter with the self.

The reality of this experience is clear to the individual who is likewise aware that it differs from auto-suggestion or poetic inspiration. In the following quotation, Karl Rahner gives his interpretation of the experience of St. Ignatius, as if the saint were writing today:

> I truly encountered God, the living and true God, who merits this name which supersedes all other names. Whether such an experience is mystical or not is irrelevant here; how it is at all possible to make such an experience comprehensible using human concepts is for your theologians to speculate. . . . My experience naturally had a history of its own. It began in a small and undramatic way; I related it and wrote about it in a manner that now seems touchingly childlike even to me and allows the true meaning to be seen only indirectly and from afar. But one thing is sure: after Manresa, from then on, I knew the inscrutable incomprehensibility of God ever more intensely, ever more purely. . . .
>
> God himself: I knew God himself, not simply human words describing Him. I knew God and the freedom which is an integral part of him and which can only be known through him and not as the sum total of finite realities and calculations about them.[9]

The awakening is also often an experience of light and darkness, of conflict and contrast. One is pulled in both directions, lifted up and cast down. A young man in prison, turning from atheism as the apparent result of reading Maritain and Merton, wrote me the following letter:

> I suppose that it is basic human nature to believe in a metaphysical being. I am sure everyone has this need to believe. I myself have tried and succeeded in the past in suppressing this need. At one time I was almost completely caught up in the atheistic point of view. Now, with the books I am reading, especially *The Seven-Storey Mountain,* this need is again emerging. This one book is like a catalyst, stimulating my thought and contemplation of my own shaky beliefs and concepts. It's

kind of hard to explain. It's like sucking soda through a straw. The soda comes up and it is refreshing, but once you release the pressure, the soda just sinks back into the depths of the bottle. This is the best way to describe how I feel. At certain times I get into deep thought and it is refreshing, but then I let myself sink back into the depths of the basic me, and then all the gains I had made seem to be lost until the next time this feeling comes upon me. It happens in periods, but they don't last. They come and stay for a while and I am a changed person, but I am just not able to make them a part of the permanent me! Well, I will keep on trying to pursue it and let's hope that eventually I will be able to grasp permanently this enlightenment which part of me wants and part of me rejects.

How similar is the experience of this imprisoned young man to that of Augustine in acquiring knowledge of the heights and depths:

> This, then, O God, was the beginning in which You created Heaven and Earth: marvellously speaking and marvellously creating in Your Word, Who is Your Son and Your Strength and Your Wisdom and Your Truth. What is that light which shines upon me but not continuously, and strikes upon my heart with no wounding? I draw back in terror: I am on fire with longing: terror insofar as I am different from it, longing in the degree of my likeness to it. It is Wisdom, Wisdom itself, which in those moments shines upon me, clearing through my cloud. And the cloud returns to wrap me round once more as my strength is beaten down under its darkness and the weight of my sins; for my strength is weakened through poverty, so that I can no longer support my good, until Thou, Lord, who art merciful to my iniquities, shalt likewise heal my weakness: redeeming my life from corruption and crowning me with pity and compassion, and filling my desire with good things; my youth shall be renewed like the eagle's. For we are saved by hope and we wait with patience for Thy promises.[10]

To the degree that a person responds to the awakening—for response is always necessary—life will be changed. One person may turn away and the experience of grace will pursue him—to borrow Francis Thompson's expression—as he flees "down the nights and down the days" until he is caught. Another person may turn away and the invitation will not be extended again, as we have seen in the case of Bertrand Russell. Yet another will be haunted by it, as James Joyce was, never being quite able to stifle the call, yet never really answering it. Still others will respond totally like St. Francis. On the basis of the single experience at San Damiano, Thomas of Celano could say that Francis had become a different man.[11]

Two of the people described so far provide us with good examples of a spiritual awakening. Jerry's case is the most typical. Until the time his girlfriend confronted him, he had simply been a religious person, that is, someone with a religious intuition. Religion affected his interests but not his moral behavior or his important convictions. The revelation of his own moral weakness and narcissism was the opportunity for him to become a person in touch with the spiritual element in his life. He was literally awakened.

Helene, on the other hand, had always been a committed Christian. Her husband's desertion made her realize she needed a deeper spiritual life. It was, indeed, a second awakening. This is not unusual. Father Carl's experience, a fresh awakening, or "renewal" as it is often called, is similar. In such cases, it is my impression that the individual quickly repeats the stages previously traversed in the spiritual journey, and then continues on, facing new tasks which had awaited fulfillment when the person was, so to speak, bogged down.

The awakening of one person may radically affect the lives of others, as with the founders of religious institutes, or with Catherine of Genoa and Catherine of Siena who brought about great changes in the Church while remaining members of the laity. Another person answering it may be so private as to be known only after death. An example of the latter type is Dag Hammarskjold whose reminiscences in diary form were never intended for publication.[12]

Despite the particular circumstances, one fact is certain: When the awakening occurs in a person of real depth and dimension, and it is accepted or rejected, that person will never be the same again.

First Stage—Purgation

It may require years for an awakening to "take hold" and it may reoccur frequently. When at last it is accepted, the individual must begin to put his or her life into some relationship with that call. The need for reordering and reevaluating life has been seen in Jerry's case. It was a struggle to change.

Leon's Story

Perhaps another personal history will illustrate purgation even more sharply. Leon had grown up in a large Franco-American family, and had several brothers and sisters. Early in life he was aware of homosexual attractions. In his little New England town he was unable to express these to anyone.

When he left there for a large state college, he actively sought out and immediately became involved in the "gay scene." He felt few inhibitions and rationalized these by saying, "God made me this way and He must want me to enjoy it." Leon did just that. He saw no need to share his lifestyle with his family. "It was not their business," he reasoned, "and they would not understand."

Leon found an excellent job after graduation and moved to a large city with a very open homosexual community. He was promiscuous with little regret, always hoping eventually to settle down with a permanent partner. Around the age of thirty, Leon started to become depressed. His life was going nowhere. One day the thought came to him suddenly: "It is because my life is messed up and I am separated from God."

Leon joined the Charismatic Renewal and takes it very seriously. In less than a year he has changed sufficiently so that he hopes he may one day marry and have a family. Leon also belongs to a prayer group of other religiously motivated people trying to overcome homosexual behavior. He admits that although nights can be lonely and difficult, his renewed faith and life of prayer sustain him very well.

An experience like Leon's, which goes far beyond conventional religious practice, may appear quite awesome to some people. The call to conversion at times causes grief and bitterness. Many will ask Thompson's question: "Must thy harvest-fields be dunged with rotten death? . . . Must Thou char the wood ere Thou canst limn with it?" Others run on and begin the task of change with great enthusiasm only to discover later that it will not always be so easy. Augustine's response to the words in the Epistle to the Romans—"I read no further. I had no need"—is related to the fact that he had already lived through much of the conflict and continued to struggle after the moment of "triumphant exultation."

Perhaps for the individual who comes to know God as person, the challenge is best summed up in the words of Christ to the disciples: "Follow Me." The call of Abraham and of Moses, of Joan of Arc and of de Foucauld, may have been more dramatic but certainly was not more imperative than that given to most people. God does not moderate His voice; we simply choose at times to be deaf.

There are several responses which can be considered in some chronological sequence. As we noted above, there is no single life map for this journey and one phase begins while another is still going on. The steps of the first, or purgative, way are basically integrating. The individual brings his or her external behavior, activities, attitudes, and desires into increasing agreement with what he or she believes and accepts as reality. For the Christian, the best guide in this pursuit is the Sermon on the Mount. If he or she can focus on that teaching, which summarizes "The Way," he or she will inevitably grow.

Moral Integration, Belief, Trust

Integration requires the renunciation of serious sin, then of all deliberate sin, and finally the confrontation of unseen omissions and responsibilities. This last consideration is so vast and appalling that many sincere Christians never manage to face up to the sins of omission and remain pious but half-hearted in their efforts toward perfection. After coping with omissions, the individual must struggle against immature attitudes and imperfection. The striving for perfection is not nit-picking, but confronts the whole value system which keeps a person from living the Gospel fully. Nit-picking or obsessive-compulsive behavior is an attempt at some kind of external perfection unconsciously masquerading as inner conversion. Despite sincere attempts to become better, we frequently fail to recognize that consistent behavior reflects attitudes and it is these we must change.

Finally, as a person's life slowly comes into greater harmony with the Gospel, he or she comes to realize the need for modification. Such a need is often at odds with all the superficial prattle of the religious marketplace. We must look for ways to minimize the control of certain egocentric aspects of the personality, and liberate the more generous, altruistic, and intuitive impulses of our being. The individual is faced with two selves. The first self is the true child of God gradually emerging in a person's life under the influence of grace and of the infused virtues. This self is ever more open to God's will and must increase. The other self is the egocentric image which can be apparently very devout but which ultimately relates everything, even the divine will, to its own preferences. This other self must decrease. If the realization of the two selves comes in one's twenties, it may precipitate a conflict temporarily incapable of resolution because the personality is still developing and the life dream has yet to be resolved. One is required to grow and decline simultaneously and, seemingly, in the same areas of development. For instance, a person may grow in ability to teach religious education and at the same time decline in concern that this teaching be favorably received by others. By the mid-forties one begins to settle down. It becomes less necessary to compete, win, or be accepted, and the process of mortification involves becoming one's own man (or woman)—to use Levinson's terminology.

The following quotation from Aldous Huxley, a lifelong student of the psychology of spirituality, sheds a good deal of light on that most maligned notion: mortification.

> Mortification or deliberate dying to self is inculcated with an uncompromising firmness in the canonical writings of Christianity, Hindu-

ism, Buddhism and most of the other major and minor religions of the world, and by every theocentric saint and spiritual reformer who has ever lived out and expounded the principles of the Perennial Philosophy. But this "self-naughting" is never (at least by anyone who knows what he is talking about) regarded as an end in itself. It possesses merely an instrumental value, as the indispensable means to something else.

That mortification is the best which results in the elimination of self-will, self-interest, self-centered thinking, wishing and imagining. Extreme physical austerities are not likely to achieve this kind of mortification. But the acceptance of what happens to us (apart, of course, from our own sins) in the course of daily living is likely to achieve this kind of mortification.

In the practice of mortification as in most other fields, advance is along a knife-edge. On one side lurks the Scylla of egocentric austerity, on the other the Charybdis of an uncaring quietism. The holy indifference inculcated by the exponents of the Perennial Philosophy is neither stoicism nor mere passivity. It is rather an active resignation. Self-will is renounced, not that there may be a total holiday from willing, but that the divine will may use the mortified mind and body as its instrument for good.[13]

The end of the purgative way for the Christian is a time of generosity and powerful rejection often bound together. A person relies on a greater life of union with Christ, with increased prayer, reflection, more listening and less manipulation of and speculation about God. Faith and hope mature. Experiential awareness of the life of grace grows in the use of Scripture, liturgy, and the sacraments. Daily prayer and frequent contact with the living Christ of the liturgy begin to transform the individual. A response of generosity and zeal overcome the conflict generated when family and friends no longer understand what one is about. The apostolic call to charity and good works opens up the healthy springs of love and altruism. As St. Vincent de Paul teaches, the love of the poor becomes the medicine of the soul.

Putting all this in abstract theological language, we may say that a person is growing in the life of virtue. The four moral virtues—courage, prudence, temperance, and justice—and the three theological virtues—faith, hope, and charity—all increasingly dominate the individual's behavior under the influence of the Holy Spirit.

Then, suddenly, the individual is terribly vulnerable. Rejection meets his openness. Attempts at fraternity are regarded with suspicion or rejected as patronizing or pathological. Self-disclosure leads to ridicule. The dishonest see him as an easy target and attack. He tries to forgive, but the ominous number 491 (seventy times seven plus one) comes into view. Under the impact of it all, doubts arise. Is it God's will? Is it God at all? Job's comforters suggest, often with good intention, that much of his life of grace is self-love in a devout disguise; that it was not an invitation of Christ but of a counterfeit Jesus. Religious experience recedes into the past. Did it ever happen at all? "Are you the Messiah or shall we look for someone else?"

The First Darkness

The individual now faces the first grave struggle in the spiritual life after the awakening. A decision to cling to God in the darkness is demanded. There is a growing awareness that one simply hasn't the strength to go on: body, self-love, even the soul cry out, "We cannot go on."

In the *Dialogue* of St. Catherine of Genoa, the body and self-love complain to their traveling companion, the soul, in the following tragicomic excerpt. The soul is speaking to self-love:

> *Yet I know that in this world*
> *there is no food that appeals equally to the two*
> *   of us.*
> *We left heaven, where my food is found,*
> *   very far behind.*
> *Will I ever find my way back to it?*
> *The day that we satisfied ourselves with*
> *   worldly pleasures,*
> *God closed those doors to us,*
> *leaving us at the mercy of our appetites.*
> *Confused and virtually desperate, we turn*
> *   to Him now*
> *because of the use we can make of Him*
> *rather than out of pure charity as He would*
> *   rather have us do.*
> *When I consider what I have lost in following you,*
> *I almost despair.*
> *I justly deserve to be despised by God,*
> *by you, by hell, and by the world.*
> *In following you, who I thought could help me*
> *   in my needs,*
> *I have become a thing of this world.*
> *I have never found the peace I sought,*
> *though possessing all that I asked for on earth;*
> *and all your appetites and joys heightened*
> *   my restlessness.*

Still, I persisted in my confusion,
hoping in a worldly future that would satisfy
* my craving.*
In acceding to the desires of the Body, under
* the guise of necessity—*
a notion that led straightaway to that of the
* necessity of the superfluous—*
in a very short time I became enmeshed in sin.
I became arid and heavy, a thing of the earth.
The appetites and food of the Body and of
* Self-Love were mine;*
and you, Self-Love,
had so tightly bound yourself to me and
* the Body*
that I almost suffocated.
In my blindness the only good left to me,
* remorse, did not work in me long.*
I continued to lose myself in things that gave
* me shame,*
and as I moved further and further away from God,
* my unhappiness grew proportionately.*
I sighed with longing, not knowing what it was
* I sought—*
and that was the prompting, the instinct for God,
that was mine by nature.
God, who is all good, does not abandon
* His creatures.*
He often sends them a sign or a word
that, if man pays heed, will help him,
and if he refuses his condition will be worse yet.
Thus, in my ingratitude I deepened my sin,
taking pleasure in it and even boasting of it.
The more grace I received,
the more blinded and desperate I became.
Had God not come to my aid I would have perished.
Wretched me, who is to save me but God alone?

Thus, after allowing the Soul to exhaust itself in a vain quest, God
illumined it. The soul realized its errors, the dangers it had fallen into,
from which God alone could free it. Fully conscious at this point of the
spiritual and bodily death confronting it, and of having become like an
animal willingly led to slaughter, the Soul was overcome with fright.
Turning to God as best it could, it said: "*Domine fac ut videam lumen*

[Grant, O Lord, that I may see the light], so that I may escape the snares of my enemies."[14]

This struggle may go on for months and years. I have chosen arbitrarily to call this experience "the first darkness" (rather than the first dark night). The latter phrase has been somewhat canonized by the writings of St. John of the Cross. When he uses the term, it is to describe an experience which comes later in the spiritual journey, at the end of the illuminative way. In order to avoid confusion, I will refer to this experience which is under discussion at present as the first darkness. It occurs, as is indicated in the *Dialogue* of St. Catherine, at the end of the purgative way.

If one is in a responsible position—clerical, religious, or lay—one is expected to smile. "A sad saint is a sorry saint. Christians always smile! And celebrate!" The *Salve Regina* with its vale of tears is said to be a baroque leftover. The exiled person often feels alone. Then, some external event usually occurs over which one has no control: It is often a failure, perhaps a betrayal, a collapse, a career failure, or even a death; and then life falls completely apart. One has nothing: *Nada*. One is fortunate at that time to be able to cry. In a very real way one dies. Many important things are laid aside as trivia. One becomes detached, objective, "disinterested," to use Loyola's word. There is a dead person lying on the stage of life; he or she looks familiar: "Oh, yes, it's me. Could someone please take me away so that they can rehearse for the next dance?" These are the sentiments of the first darkness.

Several people mentioned above experienced this kind of darkness: Father Carl, Sister Marie, Jerry, and Helene all lived through it after their awakening. John still experiences it, as his marriage does not provide all that he had hoped for. For most, this darkness ends rather abruptly.

In an hour, or a day, or a week, a new world dawns—sharp, clear, free. The basic anxiety of life has been silenced because all is lost. All is quiet because the individual is resting at the bottom of the sea. A strange light breaks; strange because it has always been there, but it has been hidden behind the hill. It is as if great doors open in the eastern sky. In the silence music is heard; it is familiar, yet it was never heard before because there was so much scatter sound, so many distractions. There is a presence at once familiar and oddly new; soft, gentle, but commanding.

SECOND STAGE—ILLUMINATION

For those who choose not to go back, the illuminative way has begun. Many people misunderstand this way and hesitate to admit that if they are not there, they have at least looked into it and had its light reflected in their eyes. The word "illuminative" sounds too exalted. Some who arrive at the second stage are afraid to go on even though the gate is open, for fear that they might find real happiness and fulfillment. Misery, suffering, and temptation have been their lot for so long that they cannot give them up. "If I am miserable, I can't be expected to do much. If I cease to be miserable, then I'll undergo an identity crisis because it will not be me anymore. If I continue on this spiritual road, I will be expected to buy the pearl of great price or sell all that I have to buy the treasure in the field. Maybe I should stay put." Such thoughts pass through the mind. "And he went away sad because he had many possessions."

If a person stops at the end of the first darkness, life becomes a long twilight. One might say that such a person commutes back and forth through the darkness. The death of self takes on the aspects of a lingering, terminal illness. The spiritual life resembles a sick room and the spiritual director can be likened to the doctor of the rich, a physician for those who never see fit to get better and manage to enjoy ill health indefinitely.

Others are generous enough, but they misinterpret the illuminative way, thinking it will be without sin or struggle. They experience both, so they suppose that they must be deceiving themselves.

There is another excuse for avoiding the illuminative way: the fear of a life without self-seeking. Augustine encountered the threat of this possibility: "You will never have us again. Can you live without us?" his vices called out. Or a person may have had a problem with scruples which he or she has managed to overcome. He or she has recently been freed from the slavish notion of external perfection or artificial purity. Does the illuminative way mean going back to all of that again?

These are not idle fears. Spiritual writers have pointed out that the relative freedom of the illuminative way is often more frightening because one may become aware of more deeply rooted conflicts. Repressed pathologies, disguised doubts, and egotism deprived of its virtuous mask all come before one's eyes. One has a bit more strength so the challenges become greater.

As one moves on, however, guilt is replaced by sorrow, and worry by tears. Not only the past with all its failures, but also the present with its imperfections are mercilessly enlightened in this illumination. The love of God, the loving call to Christ, the gifts of the Holy Spirit combine to make the presence of egotism, cupidity, spiritual immaturity, and lack of social responsibility almost unbearable. There is a growing intensity to the true pain of purgatory, which is the awareness of the obstacles one places in the way of being in love with God. The description of purgatory given by St. Catherine of Genoa takes on added significance for someone in the illuminative way. He or she may be drawn to live with the poorest and most rejected out of a need to share and to give. This need is there also to assuage guilt, to begin to take on some of the things that Christ suffered and still suffers in the poor. One is frustrated by the inability to do more—a frustration shared with St. Paul. "The love of Christ urges us on."

Consequently, good works, even monumental ones, become the hallmark of the illuminative way. Dom Chautard in *The Soul of the Apostolate* suggests that the effectiveness of the Church's apostolate is directly related to the number of Christians who have entered the illuminative way.[15] Charity, creativity, zeal are no longer seen as responsibilities as they had been in the last movements of the purgative way. They are a response that brings some peace and balance to one who has begun to understand St. Francis when, in tears, he went banging on the doors of Assisi, rousing the sleeping townsfolk with his cry: "Love is not loved." Little do most people in the illuminative way realize that in the very experience of seeing their lack of love in the light of divine love, they are beginning to prepare for the searching trial of the Dark Night.

The prayer life of those in the illuminative way is much changed. It flows like a God-given spring from the earth rather than through the valves and pumps of a human-made fountain, says St. Teresa. It has a gentle joy and release in it. God is everywhere. Christ shows Himself in the good and the beautiful and His Cross is seen in the ugly and the terrifying. The mind is filled with images; the heart greatly overflows and is set on fire. Techniques are discarded; they become "excess baggage" because He is there.

The Christian in the illuminative way lives on Scripture and is fed on the writings of the saints. Reverence and awe are growing in his inner life and the soul is now seen not so much as a shadow being but as the inner place where the Trinity abides in glory. The liturgy of the Church on earth is a vital link with the heavenly liturgy for which one longs. The moral life of the individual is epitomized by Our Lady whose prayerful life becomes the model of response. An arc of flame reaches from earth to heaven and back again. Although one suffers, at times intensely, for the Church, for the human race, for the young, the old, and the dying, the pain is at least in some way united with the Incarnate Word in the mystery of divine love.

As the illuminative way proceeds, a silence and calm envelop the individual. This is reflected mostly in prayer—"the prayer of quiet"— wherein listening brings more answers than speaking. A gentleness so well described by Father Van Kaam becomes the individual's salient emotion.[16] If he or she is going through later midlife, the Whiteheads' observations on the resolution of polarities fit in well here.[17] Such opposites as creativeness and destructiveness, attachment and separateness, masculinity and femininity begin to be resolved. Ewert Cousins has noticed a similar process on a more intense spiritual level described by St. Bonaventure in his life of St. Francis.[18] This coincidence of opposites is a characteristic of the later stages of the illuminative way. The resolution takes place in the presence of the infinite, simple Being of God. God appears to have become the *All* of the individual. The shining inner image illuminated by the candelabrum of reason, to use Bonaventure's glorious metaphor, is the center of all attention. One has given away all and seems to have all, and it has been worth it.

The Dark Night

Suddenly it all disappears. Darkness fills the inner temple. The blazing image of the divine Icon, accompanied by the lovely image of the Madonna, is totally extinguished. Beauty, honor, love, hope—even the divine Presence—are disconnected, like a power line that has come down. There is no great storm as there was in the earlier experiences of darkness; there is only a hot stuffy night without wind or air, and in the midst of it a frightened soul feeling totally alone, a complete failure, and altogether bereft, to borrow the descriptive phrasing of St. John of the Cross.[19] The first phase of the darkness is primarily an experience of aridity. The childish ego, thought to have died so long ago, returns like a specter. It wails pitifully in the night, with a repressed need to be satisfied. The flesh, long since quiet in the beauty of the inner temple, cries out, "It's not too late—come back." The parable of the man who returned to his house and found it garnished by seven devils is about the only Scripture passage that seems to suit the occasion.

If prayer can take place at all amid these distractions and strong feelings, it is a prayer of aridity. One older man, well advanced in the spiritual life, used the following analogy when describing his prayer during the dark night: His only consolation, he said, was in knowing he shared the terror and loneliness of Mary and Joseph when they hurried back to Jerusalem to search for the Christ Child who had been entrusted to them and lost through their own apparent negligence. Such a description more accurately fits what St. John of the Cross calls "the Dark Night of the Senses." It is really the beginning of the prayer of simple union with God. Psychologically, one may not be prepared for approaching

God in such simple terms. Gradually as this Dark Night is dispelled, very advanced souls may come to so profound a union with God that it is referred to as ecstasy. After that, there ensues a second Dark Night, referred to properly as the Dark Night of the Spirit. Since only the most advanced souls arrive at this state, we shall only mention it now for the phrase is often incorrectly applied to an experience of less profound darkness.

In the midst of the Dark Night of the Senses duties must be fulfilled: classes taught, people cared for, friends encouraged, sermons preached. Those who have experienced the Dark Night say that they become almost dissociated from their work, so that the Holy Spirit puts into their mouths words and wisdom which help others but never touch their own hearts.

Worst of all, the sweet penitence of the illuminative way, the healing tears for having sinned and failed to love God, are now dried up. St. John of the Cross tells us that they are succeeded by a growing, terrifying apprehension that one is lost, that one will perish and never come to taste the union with God which has been one's goal for so many years.

We are told that those who have not lived through this appalling situation cannot know what it is. We can only listen. The unwise will offer the theological observation that such a feeling is a denial of hope and good Christian optimism, thereby suggesting that they themselves have neglected to meditate on the words, "Why have You forsaken me?" (Matt. 27:46).

There is no dramatic ending to the Dark Night as there was to the first darkness. Descriptions about the end are anticlimactic. Blessed Henry Suso writes:

> And later when God judged that it was time, He rewarded the poor martyr for all his suffering. And he enjoyed peace of heart and received in tranquility and quietness many precious graces. And he praised the Lord from the very depths of his soul and thanked Him for these same sufferings which for all the world he would not now have been spared.[20]

What has happened is that everything is lost and gone. All that is left is the stripped human will, unsupported, unadorned, without reinforcement or reward. One preserves the *desire* to remain loyal to God. T. S. Eliot in the *Four Quartets* suggests that this experience is unlike any other experience of faith, hope, and love in the past. It is a simple "yes" to the simple presence of God; the simple acceptance of the grace to love. The inner icon is gone. God speaks to the individual not by "tongue of flesh nor voice of angel nor darkness of parable nor sound of thunder but in silence He speaks His word, which neither begins nor ends" (St. Augustine). Union with God has begun.

There are some indications that this passage into the unitive way is a final act of surrender, even an acceptance of the possibility of eternal loss if that could be the divine will, which, of course, it could not.

THIRD STAGE—UNION

A short summary of the unitive way is what is required by the text and yet it is not possible. Words fail and thoughts evaporate as one attempts to describe the experience of union with God which comes to the very few who arrive at this way of infused contemplation. It is rather like trying to express the idea of eternal life and merely evoking an everlasting church service—not a very helpful analogy.

Perhaps when discussing the unitive way, it is best to say what it is not. It is not spectacular in any sense. Rather, it is like the sun at high noon in a cloudless sky. One suspects that if we were able to experience it without first being purified of all egotism and imperfection, we would be bored as little children are bored with great music. According to Augustine, it is a single Word spoken by God, with neither beginning nor end, and containing all.

Without being spectacular, the unitive way is also totally absorbing, like love's quiet joy. Perhaps human love, beyond its initial powerful impulses, is a good analogy, especially when one visits an elderly couple who are quite at peace and tranquil in each other's presence. Many saints have used the analogy of the love of husband and wife as a symbol of the unitive way. But human love is finite and time-bound; the only way for lovers to make it everlasting is to link it with the reality of divine love from which it flows and which it symbolizes.

The great women mystics seem to experience the unitive way as the Lord coming toward them; men tend to see it as a journey into a new domain of being. Yet when one encounters the unitive way in its most common form, among the elderly who live lives of peaceful gratitude to God (often for what the world would scoff at), it seems to be a simple childlike hymn of praise. In all cases, there is a clear perception on the part of the one who views another person in the unitive way that it is a movement whose source is beyond all human origin or limitation.

For the sake of the present discussion and to complete our water color sketch of the experience of the three ways, perhaps the following quotation from St. Augustine can best relate our own experience gained at a much less developed level of the spiritual life to this last stage. "If this experience could continue, and all others so inferior be taken away, and this one so wrap the beholder in inward joys, that all of life might be like that single instant in which we had come to touch (the Divine Reality), would this not mean 'enter into the joy of the Lord.'"[21]

Applying Psychology to the Journey

The spiritual journey as we have briefly sketched it has been thus described by writers from different cultures throughout the centuries. As we seek in Part II to present some theoretical understanding of its psychological dynamics, we must keep in mind that this is a most limited view, only half, and the lesser half, of the picture. In the next chapter we must first pause to consider carefully the limitations and aberrations of contemporary psychological speculation before applying such a limited instrument to something so lofty and sublime.

Chapter 5

Psychology and Spirituality

Psychology in the Contemporary Religious Scene

One of the most important questions raised as a result of Vatican II is the relationship of contemporary psychological theory to the life of the Christian and the practices of the Church. The entire area of discussion has, on a universal level, deeply affected religious education, the train-ing of priests, preaching, and the whole fabric and future of religious communities. Psychological theory has also influenced legislation and practice concerning marriage and all of moral theology, especially as it relates to the norms, practice, and requirements of the Sacrament of Reconciliation. Even areas seemingly as far removed from psychology as the study of Sacred Scripture and liturgical theology have been drawn into the currents of change generated since Freud, Jung, and their asso-ciates moved the study of the human mind from the laboratory to the office on Main Street. Academic disciplines which are scarcely under-stood as regards methodology, scope, and limitations, such as social psy-chology, psychological anthropology, and even inferential statistics, have, on occasion, provided data for bishops' meetings, religious chap-ters, and parish councils—groups which had little or no means of evalu-ating the validity of what was presented to them as objective truth. This was done often with the most sincere motives to provide solutions to practical problems.

If you have ever discussed the following, or similar, questions, you have been deeply involved in the complexities of a science whose name you probably did not know. For instance, if you have investigated the possibility of achieving greater integration of ethnic groups within a dio-cese or parish because the Gospel bids us do so, or if you chose some constructive social change to improve racial attitudes, you were grap-pling with social psychology. You accepted conclusions from very spe-cific and well-documented experiments which were very narrowly defined. Later, if you wondered why you succeeded in integrating the Boy Scouts but had a school bus with broken windows and lots of wounded lives, it was because you were using powerful tools which you did not understand.

On the other hand, if, as a member of a religious community, you were guided at a chapter by professional consultants, doing all that various professionals suggested, only to see everything subsequently fall apart, you witnessed the use of techniques of social analysis, more or less valid in themselves, but specifically limited and never meant to provide the answers sought by a religious community. Window poles are helpful, useful, and well designed, but if you use them to build a suspension bridge, you must expect it to collapse.

Shifting to another area of discussion, one might objectively consider the future role of women in the Church. There are equally vocal proponents of varying opinions which are based on human rights, tradition, theology, Scripture, history, developmental psychology, and almost everyone's final criterion, common sense. Both sides can appeal to psychology; answers will depend on which psychologists and social scientists are asked for their opinions. Any discussion of the role of women must necessarily include consideration of the role of men since femininity and masculinity, to the anthropological psychologist, are not separate boxes but polarities totally related to each other and incomprehensible without one another. I am not so naïve as to think that anthropology and psychology alone can provide a quick and easy solution to the question of the role of women and men in the Church. If we are going to look for data and theoretical solutions in these disciplines, however, we have first to understand their purpose and method of operation.

Perhaps no scientific discipline has provided more information and confusion in the contemporary Church than the mysterious study of inferential statistics. Every conference of bishops and religious superiors, every order, diocese, and department of education, has been confronted at some point with a complex set of computer printouts which few, if any, really understood. An expert in some social or psychological discipline, usually not an expert in statistics, delivered the package and then went on to help the assembly arrive at practical conclusions from the arcane data. Several implicit and dangerous assumptions normally underlie such use of psychological data. They include:

1. The data presented accurately the opinion of the majority.
2. The opinion of the majority must be right.
3. Even if the majority goes against law, tradition, and previous intellectual and moral commitment, the majority must be followed (even if the rights of individuals or minorities are ignored).

Such a procedure is fascism: the absolute rule of the majority; it destroys democracy, which preserves the rights of minorities. Moreover, it is ill-informed fascism because inferential statistical data rarely, if ever, give the kind of answers on which one can base such decisions. A questionnaire or survey is as good as what one puts into it. An oft-quoted adage in computer science states: "If you put in garbage, you take out garbage." I once had the experience of being required to participate in a social psychological study of a religious community. Although conceived with apparent sincerity, the study was patently invalid from a scientific standpoint. Fortunately in this case, the common sense of most of those involved told them it was invalid. Sadly, common sense does not always prevail when people have spent a lot of money on something that is the scientific equivalent of a duck-billed platypus.

Pop Psychology

Psychology, like music, comes in classical, semiclassical, and popular modes. Classical psychology, especially experimental psychology, often has as little to do with popular psychology as Bach has to do with rock-and-roll music. But there is no doubt that popular music has more impact on most people's lives than classical. Underneath it all, the two modes of music are related. Many great musicians begin by playing what is then popular music as children. In an age when classics of any discipline are not communicated in mass media or public education, the potential classicists of today are most likely to begin learning music in the popular mode, even in its most banal forms. In spirituality, as in music, the popular model is not always invalid as an expression of reality. One has only to think of many outstanding spiritual persons who began with popular forms of piety and retained some of them throughout life. (The Rosary is a splendid example of a popular devotion that can become part of classic spirituality.)

As popular music has affected contemporary culture, so pop psychology has had a tremendous influence on the life of the Church in recent years. Like music, pop psychology has different levels, from semiclassical to the slick and trendy, and ranging from what is genuinely perceptive to simple junk. Pop psychology's overriding problem, which it shares with popular music, art, and TV religion, is that it is usually based not on what is valid or true but on what will sell. Like the fast food producers of our day, the pop psychologist may ask, "What will sell?" rather than, "What is helpful for the client?"

Having said all that, it is nevertheless true that pop psychology has done a good deal to help people live healthier lives especially when it bears a relation to some scientifically validated or at least seriously analyzed technique. Contrary to popular opinion, many of the most effective psychological techniques are really not experimentally validated, but at least they have been critically appraised and frequently tried by a variety of informed professionals. There is also a tendency with popular psychological techniques (for example, the "I'm O.K., You're O.K." slogan) to be meaningful for a short period of time, but to fade quickly. The trendiness of such techniques perhaps reflects the transitory nature of much in modern civilization.

Pop techniques are sometimes helpful within limits, particularly in assisting people to gain self-knowledge. A religious community or a parish based on them, however, would be built on sand. The best hope for a fairly honest pop psychology is that it will make some lasting contribution that will be permanently integrated into the life of a society, institution, or individual. The possibility of this happening is directly related to the amount of serious thought and intellectual honesty given to the pop movement in the first place. The fascination with group processes and group dynamics in the late 1960s was in fact based on some very serious and solid theory and experimentation. When popular enthusiasm waned, a substantial contribution to psychotherapy and human understanding remained, even though the professionals had been embarrassed by naïve enthusiasts and an occasional charlatan.

You ought to sit back at this time and ask some questions: "What do I really know about psychology? If I am going to relate it to something as important as my spiritual life or to someone else's spiritual life, where did I get my notions of psychology? Have I just accepted things naïvely? Have I bothered to understand the limits of serious psychological theory when using it? Have I opted for pop psychology and, if so, have I tested it against things of which I thought I was certain? Have I measured it against the Gospel, the teaching of the Church, my own common sense? Or have I twisted my convictions to fit what is untested and may be only a passing fancy? Worse still, have I compromised my beliefs by accepting what fits into contemporary, hedonistic, consumer culture? In a word, have I conformed to the spirit of the world? Underneath all the tinsel, have I bought the real tinsel? Have I really used the brain God gave me?

Jung's scathing condemnation of the Nazis in their early years was provoked by their tendency simply to mirror what the modern age seemed to want. He felt that any valid world vision must be rooted in the past 5,000 years of human history and at the same time engage the issues of the present situation. This is a much more difficult and worthy task than just reflecting the ephemeral needs and notions of the present moment. Contemporary issues in both Church and society should be measured critically by Jung's standards.

What Is Meant by the Term "Psychology"?

The behavioral sciences include psychology, psychiatry, sociology, and various combinations and subgroups such as social psychology and social work. The word "psychology" is used as a catch-all for studies in human behavior, even though experimental psychology often studies animals and many of the social sciences deal with groups rather than with their problems. Those interested in spirituality, by reason of their very individual orientation, usually mean therapeutic psychology when referring to psychology. Thus they often include in the term "psychology" areas related to therapeutic psychology, such as psychotherapy, personality theory, and counseling. As this book suggests, the scope of psychology has recently been extended to include developmental psychology.

If all the behavioral sciences were housed in a single building, with proportionate office space for the different schools of thought within each discipline, they would comprise the equivalent of a zoo, i.e., a little sample of everything from penguins to alligators. The followers of these disciplines would all move about and make noise like the animals in a zoo, but otherwise would share little in common. It would be unwise to think that any answer, theory, or attitude based on a hypothetical agreement among these disciplines would be of any more use than a composite picture of the "average animal" in a zoo. The average height and weight of all the creatures in the Bronx Zoo is a senseless, even misleading piece of information. (Such a figure would vary immensely from milligrams to tons were all the fleas in the zoo added.) Even more misleading and dangerous information follows the familiar words: "Contemporary psychologists say. . . ."

Nonetheless, both the behavioral sciences building on campus and the zoo in the park can be sources of beneficial information. For instance, experimental psychology, which is more uniform and cautious in its conclusions, can tell you much about the processes of recollection and behavioral change.[1] Therapeutic psychology and psychiatry can help us, provided we know the concepts underlying the therapeutic technique and use them with care. As we shall see, broken wine skins in the Church are often the result of applying good therapeutic psychological methods to living situations which, in fact, represent old wine skins. At least one community of monks has been completely wiped out because no one was thoughtful enough to look at the psychological and theological assumptions on which a particular therapy was based.

Issues are often complicated by the fact that a genuinely effective technique (for instance, psychoanalysis) may have been formulated by a person such as Freud who, according to his own public statements, was opposed to all revealed religion and especially to Christianity. Psycho-analysis frequently can be effective with believers; it can be "baptized" and many psychoanalysts have indeed done just that. One has only to think of the work of Braceland, Stock, Zilboorg, Joyce, and Stern in this endeavor.[2] But the indiscriminate and unqualified use of psychoanalysis has plunged believers many times into profound crises from which they never recovered. The authors cited above were all men whose faith was obviously strengthened by the encounter with psychoanalysis and who could separate the wheat from the chaff. This has not always been the case, however. In therapeutic psychology, as in all fields, the answer is neither to run away and hide nor to proceed with your eyes closed. History has proved again and again that the correct response is neither the condemnation of Galileo nor the canonization of Spinoza. Unfortu-nately, both procedures appear to continue in various segments of the Christian world. We might do well to ponder the parable of the dragnet and take the time to sit on the beach and sort the catch.

DEVELOPMENTAL PSYCHOLOGY

I am obviously more encouraged by contemporary trends in develop-mental psychology than in therapeutic psychology for insights in under-standing the life of the spirit. This optimism is a result of at least two factors. The general trends of thought among spiritual writers and mys-tics in the Christian tradition (and in most other religions) have been developmental, as indicated in our discussion of the Three Ways. In the past two decades, spiritual writers have been preoccupied with the con-sideration of pathology and illness, usually under the general heading of weakness and sinfulness. Secondarily, they have sought ways to encour-age continued growth, that is, developmental answers. I am attracted to developmental psychology because it is much more unified in itself and more integrated into the general field of the behavioral sciences than is therapeutic psychology, especially pop therapeutic psychology. Developmental psychology has tended to use more objective data in its construction of theory and has been more modest in its conclusions. The intellectual arrogance and intolerance that has often marred the history of therapeutic psychology, especially pop psychology, is absent from developmental psychology, as becomes an academic pursuit. Conse-quently there has been less need for caution with regard to philosophical implications underlying developmental psychology. These underlying foundations have never been Christian, or explicitly related to belief at all, but they are seldom directly opposed to religion. We will make use of both branches of psychology in this analysis. Therapeutic psychology, which will be approached with caution, is included here because many spiritual problems are linked to the need for psychotherapy and counseling.

THERAPEUTIC PSYCHOLOGY

Since many aspects of therapeutic psychology must be used for practical application in spiritual direction, we will pause here to summarize the relationships of therapeutic psychology to spirituality. This will be done by raising several questions which probably have occurred already to the thoughtful reader.

1. Are psychological adjustment and spiritual development the same thing?

The answer is no. Psychological adjustment is, however, related to spiritual development. Another way of posing the question is to ask whether I am well adjusted and growing spiritually. Psychological adjustment is a dynamic, ongoing process in which the individual seeks to make productive use of his or her abilities and at the same time fulfill personal needs adequately. Perfect adjustment or balance is an abstract ideal. Human adjustment is always made within realistic parameters of a situation. I adjust to the situation in which I find myself. Unfortunately defense mechanisms, which are unconscious distortions of reality, enable people to make pleasurable adjustments which are eventually destructive to themselves and others. Many people experience a sense of self-fulfillment and self-satisfaction while they are in fact neglecting their potential and omitting to do much of what is expected of them. Sacred Scripture often speaks of the contented man who has a fleeting but sinful happiness. In St. Luke, chapter 16, the rich man was condemned for neglecting the needs of others. Nevertheless, a mature life adjustment, including a valid perception of the human condition, powerfully contributes to the growth of a spiritually oriented person.

Spiritual development, on the other hand, is built on divine grace. God is not a psychologist and He will choose persons and means of His own. The words of the Magnificat—"He has pulled down princes from their thrones and exalted the lowly"—provide a familiar theme in Scripture and in tradition. Spiritual development relates primarily to a person's willingness to respond openly to God, and an equal willingness to embrace the truth, at least as one knows it. The dimensions of psychological adjustment are determined early in life by environment and circumstances. If you are not impressed with your early life experiences, recall that since the time of Moses and David, Providence has been calling those who might seem, from a psychological point of view, unlikely candidates for God's mission. It is also good to remember that many canonized saints struggled throughout life with scars and pathologies from childhood.

As we have noted, an obvious relationship exists between psychological adjustment and spiritual growth. A good adjustment leads to an overall decline in defensiveness and anxiety, thus bringing about a better perception of reality which certainly contributes to spiritual development. On the other hand, to grow spiritually means to grow in faith and trust, to reduce much of the self-defeating anxiety on which pathology builds. Consequently the person growing in holiness should experience an improved adjustment to reality. Genuine inner peace is a mark both of spiritual growth and of psychological adjustment.

2. In certain religious systems obedience to a higher order of reality demands self-denial and self-sacrifice. Can such systems hold out to their adherents the possibility of self-fulfillment as it is proposed in most psychological theories?

This question expresses the great conflict between therapeutic psychology and transcendent values based on revealed religion. As we saw in Chapter 1, revelation demands an obedience of faith and may even exact the surrender of one's life. Christianity, Judaism, and Islam, as well as other revealed religions, frequently require that one place the rights of God and others before one's own. The Catholic Church has often lost ground (as it did in the case of Henry VIII) because of its demand that the desires of the individual had to be subject to the needs and rights of others.

The commands of a transcendent order and the exigencies of obedience to faith in a personal God are incomprehensible to those with a world vision which is either atheistic or deistic, that is, one specifically affirming an impersonal deity, like the god of Spinoza. Atheists who follow a movement that gives a quasi-religious identity to a "divine state," are in fact better able to comprehend the need for obedience and dedication beyond oneself than those who raise the human to a quasi-divine level, as is done in secular humanism. The real question is one of dedication and commitment beyond one's own gratification, however nobly that self-seeking may be described.

The notion of self-fulfillment goes through various evolutions. For the believer, ultimate blessedness or happiness is to come to God, the unchanging, all-fulfilling Reality. Augustine's warning to those who seek happiness in less is worth noting here. "Seek what you seek, but not where you seek it. Do not look for life in the land of death." There is a kind of fulfillment in spiritual pursuits. It is very different from the self-seeking advocated in the past two decades. One can hardly say that

Father Damien or Albert Schweitzer was involved in self-actualization in Maslow's sense of the term. Any number of social and therapeutic psychologists in the late 1970s deplored the unbridled selfism of the contemporary scene. Several have seen it as the cause of the decline of Western culture, and some have not hesitated to lay the blame squarely at the door of psychology.

The following quotation from social psychologist Dr. Donald Campbell, past president of the American Psychological Association, avoids the spiritual question of selfism, but points out the dangerous effects on our culture.

> There is in psychology today a general background assumption that the human impulses provided by biological evolution are right and optimal, both individually and socially, and that repressive or inhibitory moral traditions are wrong. This assumption may now be regarded as scientifically wrong. Psychology, in propagating this background perspective in its teaching of perhaps 80 or 90 percent of college undergraduates, and increasing proportions of high school and elementary school pupils, helps to undermine the retention of what may be extremely valuable social-evolutionary inhibitory systems which we do not yet fully understand.[3]

Campbell's attack on selfism is not unique. Paul Vitz has analyzed the origins and effects of this uncritical selfism on our values and culture. Christopher Lasch in *The Culture of Narcissism* and William Kilpatrick in *Identity and Intimacy,* have both indicated how selfism has undermined the permanent commitment on which all culture and family life are built.[4] The uncritical acceptance of selfism, especially of the Rogerian type, has had very damaging effects on religious commitment in the Church.

Since these theories of selfism are so popular and so clearly dedicated to a kind of hedonistic self-indulgence, it seems that the answer to our question about the demands of a higher order must be that the two are not reconcilable. Although motivated by the most humane considerations, Rogers particularly avoids examination of a higher order beyond the individual in his or her concept of adjustment. It may indeed happen that a parent will have to deny personal desires and impulses for the welfare of a child, or a wife, or a husband. It may be that religion requires this denial. In order to avoid a direct confrontation with the Gospel, those who think of themselves as practicing Christians, when faced with a conflict between self-fulfillment and the higher order of Christian values, will generally adopt the rationalization: "I can't do it." It sounds better than saying, "I won't do it." And since psychology has revealed many areas of real but relative psychological impossibility, the rationalization is a comfortable and handy one.

A new work by Daniel Yankelovich blames a good deal of this kind of thinking on Rogers, Fromm, and especially Maslow.[5] Yankelovich points out the essentially contradictory nature of the philosophy of self-fulfillment which has obtained in psychotherapy and throughout American culture for the past twenty years. Self-seeking, as mystics learned long ago, leads to the inevitable frustration of loneliness and isolation. We have all seen that in extreme forms found among wealthy eccentrics, the ultimate self-seeking often results in schizophrenia. Yankelovich also suggests optimistically that many young people are moving toward a new culture of commitment and a sense of the sacred.

3. Is the psychological good of the individual, therefore, irreconcilable with a higher order of values?

Many psychologists who reacted to Campbell's condemnation of self-ism accused him of opposing the good of the individual to that of society, claiming that he favored the latter.

Paul Vitz, whose book is highly recommended to all who are seriously interested in the subject, has observed that the response to Campbell's condemnation represents a low-level presentation of the problem. Vitz goes on to make the following clarification: "The higher religions claim that through love of God, through transcendent experience, the individual is dramatically better off. One important consequence of spiritual transformation is greater altruistic behavior. Thus in the religious interpretation, the individual and society are not in conflict but in fundamental cooperation."[6]

The reader interested in the spiritual life had perhaps already come to this conclusion, but was afraid to say it aloud because the shibboleths of selfism are so well entrenched, even in religious communities. Vitz's answer, however, does imply the acceptance of certain spiritual possibilities which go quite beyond the ken or expectations of the science of psychology, as it is construed at present. Spiritual transformation, contemplation, and the ultimate unity of individual and social good are concepts to which psychology is usually unwilling to extend itself—except when it is moved to deny them. Contemporary psychology, as Vitz often points out, is agnostic in its principles and atheistic in its prejudices. Pop psychology demonstrates fewer of these biases because of the popularity of religion. However, it is an observable phenomenon that science in general, and psychology in particular, are permitted to move into theological and philosophical areas of discussion only when they are attempting to deny the transcendent. Normally they are not allowed to approach this field of thought when, as in the present case, the only coherent answer can be found in an appeal to a Reality which encompasses both the individual and the whole of humankind. Frankl has noted the devastating effects of this prejudice on the history of modern societies; in his opinion, such thinking built the concentration camps of the Nazis.[7]

4. In view of the widespread acceptance of selfism in therapeutic psychology, is there any hope for the adoption of spirituality or any other structure that requires self-transcendence and commitment beyond one's own pleasures and interests?

This question is asked in many ways by those interested in the survival of family life, religious life, pastoral ministry, or indeed of any society where the individual finds his or her dignity going beyond mere self-interest. For several years I too have observed a small but growing trend among the postadolescent and young adult population toward commitment and altruism. Such trends seem frequently to be reactions against the boredom of hedonism. They sometimes result from an experience of grace and faith which is totally at odds with the pleasure-oriented, self-centered values with which the young person has grown up. Unqualified pleasure-seeking inevitably reaps its own reward: boredom, alienation, ennui, and passive aggression. The teachings of spirituality, Eastern or Western, are so unfamiliar that they suddenly become attractive to the young.

Yankelovich sees that "there are now scraps and shreds of evidence that American culture is evolving toward a new ethics of commitment." I was delighted that such an outstanding social scientist had observed what I had been noticing for a while. He remarks on a growing relationship between social responsibility and the sense of the sacred which, if not specifically religious, is certainly connected to religious values. Yankelovich continues: "This embryonic ethic is now gathering force around two kinds of commitments: closer and deeper personal relationships and the switch from certain instrumental values for sacred/expressive ones."[8]

While many other signs indicate that the young are rejecting the culture of selfism, middle-aged people often fail to understand this rejection of an apparent freedom that was won less than a generation ago. They remember days of excessive control and repression. It is not so long ago that many of the serious and dedicated were, at the same time, unrelated to others. The middle-aged are well aware that moral inhibition is by no means a straight road to altruism and creativity. The task facing us today is to save what values have come from the past two decades, without holding on to reactionary "liberalism" and concepts of self-fulfillment that have proved destructive and dehumanizing.

At this juncture an appeal to well-formed and valid spirituality might be a great help. Large numbers of young people, indeed many persons of all ages and religious backgrounds, show a real interest in spiritual values and teaching. Prayer, sharing of contemplative experience, social responsibility founded on the sacredness of human life, are all values of increasing social importance. For a year or two, spirituality even became a fad, although I suspect this was a part of selfism. Now that the fad has subsided, people everywhere are discovering the social and communal appeal of transcendent meaning and beauty. It is very important that this interest lead to a well-informed, integrating spirituality, one that is committed to others and has a genuine sense of the sacred. This is the task of the churches as the second millennium draws to a close. The Church can find in psychology an ally or an obstacle. The issue, however, must be faced by the believers themselves as well as by the psychologists. If the organized religious bodies of America fail to grasp the moment of what Yankelovich calls our first cultural revolution, they will continue to lose ground. Their old partner/competitor, psychology, will be left alone to face a challenge which is simply beyond its purpose and capacity. We will then return to another round of the psychologists and psychiatrists as prophets and philosophers, with priests serving as their devout cup bearers. Lord, may it not be so!

5. Is psychology a help in understanding spirituality?

Yes, when it is properly and cautiously used. Spirituality does not exist in a vacuum. It is a phase of human growth and development, albeit responding to the impetus of grace, a help that comes from beyond any human source. Human beings respond to many forces outside themselves. All responses, including the response to grace, are best studied in a way that uses all the behavioral sciences.

A person responds to grace and revelation in a social context, and both sociology and social psychology open up great areas of understanding. A person responds with his or her personality as it has developed, with many scars and wounds; thus therapeutic psychology can be very helpful. Human beings respond in different ways at different phases of development, and therefore developmental psychology and experimental psychology can provide a good deal of insight. With this in mind, we turn now to a psychological consideration of the spiritual road.

PART II

A PSYCHOLOGICAL UNDERSTANDING OF THE THREE WAYS

Chapter 6

The First Stage
of the Spiritual Life:
The Purgation

First Phase—Moral Integration

The most important and, to the uninformed, most discouraging phase of spiritual development is the initial step in the purgative way: moral integration. The new convert or the Christian recently aware of the life of the Spirit is drawn inexorably to change, growth, and a complexity of seemingly contradictory behaviors: the healing of old wounds and inflicting of new ones; growth in the Spirit and a decline in egotism; being filled with the strength of God and at the same time becoming utterly helpless. The precious gifts of life and time are not less important, but take on a transcendent importance. Sin is more and more abhorrent; yet, just as the person becomes more free, the possibility of sin, even the repressed and long-forgotten primitive tendencies toward rebellion and self-seeking, come back to life. Pain and pleasure, virtue and sin, belief and unbelief swirl around the person as he or she emerges from the awakening into the long journey of the spiritual life.

THE WORK OF PURGATION

When the call of God comes, it is abundantly clear that there is much work to be done. This is evident from our discussion above concerning the particular aspect of God that speaks to us depending on our personality (the Four Voices of God), as well as from what we have seen of the developmental needs of individuals, and the constant pull of pathology against our complete development. The God who calls us in the awakening is Absolute Being. He accommodates His call of grace to our needs so that eventually we may totally accommodate ourselves to Him. As the followers of all schools of spirituality have remarked, this accommodation to the Absolute is the essence of growth in holiness.

In Christianity the development of the individual toward conformity with Absolute Being is not accomplished haphazardly. It can be achieved only by the grace of the Son of God and according to His teachings. Its dynamism derives not from some exotic array of divinelike qualities, but from adoption as children of God. The startling document called the Sermon on the Mount, which flows from the Law and yet transcends it, provides the foundation for the code by which the Christian must live.

It is not appropriate here to review the entire body of teaching on Christian morality or add a comprehensive summary of Christian ascetics, but it is necessary to affirm that they operate today as they did when the bewildered multitude found their way home after Christ had given one of His moral teachings. Thus, we come to the question:

1. Do I live by the moral teachings of Christ?

This question is of permanent importance to us as we examine our own lives in reference to the purgative way. It is of particular importance at the present time when there is a good deal of moral relativism among Christians; it is also timely because of the current vogue to learn methods of meditation aimed at producing religious experience apart from the imperatives of moral conversion. The tendency to separate religious experience from rectitude of life represents an old and dangerous tradition of gnosticism at its worst—a tradition which, by the way, is contradicted by the lives and teachings of the saints.

The moral question posed has, therefore, two parts: accepting responsibility and a positive effort to fulfill that responsibility. The acceptance of objective moral norms needs constant personal review. It is not enough to say, "I accept the whole thing," or "I follow what is probable," or "Basically I try." Living according to the Christian moral law is a process of becoming. If one is growing, there are ever new horizons and challenges. Yesterday's good works may be seen as today's ego-trips. Yesterday's imperfections may be today's sins of ingratitude or negligence. Even more surprisingly, previous acts of trust may suddenly appear as flagrant presumption or self-deception.

In addition one must contend with the most common and insidious defense mechanisms: rationalization and intellectualization. The first provides good reasons for doing evil or omitting good, and the second provides many types of involved subterfuges which are essentially a corruption of the truth. These defenses must be carefully examined because they are the trump cards in the devil's deck which may be played against the very people who will read this kind of book.

An appreciation of the effect of these defenses and their ability to subvert whole schools of thought and even to destroy the Church in entire nations is a very useful piece of mental equipment. Defenses are usually ingrained in our thinking and, at times, may be considered necessary. It is important to be vigilant so that one may notice when the defensive character of our behavior becomes conscious. We live in such an un-Christian world and are immersed in its values to such a degree that if we were deprived of these two defenses in an instant, we would probably despair. Simply think of the social injustice of which we are unconsciously a part since we live in the affluent nations, and ponder the sources of that affluence so nicely covered up by rationalization and denial. This will give us a brief and striking insight into the reality behind our own defenses. We need the courage born of belief in divine forgiveness to enable us to look at reality in its ever clearer dimensions.

Such a sobering glimpse at reality is often provided by personal work with the poor. It is difficult for me to think of anyone making real spiritual progress who has not closely examined the plight of those who carry the burden of the world's greed. To be delivered from self-centeredness, the saints tell us, we must work with the destitute. In the same vein, it is certainly true that very effective sermons on chastity are preached by those who have been the victims of lust; similarly, delinquents can remind us that we are all capable of dishonesty. The poor, too, are often very edifying and approach dimensions of love and generosity which the well-encamped Christian may find astonishing and humbling.

The need for an objective moral order, and for a Church which interprets that moral order, becomes urgently clear to someone seeking to purify his or her heart. Whereas many see the moral teaching of the Church as a burden or imposition, the person who is becoming a spiritual Christian will welcome gratefully the guidance of the pastoral office. Those who work with young adults growing in the spiritual life constantly find them not simply docile but eager to establish norms of behavior in our self-centered, pleasure-oriented society. The young are quite able to deal with the fact that new norms must be worked out for new situations. They realize that even those seriously committed are often in conflict with each other. But the young, newly awakened Christians are scathing in their rejection of religious enterprises without moral norms and vitriolic in their criticism of those who claim to lead other Christians but who are themselves blind guides. I have heard them complain about this for years—and the complaints are becoming louder.

The larger question, of course, is not, "Do I accept a law beyond my own defenses?" but, "Do I live by the law of Christ?" Unless you are already a saint, the answer will be, "only in part." This is the very meaning of development or becoming. Children preparing for First Communion were once taught prayers that began, "Dear Lord, I give You my heart and my soul." It is a great idea, but doesn't convey the real situation. The child is no more prepared to surrender himself to God than are most adults. If you surrender completely to God ten minutes before you die, you will have accomplished more spiritually than anyone ever expected.

Growth as a Christian or, indeed, as a sincere believer of any kind, requires a constant effort. It involves an endless attempt to purify motives, improve behavior, use potentials more effectively, and become more and more sensitive to the rights of others. It is indeed a narrow gate we must enter. The importance of following Christ's moral teaching is illustrated from a somewhat different perspective in each of the Gospels. Perhaps St. John's Gospel most dramatically relates the moral law to the spiritual life with the relentless message, "If you love Me, keep My commandments" (Jn. 14:15). But it is obviously a task of long duration; the experience of the apostles has shown it to be a process of becoming.

2. What about sins of weakness?

Our discussion of pathology in Chapter 3 now takes on a special relevance. Most people who have experienced an awakening and begun to grow recognize that at least their conscious and deliberate sins are deeply entwined with pathology. We describe them with the phrase "sins of weakness." Sin linked to pathology covers the whole spectrum of immoral behavior, from intemperance to injustice, from sins of vanity and selfishness to sexual sins.

Frequently struggles with sin are struggles with what Jung aptly called the Shadow, the dynamic complexity of *id* demands organized and given coherent expression as they become integrated into conscious life. Since grace builds on nature, it is not illogical to suppose that sin does too; thus our pathologies become the very working ground of our spiritual foes. They are not inappropriately identified as the world, the flesh, and the devil.

Paradoxically, one of the most devastating effects of sins of weakness (and even of partial malice) is the production of psychological guilt. The word "guilt" is charged with meaning; it can signify moral responsibility, the effects of a person's fall, or a nagging state of mind arising from illusory sins. Here we take it to mean the whole range of negative, self-destructive feelings which deprive an individual of an awareness of the hope of divine adoption and drive him or her toward further sins and evil deeds.

During His earthly life, Christ worked as strenuously to pardon sin as He did to teach the law of God. He did not bury guilt, or wish it away, or say to some that they judged themselves too harshly. In a word, He did not play the role of many therapists who think they can talk or wish away something as deep as a person's guilt. Christ pardoned guilt. It was the very first sign of His divinity in His public life. "Who can forgive sins but God. . . . But to prove to you that the Son of Man has authority on earth to forgive sins . . . get up, pick up your stretcher . . ." (Mk. 2:7–11).

Christ destroyed sin and guilt. "Your sins are forgiven" (Lk. 7:48); "Go and don't sin any more" (Jn. 8:11). This healing summons was unique. And it works now to the degree that we are able and willing to let it work. Most spiritually minded people want more than anything else to respond to this summons. But because of pathology and defenses, they can follow it only partially. And that is the drama of *becoming*. We respond each day when we become a bit more free, a bit more delivered from guilt.

A great tool in the struggle for deliverance is Confession, in the sacramental or nonsacramental way. The Sacrament of Reconciliation is a most powerful means for personal perfection when used wisely and well. Christians who are without this sacrament or unable to celebrate it, may confess to another informed and prayerful person whom they trust. This is similar to the confession required in the fifth step of Alcoholics Anonymous. Confession is a great relief and opens the soul to the forgiveness of Christ.

One of the great contemporary proponents of Confession is Brother Roger of Taizé. Although raised in the Calvinist tradition, where the practice of Confession had fallen out of use, he has discovered its meaning and value. "The Catholic is above all the Church of the Eucharist, but she has another special gift. She has known how to set apart men to bestow forgiveness, to loose on earth what is immediately loosed in the Kingdom, to lift from our shoulders the burden too heavy to bear, to wipe away the past, even the most recent past. Confession gives us the opportunity of expressing as spontaneously as possible all that weighs on our conscience. No one is able to say all there is to say about his faults" (Brother Roger of Taizé).

3. What do I think about mortal sin?

Perhaps the most painful experience for someone in the purgative way is to commit a mortal sin. Such a fall can be so unnerving and disorienting that several unfortunate consequences may result, apart from the sin itself. The person who commits mortal sin or thinks she or he has done so, may suffer great depression, and in some cases, despair. This very situation, especially when it is a question of compulsive sin, may precipitate more unacceptable behavior. An even greater calamity is to rationalize the sin as indifferent or virtuous behavior. "I did it out of love." So did David when he killed the husband of the woman who had caught his eye. Honesty is certainly required if any real insight is to be gained.

It is important that both the beginner in the spiritual life and the spiritual director be able to cope with this tragic situation. It might be said that success, especially in the early stages of the spiritual life, is largely related to a person's ability to cope with sin in a constructive, Christian way and, if possible, to make temptations and sins work as dynamic motivations for spiritual development.

The following question may be a useful guide.

4. How do I use my sins?

You are asked to ponder carefully the following proposal drawn in part from classical moral theology, contemporary speculative moral theology, the sounder elements of contemporary psychological theory, and traditional practices of past spiritual directors. All of these can provide a path through the desert, not unlike the way to the Promised Land when the children of Israel tempted the Lord.

Perhaps we should first reaffirm the possibility of mortal sin, a sin unto death. Sacred Scripture as well as every great spiritual writer of the Church clearly enunciates the possibility of a morally lethal human act which disrupts relationship with God. Such grievous behavior leads to everlasting spiritual ruin and separation from our eternal destiny as children of God. Despite this, contemporary society denies the possibility of sin unto death. In a statement of outstanding insight, which blended moral teaching with the values of the spiritual life, the American bishops in 1978 firmly restated the biblical imperative to avoid serious moral failures in the many areas of human conduct.[1] In his address to the bishops in Chicago in 1979, Pope John Paul II praised this statement and reiterated the necessity for pastoral instruction based on the moral imperatives of Christ.[2] Several years earlier, Dr. Karl Menninger, one of American's outstanding psychiatrists, had asked the ominous question, "Whatever Happened to Sin?"[3] In his book Menninger challenged the moral subjectivism of our culture and suggested that a recognition of the reality of sin would alleviate much of the gloom and anxiety brought about by moral relativism and pop psychology.

The dogma of the possibility of mortal sin (and it is a dogma) is the dark side of our belief in adoption as children of God.[4] In order to be God's child one must be able to say "yes" freely. Being able to say "yes" freely implies the freedom to say "no" as well. To say "no" to God's love is the beginning of hell.

MORTAL SIN AND SIN DONE IN CONFLICT

Moral theologians have defined "material sin" as an act (in this case no real sin at all) which, if done knowingly and deliberately, seriously violates the moral law. I know many poor, socially disadvantaged people who have no realization that they should enter a stable marriage or that living together without marriage is morally wrong. This is usually the result of years of sin committed against, rather than by, the poor. There is no need to dwell on this kind of behavior, except to say that many apparently sinful deeds fall into this category, particularly in secularized cultures. Such acts contradicting the moral law that is unknown and therefore without influence, damage both individuals and society, family life and children. They take a terrible toll in human suffering. (But where is the real moral responsibility in such cases?)

As we grow in the spiritual life, we gradually become aware of aspects of personal behavior whose damaging consequences had previously been denied or rationalized. For example, we question whether we have faced our responsibility to the poor. On this subject, constant self-examination, change, and conversion are necessary if we are to escape the rationalization of the affluent.

There is another sin of greater significance, even though it is without a simple term of designation owing to a fault of language. It was once couched in an almost liturgical term: "sin imperfectly committed." It is an act or habit so ingrained and linked to self-destructive pathology, or so much a part of a person's life adjustment that freedom to act otherwise is greatly diminished. Even confessors using the severe morality of days gone by never overlooked this phenomenon. The complex issues that minimize freedom and, consequently, real responsibility were summed up in the frightening package labeled "concupiscence." With the advent of modern psychology, the contents of the package were examined; the superficial conclusion often reached was that almost no one was seriously responsible for anything. Sophisticated moral systems that focused primarily on the individual's situation and gave less attention to Scripture and Tradition or the teaching authority of the Church, created the impression in people's minds that formal, serious sin was a relative impossibility. It is true that an understanding of pathology and of developmental psychology sheds much light on the meaning of concupiscence, but the light has frequently come from psychologists like Freud. A most influential thinker, Freud was deeply convinced that human beings are completely and perversely driven to pleasure; moreover, he considered as a neurotic illusion the notion that a personal loving God created human beings capable of saying "yes" to Him. Because of the influence of Freud and others, insights regarding a person's limitations to commit serious sin have often been invalidly applied.

Finally, there is another question related to the classical idea of virtue: Does a good Christian, by a single instance of sinful behavior, forfeit salvation and say a true "no" to God and to the grace of adoption? For centuries, spiritual directors have been familiar with this question as a practical reality. In most cases the director is wise enough to leave aside the question of actual mortal sin while working with the person's sincere desire to be a good Christian. The occurrence of seriously forbidden behavior linked to developmental crisis or pathology is common enough; such acts as anger, sexual indulgence, dishonesty, or resentment have plagued the committed Christian since the Acts of the Apostles. Confessors commended the person to God's mercy, suggesting that repentance for these failures was an added motive for trust, gratitude, and understanding others. The impact of psychology, however, made it necessary to seek intellectually articulate answers to what seemed a rather untidy system to the logical minds of many theologians. Various solutions involving what is known as the fundamental option were proposed with great skill and pastoral concern. Perhaps this sin of the well-intentioned is the most profound mystery in spiritual theology. The last mystery Christ revealed in the Johannine Gospel concerned the personal anomaly of the apostles, "Do you now believe? The time will come—in fact it has come already—when you will be scattered, each going his own way and leaving me alone" (Jn. 16:31–32). Yet He prayed for and relied on them to repent and lead His Church.

There are two problems with the fundamental option theory: It is psychologically inadequate in its explanation of how one can choose diametrically opposed things at the same time; and it lends itself to rationalization. Martin Luther confronted the same problem with soldiers who, convinced they had been saved, went on behaving as badly as they had done before. To their simple way of thinking, they were God's children and sins were not held against them. One wonders what the great reformer would say about the fundamental option.

As someone more interested in spiritual development than in abstract moral theology, I hope that the theologians never completely solve the puzzle of the sinning and struggling believer. What would Peter and

Paul amount to without their sins? How artificial they would look. Even late in life with martyrdom not far off, they showed signs of inconstancy and aggression. Certainly, their tendencies were not mortal sins, but if they had surrendered to the tendencies—Peter to his life-long vacillation and Paul to his Olympian wrath—we might have been deprived of two outstanding models of the spiritual life. The sins and failings of the apostles, especially early on, like the sins of all others on the spiritual journey, are an untidy element in the spiritual life. They are also a necessary background to such words as, "For those who love God, all things work together for the good." Rather than concentrating on whether past sins were truly mortal, we should be deeply stirred to repentance by our manifest inconsistency in seeking to love God. We must avoid all sin; we must repent of all sin.

5. How do I use my venial sins as opportunities for growth?

The very confusing reality of venial sin is another mystery which we encounter early on in the spiritual life. Venial sin boils down to saying "no" to God in little things. Just how saying "no" to God can ever be a venial sin or of lesser importance is beyond the greatest theological minds. Most theologians see it ultimately as a reflection of the immense mercy of God. He not only forgives when He is rejected in favor of things He has made, but He also allows Himself to be slighted. I am convinced that the fact of venial sin, always recognized by the Church, is a reflection of Christ's gentleness, a memory of an indulgence that neither Judaism nor Islam has ever been quite able to understand, although their spiritual leaders have, in fact, learned to cope tacitly with slights to the Eternal Being.

Venial sins fall into the same categories as mortal sins: deliberate sins, and sins of weakness or sins committed in conflict. Sins of both categories abound, ranging from more or less harmless gossip to careless participation in the liturgy. Swearing, cheating at bridge, and telling white lies are typical. Counting these sins can lead to severe depression, but we should examine our conduct carefully and daily repent of these failures.

Of particular importance are sins resulting from driven needs and compulsions. Simplistically, they may be called mortal sins poorly committed. Compulsions are pleasure-producing, self-destructive habits which can seriously impede progress in the spiritual life because they bring about their own unhealthy forms of penance. Augustine's "let it be now" may alternate with "not yet." At this point a spiritual director can greatly assist with insight, encouragement, and support. The individual in crisis may suffer depression, self-doubt, and bitterness, while prayer may become a time of complete aridity.

In a forthright document, Pope John Paul II gives the following advice to priests (who were once considered so sinless they went to Confession clandestinely); it may be of help to anyone in the purgative way.

> We must all be converted anew every day. We know that this is a fundamental exigency of the Gospel, addressed to everyone, and all the more do we have to consider it as addressed to us [priests]. If we have the duty of helping others to be converted we have to do the same continuously in our own lives. Being converted means returning to the very grace of our vocation; it means meditating upon the infinite goodness and love of Christ, Who has addressed each of us and, calling us by name, has said: "Follow Me." Being converted means continually "giving an account" before the Lord of our hearts about our service, our zeal and our fidelity, for we are "Christ's servants, stewards entrusted with the mysteries of God." Being converted also means "giving an account" of our negligences and sins, of our timidity, of our lack of faith and hope, of our thinking only "in a human way" and not "in a divine way." Let us recall, in this regard, the warning that Christ gave to Peter himself. Being converted means for us, seeking again the pardon and strength of God in the Sacrament of Reconciliation, and thus always beginning anew, and every day progressing, overcoming ourselves, making spiritual conquests, giving cheerfully, for "God loves a cheerful giver."
> Being converted means "to pray continually and never lose heart." In a certain way prayer is the first and last condition for conversion, spiritual progress, and holiness.[5]

These suggestions set forth by the Pope apply to all sinners and all sin with the single exception which we will take up presently. They serve as practical advice in the case of mortally sinful behavior or in the case of what are termed life's peccadillos.

The attitude of repentance for one's sins brings the Christian to Jesus Christ who alone can forgive. Christ does not brush sin away; He does not deny it, saying "Boys will be boys and girls will be girls." He is deadly serious about it and, after all, it cost Him His life. But He destroys it with His love and bids us with Peter and Paul constantly to start over.

SINS UNTO SORROW AND SINS UNTO DEATH

The phrase "sin unto death" refers to any mortal sin, that is, any serious violation of the divine law. I use the term here in a more restricted, literal sense to describe the sin that can kill spiritually. This is truly the "unforgivable sin" because its existence as a sin is denied and, consequently, it cannot be repented of.

There is a sin unto sorrow known to any spiritual director who has worked with persons beset by seriously sinful habits. One person recognizes the sin as a chain that binds him and leaves him confused and in pain. Another accepts it as an inescapable servitude. He may have tried everything from daily holy hours to psychotherapy and finally rationalized himself into the belief that "God made me this way." He lives in the hope that some providential turn in the road, like terminal illness or martyrdom, will free him from his slavery. One hopes and indeed believes that the Father of Mercies will deliver him sooner or later. However, like the men in Levinson's *Seasons,* he is caught in erratic behavior and unproductive habits, and may eventually burn himself out. Such persons can do serious harm to themselves and those who depend on them and waste most of the only life they will ever have. Often they receive a bolt of grace and become like Augustine, twisting and turning in their chains, at war with themselves, after which they embrace a sincere conversion. But whatever may happen to cause a turning to God (and one prays daily for this), they are not, in their present bondage, capable of much substantive progress in the spiritual life. They are most often firmly fixed at the beginning of the purgative way except that they can struggle to achieve a greater faith and trust. Encounter experiences or the Charismatic Movement are sometimes the source of a wave of grace that lifts them off the sandbar. Like Augustine,[6] they hear clearly for the first time the words of St. Paul to the Romans: "Let us live decently as people do in the daytime: no drunken orgies, no promiscuity or licentiousness, and no wrangling or jealousy. Let your armor be the Lord Jesus Christ; forget about satisfying your bodies with all their cravings" (Rm. 13:13–14).

Both Jerry and Leon are representative of this kind of person, although they were able to accept grace with considerable difficulty. I have known others who had to struggle for years to get as far as Jerry went in several months.

People who are fixated at the beginning of the purgative way must come to realize that their first mistake is to pay constant attention to the cravings of the flesh. They may no longer keep their temptations tucked away in some little corner, like a ticket or telephone number or pleasant piece of candy that would lead them to temptation and a fall. Temptation must be faced.

Since many sincere people find themselves in states of deep conflict, it is perhaps worthwhile at this point to examine another case history.

BILL'S STORY

Bill was raised in a strict, Irish Catholic home. He describes himself as a "go-getter" early in life. Behind his aggressive business sense lurked a strong need to win the recognition he had not received at home from his father. Bill's boundless energy was based partly on a great deal of suppressed anger.

Bill married a girl who, he says, "was and is still a saint." She is the best Catholic he has ever known. While this may be an exaggeration, his wife is, in fact, a fine person with much patience and common sense.

Bill's drinking problem began on the job. He was a salesman of construction equipment and had a good expense account. He turned to alcohol to control his temper when his teenage sons began to rebel against him. They had grown up in awe of their father, but grew tired of his domineering ways and ashamed of his emotional outbursts. Love turned to hate; at least one son developed symptoms of a seriously antisocial personality.

Bill states: "I got down on everything. I was mad at God, at the Church, at my family, my wife's family, and my company. I got louder and louder. One day, Rose, my wife, told me I was an alcoholic and should join AA. I had never been really angry with Rose; I came close to hitting her that day. Thank God, I did not. She told me that she had been going to Alanon and that for my own sake she would not cover up for me any more.

"I tried to get control of my drinking; I could not. I went to Confession; I made a retreat; I did everything because I did not want to join AA. I hate weakness and thought only weak people needed that kind of help."

Bill continued to drink for two years. He had week-long periods of sobriety and religious devotion. He tried to make up to his sons, but would slip back to drinking in a few days and have a blackout. Finally Bill went to AA. Fortunately it was the beginning of a new life for him, but it took him a long time to achieve three months of sobriety.

Bill took his twelve steps very carefully. He spent hours on the fifth step going over all his sins with a religious brother in the program who offered this assistance. Those who know Bill say he is a different man now. He is open to others and much more in control of his temper; most importantly, he is happy. He does not need to prove himself. He reads Scripture and finds the books of Henri Nouwen very helpful. He works hard helping others in AA. His son has yet to recover and Bill tries patiently to assist him. He struggles with guilt which could destroy him if he allows it to. Bill's battle for sobriety went on for a year after he joined AA. He is an example of a man caught in a "sin unto sorrow."

Frequently, Christians trying to overcome problems that combine psychological and moral elements, like alcoholism, must struggle for a long time after an initial decision to change. Apparently, the length of time is proportionate to the depth of the problem. Any compulsion is a severe problem, be it an addiction, like alcohol or drugs, or a behavioral difficulty, like sexual deviation or gambling. Certain compulsions, such as compulsive negative speech, are sometimes unrecognized. They are often linked with other problems like neurotic depression or manic-depressive tendencies. A person struggling with compulsion needs to be patient and absolutely convinced that it must be overcome. Making deals with compulsive behavior is useless and as dangerous as telling an alcoholic that he can drink a little.

A spiritual director or fellow Christian should not be surprised that someone desiring to advance in the spiritual life struggles with a compulsion. The compulsion itself may be the opportunity for taking the spiritual life more seriously. Someone already committed to the Christian life may encounter a compulsion after having made appreciable spiritual progress in the purgative way.

After having worked with many such persons, it is my impression that two common mistakes prevent people from overcoming compulsion as quickly as they might:

1. The failure to deal effectively with deep anxiety manifested as loneliness, anger, or frustration. We will examine the spiritual dimensions of anxiety in the next section of this chapter when we consider faith and trust.
2. The failure to reject every element of life that feeds the compulsion. Even when they decide to do better, compulsives usually retain the possibility of indulgence.

Psychotherapy or counseling is often needed to overcome a compulsion and will be most effective when the spiritual director or guide is in communication with the therapist. A program like AA precludes the need for therapy but not for a spiritual director, if the person is interested in growth. If the compulsion has moral overtones, the individual should, in my opinion, have a steady confessor who at least knows him or her by sight and first name and to whom he or she resolves to confess in the case of every fall.

TRUE SIN UNTO DEATH

There is another group to be considered in relation to the sin unto death. These are the most unhappy of mortals, those who have changed their sins into virtues. They really cannot repent because they do all things so "virtuously." They say they do evil out of love of God and their fellow human beings. Their preaching of the Gospel is a handful of confetti because it omits all references to "vices and virtues, punishment and glory," to borrow a phrase which St. Francis used when directing the preachers of his order.[7]

Changing vices into virtues is certainly no new phenomenon. In the opening chapters of the Epistle to the Romans, St. Paul rails against those who had deceived themselves by rationalization and denial. The ever-present tendency to deny sin constitutes an entire "antitradition" in the Church, made up of people like the Borgias and their camp-followers who by word and example denied the reality of sin in a very personal and consistent way. Oddly enough, it happens that such people evidence an interest in things spiritual. There is, of course, no possibility of progress in such circumstances. Certain methods of meditation may give the appearance of spiritual progress but are, in fact, a form of self-hypnosis. The superficial impression of progress in these cases actually compounds the individual's spiritual peril because it reinforces the denial of sin.

Thus we come to the most dangerous situation of the person whose sins God cannot forgive. God has forgiven billions of sins; however, His omnipotence will not contradict His decision to give human beings freedom. There is the case when the individual uses his or her free will against the Holy Spirit and refuses to repent. God Himself cannot forgive an impenitent sinner. Since impenitence is so terrible and contrary to human nature, and since it contradicts our elemental search for happiness and the attraction of the "four voices" of God, it is almost never an explicit choice. An individual refuses implicitly to repent by denial, pretense, or other defense mechanisms. Christ calls it a blindness protesting that it really sees.

NEUROTIC FEARS OF SIN AND LOSS

If you are moderately sincere (total sincerity being the preserve of the saints), you should not be unduly concerned with the neurotic fear of being spiritually blind. Such fears could be a symptom of spiritual neurosis and a lack of trust in God's love and mercy. Surely the Holy Spirit reveals the truth to those who ask for it. But one should be aware of spiritual blindness because our spiritual vision is imperfect. The destructive elements of total spiritual blindness and the denial of personal sin and repentance are constant themes in Church history. History has at times harshly judged certain eras and events in Christendom as well as activities of those who claimed to be Christ's disciples. Pre-Reformation Europe was filled with a great deal of behavior contrary to the Gospel. Most of those who caused scandal went blindly to their graves denying the evil they had done. The West would have continued its downward course, had it not been for those courageous enough to see their own sins and face up to the faults of their times. Perhaps the greatest responsibility of those aware of the interior life is to confront spiritual blindness gently, yet firmly. And the saints suggest that we begin with ourselves.

Transition to the Second Phase of the Purgative Way

The second phase of the purgative way focuses on the development of mature faith and trust. As moral integration is established, we notice a decline of fundamental anxiety. Like a traveler who has recently begun a long journey, we can now draw on personal experience to assess future stages of the journey. The struggle to accept the pardon and grace of Christ has made us experientially aware that we are loved by God and this new level of consciousness is a very powerful motive in giving up sin. The traveler feels the first winds of the freedom of God's children. As sin and its compulsion recede, he or she is filled with a greater counterforce: spiritual freedom and inner peace. Sin, at least as a possibility, will never be totally eradicated from this life, but its powerful hold has been substantially broken and new opportunities for integration begin to appear.

A Theory of Fundamental Anxiety and Inner Peace

This appears to be the appropriate time for me to introduce a theory of anxiety and inner peace on which I have been working for a number of years. This view is tentative and open to correction. Neither completely original nor very sophisticated, it offers a mental device that can be used consistently to sort out the psychological phenomena accompanying spiritual growth.

The great psychologists from Augustine to Freud, and St. Paul before them, recognized in human beings a terrible anxiety, a fear of futility and travail that haunt the person from infancy. As we become conscious of the spiritual element in our personality, our growing awareness of the possibility of a transcendent meaning to life begins to allay the anxiety. Life takes on a meaning beyond a series of random events. Two things happen which are opposite correlations of each other: anxiety declines and peace begins to reign within. Since pathology, which we have defined as driven need, is a way of discharging anxiety, pathological desire relaxes its grip and we gradually experience freedom. Defensiveness had obscured reality; as fear and anxiety recede, so does the need to be defensive, and we begin to see the truth. The following chart suggests that these opposite correlatives, symbolizing anxiety and peace, summarize much of the psychology of spiritual development.

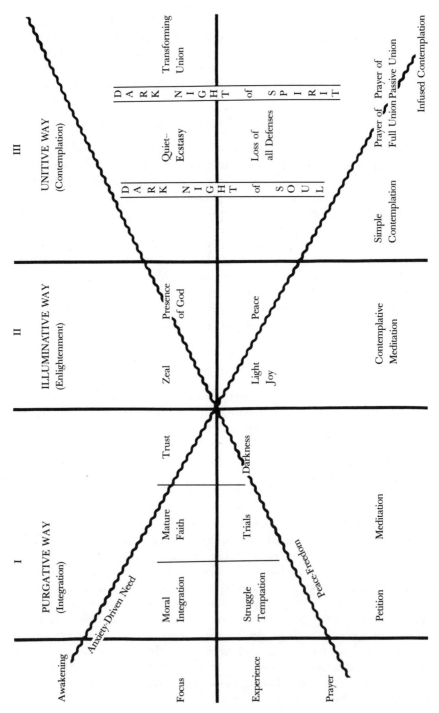

The reader will observe that a single undulating line (undulating or waving because the tendencies in life wax and wane) theoretically describes declining anxiety, driven need (pathology), and defensiveness. This line crosses its opposite, a line describing inner peace, freedom from pathology and the ability to face reality (truthfulness) at the end of the soul's first darkness. This chart can also provide some psychological understanding for the illuminative way, a period when the individual experiences substantial freedom and inner peace never before enjoyed so continually.

With regard to such a theoretical chart, it is important to note two features related to observations made earlier about the doctrine of the Three Ways. First, such a chart represents a vast oversimplification, similar to a road map. An individual's experience will be far more complex than the chart indicates. The wavy line may represent numerous falls and recoveries. There will be many instances, even early on, when freedom may be greater than driven need. Second, a person may regress or tarry along the way and therefore go through the same phase several times.

Any life map (as we have indicated) will place a person primarily or modally at one point on the journey; yet he or she is at all stages in some way. Someone at the end of the first phase of the purgative way may already experience aspects of illumination, but may also regress to the beginning. This illustrates the very interesting concept discussed above, namely, *becoming* or *being-in-time*.

TIME OF CRISIS

Crisis is ultimately a crossroad. As several writers (especially the Whiteheads) have pointed out, it is a time of pain and special opportunity for growth. As moral integration increases and new tasks of the second phase of the purgative way emerge, certain challenges arise that are worth mentioning.

The first of these is the impulse to go back. As Augustine recognized, the pleasures one is accustomed to have a stronger pull than the spiritual goals ahead which are not so well known. The question of St. Peter, "We have given up all things to follow You; what are we to have?" (Mt. 19:27), is very real. For the moment the individual must go on faith alone.

Secondly, the moral integration is still rather tenuous and the individual, therefore, may experience infrequent but more painful falls from grace. This is particularly true of those troubled by severe neurotic conflicts stemming from childhood.

At this juncture the most important question is "What do you really want?" The most encouraging reading is the Gospel understood from the viewpoint of the apostles. The Gospels reveal their long training and passage through difficult stages, during which Christ constantly confronts them with their subtle, worldly goals and selfishness.

Finally, it is during this long transition that the person has the second real experience of grace. The first experience was the beautiful call, "Follow Me," already described as an awakening. We have learned that we cannot really follow Him by our own power. Grace, the free gift of God making us children of adoption and capable of accepting Christ as our Lord and Savior, is the vital power of the spiritual life. In tracing the psychological development of a person, one often hears the expression, "I didn't know I was alive until I was thirty," or some other age when they became aware of the struggle to succeed and mature in life. An individual makes a similar discovery as the battle for moral integration comes to an end; but now the statement should be: "I didn't know I was alive in Christ."

The person has the first realization of the great truths of faith during the transition period. During the bitter conflict with the pathological self, he or she comes to recognize the absolute necessity of faith, the impossibility of following the divine will without it, the utter sovereignty of God, the inadequacy of all human expression of the truths of faith, and the meaning of the Incarnation and Redemption. At that point a figure begins to appear in the inner life of the individual, the figure of Christ. There is nothing abstract about this experience. One recognizes that indiscriminate use has trivialized the word "Christ," as in "Do this for Christ," or "The cause of Christ." All such expressions, once meaningful, are silenced. The person enters the new phase of the purgative way completely aware of a Presence, of an Individual who has suffered. "It is the Lord."

Second Phase—Mature Faith and Trust

As we begin to relinquish our defense mechanisms and see through our rationalization and intellectualization, we come to face two tasks which are usually accomplished simultaneously because one relies on the other. They were indicated in Chapter 3 where von Hügel's analysis of religious development was discussed. The tasks are the transcending of juvenile religiosity and adolescent religious speculation. Both behaviors are developmentally proper at a certain stage; both represent spiritual growth up to a point and both respond to human needs. The child attempts by cultic faith to manage the fear of life by attempting to control God with good works; the adolescent uses curiosity and rational analysis to control the divine by deciding what God can and must do. We have also seen that the experience of these developmental stages must be transformed in order to perdure in a mature spiritual life. The child's cultic works become the good deeds of charity; the adolescent's questioning becomes a reverent philosophy and theology. Unfortunately, both good works and speculation can provide a camouflage for those who choose not to mature, so that they become trapped in their own works or ideas.

FAITH—THE METANOIA OF REASON

The transition from the faith of adolescence to that of maturity is less difficult than the transition from childhood religiosity to trust, because religious rationalization is secondary as a life adjustment. In some ways it is easier to believe in God than to trust in Him. Paradoxically, therefore, the transcendence of adolescence usually occurs prior to that of childhood.

The religious belief of adolescence is based on clarity of ideas, or "what makes sense." Certitude or clarity in the last analysis is mostly a subjective experience. This may not be philosophically true, but it is unquestionably true psychologically. What is clear to one person is not clear to another. Since clarity is relatively subjective, it is also intrinsically tentative and its tentative quality can be observed in two maladaptive attitudes: fanaticism and chronic uncertainty. When adolescent faith is fueled by fear, it can be a very powerful experience and can precipitate very defensive and paranoid attitudes. Religious fanaticism (which is really a very threatened paranoid experience of belief) denies the individual's underlying uncertainty and projects his or her inner conflicts onto others. Usually the target is the devil or those thought to do his work. Fanaticism is forgivable in adolescents who are threatened by their own inner turmoil and need patient and gentle understanding. It is part of a common understanding of human nature to know that a basically healthy person may experience some paranoid ideation. (Haven't we all?) To assist the individual in such situations, however, it is necessary to enter his or her somewhat distorted world vision and try to allay his or her fears. Frequently adults who are themselves threatened attract adolescents and magnify their own fear as well as that of the young people. This is the origin of youth cults. Others who have failed to achieve a completely mature faith may join the adolescent in his or her fanaticism, forming a relationship which is doomed to dissolution if the young person continues to move toward a less threatened and more mature faith.

The greatest pitfall in moving toward mature faith, however, is not the

false certitude of fanaticism, but rather a permanent fixation in an endless series of more sophisticated speculation. Some rather intellectually
gifted people fall into the trap of repetitive experiences of tentative
clarity, and interminable defense of these experiences. This is a particular problem for adults who as children or adolescents endured rejection
or scorn because of their intellectual gifts. Understandably, they learn
early in life to build their self-esteem on their intellectual powers. Like
their competitors who become addicted to athletic achievement, they are
overly involved with self-expression through games of the mind. It is not
unusual to find Christians of real intelligence and sensitivity wasting
years formulating subtle theories and distinctions, yet failing to make the
leap into faith which is beyond such exercises.

The traits of both types of believer trapped in adolescence (the fanatic
and the overly speculative) are strangely similar. Although they may
fight with each other, trading names like skeptic and obscurantist, they
are both capable of sincere, intense commitments to religion and spirituality. Each group, however, failing to get beyond adolescence, demonstrates the signs of psychological stagnation: bitterness, boredom, and
escape into frenetic, unrewarding stereotypic activity.

The solution to the dilemma is the leap into mature faith. This phrase
may annoy those who need most to take the leap; thus a psychological
analysis of mature faith may be helpful. We will examine, first, the
subjective qualities of mature faith, then, its source and process, and,
finally, its relationship to the decline of anxiety.

As we have seen, the faith of adolescence is based on clear ideas
tentatively held until better explanations are found. Mature faith, according to St. John of the Cross, is the opposite. Instead of being tentative it is certain because the author of this faith is God. In the case of
mature faith, divine grace breaks into the ordinary processes of cogni-
tion through revelation and the personal enlightenment which enables
the individual to believe. One cannot stress enough that mature faith,
like the final struggles with moral integration, reveals personally and
unmistakably the power of a dynamism outside self, namely, grace. I
seriously question whether anyone who is subjectively unaware of this
experience has arrived at the later phases of the purgative way.

More importantly, mature faith is mysterious and obscure. It transcends ordinary theological speculation, which is based on clear ideas
drawn from analogies manageable by reason. The source of these analogies used in adolescent faith and in intellectual speculation should be
rooted in Revelation. Analogies make possible the task of positive theology. However, the faith of which St. John of the Cross speaks is faith
beyond all analogies, and is usually called "apophatic faith," i.e., faith

based on denial of what is not true rather than on affirmation of what is true.

A single example may clarify the distinction between analogous and apophatic faith. It is revealed that God is a living, personal God. The notion we share as human beings of a human person is therefore applied to God as an analogy. It is a useful analogy which every child and adolescent can comprehend, although the young adolescent, newly capable of abstract thought, will do better than the child for whom God is an old man, the Ancient of Days. The theological student will go much further, remove the anthropomorphisms, and come to the most sublime and unlimited notion of person. The theologian can examine the concept of person, and the Scripture and dogma related to the analogy, and proceed to an almost limitless refinement especially as psychology refines its definition of person.

Then the student or theologian grows silent in inner prayer and experiences a mysterious relationship with and knowledge of God. The individual experience goes beyond all concepts of person. God becomes not less than person nor more than person but beyond person, as we understand the term.

St. John of the Cross's teaching on this subject is worth studying in his own words.

Faith, the theologians say, is a certain and obscure habit of soul. It is an obscure habit because it brings us to believe divinely revealed truths which transcend every natural light and infinitely exceed all human understanding. As a result the excessive light of faith bestowed on man is darkness for him, because a brighter light will eclipse and suppress a dimmer one. The sun so obscures all other lights that they do not seem to be lights at all when it is shining, and instead of affording vision to the eyes it overwhelms, blinds, and deprives them of vision, since its light is excessive and unproportioned to the visual faculty. Similarly the light of faith in its abundance suppresses and overwhelms that of the intellect. For the intellect, by its own power, comprehends only natural knowledge, though it has the potency to be raised to a supernatural act wherever our Lord wishes.

A man of himself knows only in a natural way; that is, by means of the senses. If he is to know in this natural way, the phantasms and species of objects will have to be present either in themselves or in their likenesses; otherwise he will be incapable of knowing naturally. As the scholastic philosophers say: Knowledge arises in the soul from both the faculty and the object at hand. If a person were told of objects he had never known or seen resemblances of, he would in the end have no more knowledge than before.

For example, if a man were informed that on a certain island there was an animal whose like or kind he had never seen, he would then have no more idea or image of that animal in his mind than previously, no matter how much he was told.

Another clearer example will shed more light on this subject: If a man born blind were told about the nature of the color white or yellow, he would understand absolutely nothing no matter how much instruction he received. Since he never saw these colors, nor their like, he would not have the means to form a judgment about them. Only their names would be grasped since the names are perceptible through hearing; but never their form or image, because these colors were never seen by him.

Such is faith to the soul—it informs us of matters we have never seen or known, either in themselves or in their likenesses; in fact nothing like them exists. The light of natural knowledge does not show us the object of faith, since this object is unproportioned to any of the senses. Yet, we come to know it through hearing, by believing what faith teaches us, blinding our natural light and bringing it into submission. St. Paul states: *Fides ex auditu* [Rom 10:17]. This amounts to saying that faith is not a knowledge derived from the senses, but an assent of the soul to what enters through hearing.

Faith, moreover, far exceeds what these examples teach us. Not only does it fail to produce knowledge and science, but, as we said, it deprives and blinds a person of any other knowledge or science by which he may judge it. Other knowledge is acquired by the light of the intellect, but not the knowledge that faith gives. Faith nullifies the light of the intellect, and if this light is not darkened, the knowledge of faith is lost. Accordingly, Isaias said: *Si non credideritis, non intelligetis* (If you do not believe, you will not understand) [Is 7:9].

Faith, manifestly, is a dark night for man, but in this very way it gives him light. The more darkness it brings him, the more light it sheds. For by blinding it illumines him, according to those words of Isaias that if you do not believe you will not understand, that is, you will not have light. [Is 7:9][8]

"Intuition" is probably the best word to indicate the experience St. John of the Cross describes in this passage. Intuition is a form of intelligence beyond rational analysis; it perceives a whole reality without analyzing the parts as is done in the appreciation of great art or music. Since faith has its sources beyond the human psyche, the mere introduction of the notion of intuition does not explain or account for the phenomena associated with mature faith, especially certitude. Any analysis of intuition must essentially be limited because of its mysterious mode of operation. Description based on experience is the best guide. As St. Bernard states in another verse of the hymn given as the inscription of this book, "No tongue can say, no word express, but only experience can believe." Pascal's "Memorial" is an attempt to describe an experience of mystical intuition. He wrote the "Memorial" to assist him in reviewing and reexamining what had happened. When reading this account in which words and thoughts are so obviously insufficient, it is important to recall that Pascal was a genius; his literary and mathematical works are renowned for precision of expression and clarity of thought.

Memorial
In the year of grace 1654
Monday, 23 November, the day of St. Clement,
Pope and Martyr, and others in the Roman Martyrology,
the eve of St. Chrysogonus, Martyr, and others. . . .
From about half-past ten in the evening
Till about half an hour after midnight
FIRE
God of Abraham, God of Isaac, God of Jacob
Not of the philosophers and the learned.
Certitude joy certitude emotion sight joy
God of Jesus Christ
Deum meum et Deum vestrum.
Thy God shall be my God.
Forgetfulness of the world and of everything
    other than God
He can be found only in the ways taught
in the Gospel. Greatness of the human soul.
Good Father, the world has not known
Thee, but I have known Thee.
Joy Joy Joy and tears of joy
I have separated myself from Thee
Dereliquerunt me fontem [aquae vivae]
my God wilt Thou leave me?
let me not be eternally separated from Thee
They have life eternal, they that know Thee
Sole true God and He Whom Thou hast sent
Jesus Christ
Jesus Christ
I have separated myself from Him, I have fled,
    renounced, crucified Him.[9]

Perhaps more than any other document in the literature of mysticism, Pascal's "Memorial" illustrates the mysterious quality of the knowledge of mature faith. We might well ask the question: Can human knowledge grow under such circumstances or is the mind merely operating passively like a mirror? St. Augustine clearly defines a process of development in this kind of knowledge. He indicates that the intuition of faith is correctly considered real human knowledge in which the individual's powers are not merely passive.[10]

The following steps make up Augustine's analysis of faith: First, we use reason to come to mystery which is beyond reason. We know by reason (in this case deducing from Revelation) that God is person. But how is He person? He neither changes, nor grows, nor declines; yet all the persons we know do these things. We are confronted with a mystery; we appeal to God for faith, implicitly or explicitly, and the gift of faith helps us accept the mystery and then pass into it.

A new intuition of Person-beyond-person fills our consciousness like a great symphony. God is now known to be Person-beyond-person; reason can ask several new questions. For example, how does the insight of faith affect my relationship with other persons who receive their personhood from God? Or how do I begin to relate to Person-beyond-person? This, according to St. Augustine, is the meaning of "I believe so that I may understand even more."

The remarkable possibilities for growth in the knowledge of faith are available to all. However, the person who has studied theology in one or several forms has both an advantage and a disadvantage: his or her understanding of the content of Revelation brings many opportunities to grow in faith, but the possibility of getting caught in intellectual games is correspondingly greater. For this reason, the Church has given special honor to such theologians at St. Augustine and St. Thomas Aquinas who used their minds in the service of positive theology and in the intuitive perception of the mysteries of faith.[11]

THE SOURCE OF FAITH

Perhaps the most perplexing question in the psychology of religion concerns the origin of faith and the process of belief that follows the experience of faith. Informed Christians sometimes reinforce their own commitment to the faith of Christ by the fact that many secular scholars study the phenomenon of religious belief and pay homage to Christianity's cultural and moral contribution to civilization. Everyone admires the cathedrals of the ages of faith. Human beings appear to be naturally religious, as indeed they are. It is important to recognize that religious experience psychologically may be the result of many factors. Some religious experience is rooted in faith; it would be a misconception, however, to assume that all religious experience originates in the grace of faith.

Does the human being naturally believe in God—if not in the God of Revelation, at least in the God of the philosophers? Some disposition to religion would seem to be natural. In the Epistle to the Romans, St. Paul appears to condemn the pagans for their unbelief because there were so many rational motives for accepting the existence of God.

The root of the question is the word "nature," which can mean two different things. It can pertain to a view of the cosmos, the material world known through the senses and synthesized by the powers of human understanding; in this sense it refers to "natural science." Such a view always contains the assumption that the world exists on its own. It places the human being in a closed system as part of the great mechanism or "clock" which may or may not have had a great clockmaker. This meaning of nature prevails in almost every form of study and entertainment in our culture. It is regrettably so much a part of us that the reader is perhaps puzzled that nature could mean anything else. The material definition, however, leaves the human being imprisoned; it implies that knowledge of anything beyond the cosmos is unessential or contrary to human nature.

"Nature" may also describe that which flows from the essence or basic being of a thing; what it is in itself. In this sense, it is "natural" or of the essence of the human being to reason, and of the essence of all living things to preserve that life. It is also natural for angels not to be part of the cosmos or of what the first definition defines as nature. Angels cannot commune with "nature" in a garden; yet they have natures of their own.

The second meaning of nature should be kept in mind when discussing the origin of faith. According to St. Augustine, it is natural for human beings to believe in the living God who is their Creator. It is in accord with their nature, for belief in the true and unchanging source of being is a psychological exigency of the human creature who longs to love what is not destroyed by chance or diminished by time. It is also a social necessity: Society must be built on love between human beings. This love requires a loving Being whose love goes beyond human nature, which is capable of such hateful deeds. This loving Being calls for a response of generosity, mercy, and forgiveness. In every way the human being, by his or her very nature, is called to believe in this loving Being.

The thought of the ancient Church is summed up in the phrase *anima naturaliter Christiana:* The human spirit is naturally Christian. The human being is not just a believer but a Christian. This ancient Christian concept, which is incomprehensible to those who live with a vision of a closed "natural world," has been preached consistently by the Church and, in our own time, by the highest pastoral authority.

How is a person naturally Christian? Human beings, individually and collectively, show obvious signs of disorder and disorientation which we call the "effects of original sin." Even unbelievers like Freud grappled with this phenomenon. Within the framework of the Fall, we can consider the human being naturally Christian because all he or she does or experiences echoes a cry for redemption and salvation.

Man's natural need to be saved is reiterated dramatically for our times by the chief Pastor of the Church. The theme of Pope John Paul II's first encyclical is precisely this "natural" need:

> The Redeemer of the world! In Him has been revealed in a new and more wonderful way the fundamental truth concerning creation to which the Book of Genesis gives witness when it repeats several times: "God saw that it was good." The good has its source in Wisdom and Love. In Jesus Christ the visible world which God created for man— the world that, when sin entered, "was subjected to futility" (Rom 8:20)—recovers again its original link with the divine source of Wisdom and Love. Indeed, "God so loved the world that he gave his only Son" (John 3:16). As this link was broken in the man Adam, so in the Man Christ it was reforged (cf Rom 5:12–21). Are we of the twentieth century not convinced of the overpoweringly eloquent words of the Apostle of the Gentiles concerning the "creation (that) has been groaning in travail together until now" (Rom 8:22) and "waits with eager longing for the revelation of the sons of God," (Rom 8:19) the creation that "was subjected to futility"?[12]

This expression of the natural human need for Christ is apt to leave many believers uneasy as a result of the philosophy of a closed world (the other meaning of nature) which is so much a part of our own thought. It will surprise these believers to realize that the Pope's teaching is ultimately only a commentary on the Pastoral Constitution on the Church in the Modern World (*Gaudium et Spes*) of Vatican II. Bearing in mind the description above of the word "nature," the reader may understand the following in a new light:

> The truth is that only in the mystery of the Incarnate Word does the mystery of man take on light. For Adam, the first man, was a type of Him who was to come (Rom 5:14), Christ the Lord. Christ, the new Adam, in the very revelation of the mystery of the Father and of His love, fully reveals man to himself and brings to light his most high calling. He who is the "image of the invisible God" (Col 1:15), is Himself the perfect man who has restored in the children of Adam that likeness to God which had been disfigured ever since the first sin. Human nature, by the very fact that it was assumed, not absorbed, in Him, has been raised in us also to a dignity beyond compare. For, by His Incarnation, He, the Son of God, in a certain way united Himself with each man. He worked with human hands, He thought with a human mind. He acted with a human will, and with a human heart He

loved. Born of the Virgin Mary, He has truly been made one of us, like to us in all things except sin.[13]

TRUST—THE METANOIA OF BASIC ANXIETY

The final struggle along the way of purgation consists in the substantial relinquishment of the anxiety of life. We are driven and controlled by anxious fear more than by any other element of our psychic life. By anxious fear we mean a constant apprehension that we are threatened by uncontrollable forces. Even when human beings are consciously motivated by pleasure, the desire for good, or even spiritual blessings, a strong element of fear and anxiety prompts their actions. Pleasure offers only a temporary cessation of anxious fear; the possession of some good thing brings with it a feeling of security for a while; religious consolations ward off for a time the fear of oblivion or eternal loss. But so long as we know that fear will return, it will continue to color our desires and actions.

Leaders of spiritual movements have consistently recognized that growth in the life of the spirit does away with anxious fear. The motives for fear have been seen either as illusions, or as obstacles which are temporary and surmountable. None of the great spiritual religions has regarded the sources of fear as having a transcendent reality of their own. What about the fear of hell? Even the fear of eternal loss is properly understood as a deprivation of everlasting good which is based on the decisions made in time, not after this life. Nevertheless, the fear of eternal loss is universal and is not lightly to be dismissed. It is the most deeply rooted of fears and thus often improperly called the "fear of God." But in the ultimate analysis it is a fear of the loss of what is transcendent rather than a fear of a transcendent evil, which can be conceived only in a truly dualistic religion like Zoroastrianism.

So profound is this elemental fear of eternal death that most people don't even allude to it. As we seldom think of heaven, so we seldom think of hell. Our fears are related to lesser things: to the loss of physical health or of economic security. We fear threats to the well-being of those dear to us, and in this fear both they and we are often well aware that there is a strong element of self-interest: "I need you, so stay well" is the attitude underlying much of our concern. We fear the loss of social status and the good opinion of others. More than anything else, we fear ourselves; the loss of our powers through age or illness, the loss of control or mental balance. We fear the collapse of our world through natural forces or catastrophes precipitated by the insanity of our race; we fear war or environmental destruction; in short, we fear life and we fear death. Those of us who read books such as this one are generally better defended than others and thus we deny our fears, and then we fear because we do not fear. Many sincerely religious people who make unduly slow progress are dominated by fears denied or fears superficially projected onto other things.

In the formation of His apostles Jesus Christ constantly taught them the necessity of trust, and yet He told them fearful things; warned them of the wrath that was to come; predicted His own death; told them that they would be sifted as wheat. But despite all of this He told them to trust God, have faith and hope, and believe that the Father would look after them. The trust taught by Christ is not based on a denial of the reality of suffering or evil. Jesus of Nazareth was too much of a realist for that. Even though evil would pass away, it was real while it lasted and He taught His disciples to overcome it by loving fidelity. He never taught them to deny the existence of evil forces in the world, but He did teach that trust in God would outlast the evil and would lead to realities that do not pass away.

In ancient times the danger of death was constant. Illness, war, cruel civil punishments all made life a tenuous affair. Suffering and death were more obviously a part of everyday existence than they are now. Most ancient people dealt with these fears by the notion of fate. The Jews often tended to see misfortune as a punishment from God, although, as we see in the Book of Job, its other meaning was part of the mystery of the creation. Christ went beyond these ideas and taught that true trust and hope were focused on the Kingdom of God. He did not deny the value of human hope for ordinary human needs. He advised prayer for the fulfillment of human needs for daily bread. But when all was said and done, Christ confronted fear in Himself in its most awesome form. He obviously reflected His fear in the agony in the garden and in the moments before His passion and death. He did not pretend that these terrible happenings were not real at all. He confronted evil in its grossest form and suffered in ways that are beyond the imagination of human beings who do not have His extraordinary powers of perception.

The ultimate message of Jesus Christ is to trust God and His ability to bring good out of evil. The message of Christian trust is to trust when there is no hope and to gain the strength to trust in this way from the only source that it can come from, namely, the power of the Holy Spirit.

Romano Guardini has seen clearly that this kind of trust challenges the existential anxiety of human beings.[14] Such trust goes by many names: confidence in God, abandonment to divine providence, perfect joy, spiritual disinterest and detachment. Each of these terms has generated a spiritual literature about it and in each case it has been identified with the beginnings of a more perfect love of God. Often these terms sound contradictory, but their common base is that they lead us to attempt to respond totally to the absolute love of God. The idea of St. Francis's perfect joy, which prompted him to rejoice at the abuse and hostility of a confrere, is the same as the absolute renunciation of St. John of the Cross when he says, "think only that God ordains all things and where there is no love put love and you will find love." The *omnia* of St. Francis is the other side of the *nada* of St. John of the Cross. Confidence and abandonment are the same thing although the latter term has a more ominous ring to it. Often Christian piety has linked the idea of trust to a certain devotion, usually because of the inspiration of a particular saint. The devotion to the Sacred Heart of Jesus became the practical expression of perfect trust as a result of the teaching of St. Margaret Mary and her spiritual director, Blessed Claude de la Columbière. St. Louis de Montfort would link the same idea to the devotion to Our Lady. Parallels with this very Catholic devotional expression of trust are found in the spirituality of most spiritual movements, although they may be expressed in various ways.

Christian theology has always had to struggle with this insight of total confidence and abandonment because it could lead to a heretical quietism. One has the impression that theologians would often have been delighted if the whole idea went away. This is because they had not reached a level of spiritual development permitting them to understand the need for total abandonment. It is my guess that both the absolute nature of the mature faith described by St. John of the Cross and the absolute quality of trust given by so many mystics will continue to make many academics uneasy until the end of time. Yet the spiritual idea of trust will continue to be accepted because of the intuitive expression of anyone who comes this far and passes beyond the cultic religiosity of childhood and the intellectualized religious sentiment of adolescence.

SPIRITUAL DARKNESS

A term that needs to be introduced at this point is "spiritual darkness." A thorough analysis of this term is beyond the scope of this book and is provided by a number of eminent spiritual writers. For our present purpose it is sufficient to describe the experience. Spiritual darkness is a psychological state of great discomfort, precipitated either by external causes like a painful loss or trauma or by inner conflicts leading to depression and a feeling of profound alienation. It can come from without like the death of a loved one or the failure of a cause; it may be from within, in which case it is really a breakdown of our defense pattern or a burnout, a kind of emotional and psychological exhaustion. It can be caused by sickness or imprisonment. It is important to take note of this because often people associate the spiritual darkness exclusively with spiritual aridity or some inner state. This misapprehension is probably caused by the fact that most books on the subject are written by people who have nothing else to lose but their spiritual consolations. Hence the image of the cloistered nun kneeling on the flagstone floor in the frozen cloister is the popular image of the Dark Night. But I think most dark nights are experienced at kitchen tables and at office desks.

Any trying circumstance offering the opportunity to trust and confide in God is properly called a "darkness." The experience becomes a spiritual one because the virtues of faith, hope, and love are exercised. A monk going through a trial in prayer may fail to trust God and accept His will and so the darkness will be an unproductive religious experience. On the other hand a young mother may turn to the plaster statue of a saint in her little kitchen in a crowded industrial neighborhood and accept the death of her child with painful but loving trust. This will be a Dark Night and many contemplatives have been formed in just this way.

It is interesting to speculate about the common element in all such experiences. Perhaps the following explanation may suggest a common factor in experiences of spiritual darkness. As we have seen, human beings perceive reality through the filter of their defense mechanisms. If for a blinding moment the defenses are dissipated by a painful breakthrough of reality, the individual may, with the help of grace, be able to seize upon reality and accept it.

The Danish philosopher and Lutheran spiritual writer Kierkegaard points out with startling clarity that only darkness strips away our inner psychic defenses. It stills all the voices within except the voice of God. Surely every reader has had the experience when the illusory dreams of life have been shattered by the darkness of adversity.

> He who dreams must be awakened, and the deeper the man is who slumbers, or the deeper he slumbers, the more important it is that he be awakened, and the more powerfully must he be awakened. In case there is nothing that awakens the youth, this dream-life is continued in manhood. The man doubtless thinks that he is dreaming no more, and in a sense he is not; perhaps he scorns and despises the dreams of youth, but precisely this shows that his life is a failure. In a sense he is awake, yet he is not in an eternal sense and in the deepest sense awake. And so his life is something far less significant than that of the youth, and it is his life rather which deserves to be despised; for he has become an unfruitful tree, or like a tree which has died, whereas the life of youth verily is not to be despised. The dream-life of childhood and youth is the time of blossoming. But in the case of a tree which is

to bear fruit, the time of blossoming is a time of immaturity. It may indeed seem like retrogression when the tree which once stood naked and then burst into bloom, now casts off its blossoms; but it also may be progress. Fair is the time of blossoms, and fair is the blossoming hope in the child and in the youth; and yet it is immaturity.

Then comes affliction to awaken the dreamer, affliction which like a storm tears off the blossoms, affliction which nevertheless does not bereave of hope, but recruits hope.

Affliction is able to drown out every earthly voice, that is precisely what it has to do, but the voice of eternity within a man it cannot drown. Or conversely: it is the voice of eternity within which demands to be heard, and to make a hearing for itself it makes use of the loud voice of affliction. Then when by the aid of affliction all irrelevant voices are brought to silence, it can be heard, this voice within.[15]

In most of the case histories we have used, a period of darkness or trial was the occasion of substantial spiritual growth. Sister Marie and Father Carl passed through a period of real alienation from the communities to which they had given so much. Jerry's struggle began in darkness, but he went on to surmount even more experiences of disappointment. Helene decided that the desertion of her husband would become an opportunity for spiritual growth.

But darkness and trial were not enough. Learning a basic trust in God, and an equally important declining interest in worldly comfort and success, were necessary for all. You can't grow from the experience of darkness until you learn that some things are more important than others and that the loss of some good things leads to the gain of greater spiritual goods.

The essential lessons of the Dark Night are learned only when one takes the first halting steps toward hope and trust. These steps are totally impossible without the acceptance of grace in the form of the theological virtues. The first step to be taken, the first thing to be learned, is the sovereignty of God. This is learned only in darkness when we come to the realization of our absolute insufficiency. We simply cannot do anything alone. We are for the first time in our lives faced with the possibility of genuine humility. The English spiritual writer Gerald Heard gives the following description. It seems to me to be a bit of a hyperbole to say nothing has been done of any real value before this phase, but I cite Heard's teaching in its entirety because, even if theologically inaccurate, he does at least communicate what a person may subjectively experience:

We must start without delay on the painful, steep, humiliating path of undoing our busy, deliberately deluded selves. So only will the King-dom come, where it must come fully and where we alone can decide whether it shall come—in ourselves. "The Kingdom of God is within you," yes, but only if we are prepared to let that powerful germ of eternal life grow. . . . Unless we, this person with his tightly bound triple self-love—love of his physical appetites and comforts, of his possessions, of his place, rank, and recognition—unless that hard and hardening nut is buried and rots and is eaten away by the new life's germ, there is no hope. Indeed we may say that the whole secret of the spiritual life is just this painful struggle to come awake, to become really conscious. And, conversely, the whole process and technique of evil is to do just the reverse to us: to lull us to sleep, to distract us from what is creeping up within us; to tell us that we are busy workers for the Kingdom when we are absent-mindedly spreading death, not life.

That, then, is the first step, known by the grim technical term, purgation. I must start with myself, and stay with myself until some intention appears in my actions, some consistency between what I say and do. I must not escape into denunciation, coercion, or even superior concern for anyone else. I shall do so if I can; that is the invariable trick of the ego. . . . Then, after complete abandonment of serving two masters—my view of myself as a masterbuilder gaining recognition by my active goodness, and of God—then comes the next step, illumination. I am still far below being capable of a creative act. That is God's prerogative. But I am permitted at last to see things as they are. Fear and hurry and anxiety leave me. Why? Because, though still extremely ignorant, I know one thing at last. I know that God exists. There is utter Reality, complete creative power holding the entire creation in its grasp. The whole of time and space is no more than an incident, a minute episode in the immeasurable order, power, and glory of complete Being. Once I have seen, really seen, that, once I am illuminated, then I have fully attained one step in approaching God's Kingdom and in letting it approach; I no longer am standing in the way. I cease to be a reason for people not believing in God.[16]

The most important experience of the Dark Night, however, is the rescuing by God, which marks the end of the darkness. It is like the resurrection on Easter morning. We arrive like Mary and often at first do not realize what has happened. The light dawns upon us gently and slowly until we realize that indeed we have learned something that we never really knew before. The lives of the saints abound with examples which unfortunately are often presented by hagiographers as Hollywood-type happy endings. Of course the actual working of God is very different. The causes of darkness may still remain and tears of sorrow may still flow, but in spite of it all a new soft and gentle light is rising in the inner being of the individual.

Of the many passages I could use to illustrate this final phase I have chosen the one below from Cardinal Newman because it was written when much darkness still remained in his life. Newman had left his beloved Anglican Church at the very crest of his influence. He had been part of one of the most effective friendships in human history, that of the founders of the Oxford Movement. He was received in the Roman Catholic Church with suspicion and, if the truth be told, with hostility apparently based on jealousy. He had lost his friends and been thrown in with strangers. It would be many years before he would be vindicated in the eyes of the world. In that darkness he wrote this powerful meditation. It seems to me one of the most telling statements of trust and humility ever written in the English language.

> God has created me, to do him some definite service; he has committed some work to me which He has not committed to another. I have my mission—I may never know it in this life, but I shall be told it in the next. I am a link in a chain, a bond of connection between persons. He has not created me for nothing. I shall do good, I shall do his work. Therefore, I will trust him. Whatever, wherever I am. I cannot be thrown away.[17]

We cannot draw our discussion of the Dark Night to a close without some mention of a common problem, that of the person who passes through darkness, gaining the freedom of detachment, and then goes back again to where he or she had been. I suspect that many of us have passed through enough dark nights to ensure our entrance into the illuminative way several times over. We see the light and yet we go back. My suspicion is that we are so accustomed to our own narcissistic melancholy, so guilt-ridden and attached to our own self-deprecation, that the very thought of being at peace in the light of God, is terrifying to us. To use a cliché, it would precipitate an identity crisis if we found ourselves at peace. And so we tarry along the way. We shrink back because we know that if we experienced real detachment and abandonment, we would have to give up our cherished ambitions, our earthly and spiritual goods, and a good deal of self-determination. Like Israel we would like to rejoice in being God's servant, but we would like to keep control ourselves. Like the apostles we would accompany Christ wherever He goes, but would prefer Palm Sunday to Good Friday. We would like to keep our options open and so we must pass through darkness again and again until at last we surrender.

Chapter 7

The Second Stage
of the Spiritual Life:
The Illuminative Way

At the end of the darkness, when the level of anxiety has finally fallen below the individual's degree of peace and trust, when driven need is substantially less compelling than the freedom of the person, a new experience begins, which, in most spiritually oriented religions, is known as "enlightenment" or "illumination." The latter term used by Augustine to name the middle phase of the spiritual journey has become conventional in Christianity.[1] He saw the creation of light in Genesis as the symbol of the spiritual illumination of the individual. The image underlies the most important aspect of the Christian view of the illuminative way, namely, that we do not have within us the source of light. Light is given to us. Speaking of the similarity between the creation of the world and the illumination of the soul, Augustine says:

> It does not seem proper in Your eyes that immutable Light should be known by the mutable being which it illumines, as that light knows itself. Therefore my soul is as earth without water unto Thee for just as it cannot of itself illumine itself, so it cannot of itself quench the thirst that it has. For with Thee is the fountain of life, and in Thy light we shall see light![2]

The subjective experience of light or enlightenment seems to be typical of the middle phase of the spiritual journey in most religions. Despite the universality of this experience it is important to note that our presentation is intentionally Christian. In the following pages I will make two assumptions: The spiritual illumination resulting from God's grace is possible to members of all world religions and all spiritual seekers; secondly, it is most correctly and fully understood in its constitutive elements only when one is guided by Scripture and Christian tradition. It would be dishonest of me not to state these two assumptions. This presentation is very specifically based on the teaching of the Church and the lives of Christian saints. The most salient feature of Christian (as well as Jewish) teaching on illumination is that the light is God's light, not our own. "In Thy light we shall see light" (Ps. 35:10).

THE EXPERIENCE OF ILLUMINATION—A CONTEMPORARY DESCRIPTION

Those in the early stages of the spiritual life become ever more conscious of the reality of God "out there." His transcendence and our relation to Him, our struggle toward Him through faith and hope, are clear experiences. As the barriers to freedom fall and the most powerful defenses are relinquished, we slowly become aware of God's presence within. Thomas Merton has provided an excellent description of this experience and all that results from it in his posthumously published essay *Contemplation in a World of Action*:

> The real point of the contemplative life has always been a deepening of faith and of the personal dimensions of liberty and apprehension to the point where our direct union with God is realized and "experienced." We awaken not only to a realization of the immensity and majesty of God "out there" as King and Ruler of the universe (which He is) but also a more intimate and more wonderful perception of Him as directly and personally present in our own being. Yet this is not a pantheistic merger or confusion of our being with His. On the contrary, there is a distinct conflict in the realization that though in some sense He is more truly ourselves than we are, yet we are not identical with Him, and though He loves us better than we can love ourselves we are opposed to Him, and in opposing Him we oppose our own deepest selves. If we are involved only in our surface existence, in externals, and in the trivial concerns of our ego, we are untrue to Him and to ourselves. To reach a true awareness of Him as well as ourselves, we have to renounce our selfish and limited self and enter into a whole new kind of existence, discovering an inner center of motivation and love which makes us see ourselves and everything else in an entirely new light. Call it faith, call it (at a more advanced stage) contemplative illumination, call it the sense of God or even mystical union: all these are different aspects and levels of the same kind of realization: the awakening to a new awareness of ourselves in Christ, created in Him, redeemed by Him, to be transformed and glorified in and with Him. In Blake's words, the "doors of perception" are opened and all life takes on a completely new meaning: the real sense of our own existence, which is normally veiled and distorted by the routine distractions of an alienated life, is now revealed in a central intuition. What was lost and dispersed in the relative meaninglessness and trivi-

ality of purposeless behavior (living like a machine, pushed around by impulsions and suggestions from others) is brought together in fully integrated conscious significance. This peculiar, brilliant focus is, according to Christian tradition, the work of Love and of the Holy Spirit. This "loving knowledge" which sees everything transfigured "in God," coming from God and working for God's creative and redemptive love and tending to fulfillment in the glory of God, is a contemplative knowledge, a fruit of living and realizing faith, a gift of the Spirit.[3]

This passage, with its intelligent concern for those on the spiritual road, succinctly summarizes the Christian view of the illuminative way. The meaning and description of the illuminative experience should be of vital interest to every Christian on the road because, frankly, it is as far as most sincere travelers ever reach. The later darkness, properly called the Dark Night, and especially the unitive way are beyond most of us at the time of death. Perhaps the night of death will be much of our purgatory followed by the experience of the unitive way in the Kingdom of God. The illuminative way is the preparation for, or preface to, union with God. Even those who reach the unitive way in this life will have spent many years in the illuminative way. Enlightened self-interest, to use a pun, suggests that we pay close attention to this description of the illuminative way because of the various ways in which it can be experienced and the possibility of losing one's direction in its complicated paths.

The Experience of the Illuminative Way

While the word "illumination" suggests a passing experience of enlightenment, a "peak" experience, the illuminative way is not like that at all. It is a sustained state in which it is easier to pray, give up things that are superfluous or obstruct progress, and work to accomplish more for the Kingdom of God. Doing good becomes easier because a step has been taken in the right direction. In our struggles and accomplishments we recognize the power of grace and the goodness of God enabling us to do good. This recognition makes a person less judgmental, less demanding upon others and more accepting. The ability to do good easily continues to increase so that one on this way does not stop growing even if mistakes are made. It is quite possible to get off the track and even to take a bad fall, but so long as one does not turn back, progress will continue. From what has been said, the illuminative way appears to be a trouble-free experience and a person at this stage should be a friend to all. In fact, the opposite is true. The person who does good with ease is likely to annoy many others. Those who have never started the spiritual journey will probably dismiss the whole situation as a harmless fanaticism. Those in the purgative way will be jealous even though they are good Christians and destined one day to be in the illuminative way themselves. Imprisoned as we are in the present moment with its limited perceptions, we often despise those who have accomplished precisely what we aspire to do.

Perhaps the most discouraging part of the illuminative way is not the envy of others but the revelation of our own inner turmoil. As the defenses of denial and rationalization are gradually abandoned, the person must cope with unruly aspects of the unconscious that were previously unknown. In return for the newly found freedom, the illuminated person faces possibilities of sin and betrayal of God which he or she never experienced. The illuminative way is not a cloudless summer day. It is a spring morning after a bad storm. Even though everything is washed clean and the sky is filled with clouds and sunlight, there are many fallen trees and an occasional live wire blocking the road. We will examine this experience from different aspects: affective prayer, the sacraments, the gifts of virtue, the ease and productivity of apostolic work, dangers and trials and ways of coping with them.

Affective Prayer and Contemplative Meditation

Nothing so clearly indicates the beginning of the illuminative phase of the spiritual journey as the onset of affective prayer. Often the change of prayer style happens abruptly. In *The Confessions*, St. Augustine sums up the effect of his conversion from vice in words suggesting the very essence of illuminative prayer:

> O Lord, I am Thy servant: I am Thy servant and the son of Thy handmaid. Thou hast broken my bonds. I will sacrifice to Thee the sacrifice of praise. Let my heart and my tongue praise Thee, and let all my bones say, O Lord, who is like to Thee? Let them say and do Thou answer me and say to my soul: I am Thy salvation. Who am I and what kind of man am I? What evil has there not been in my deeds, or if not in my deeds, in my words, or if not in my words, then in my will? But You, Lord, are good and merciful, and Your right hand had regard to the profundity of my death and drew out the abyss of corruption that was in the bottom of my heart. By Your gift I had come totally not to will what I willed but to will what You willed. But where in all that long time was my free will, and from what deep sunken hiding-place was it suddenly summoned forth in the moment in which I bowed my neck to Your easy yoke and my shoulders to Your light burden, Christ Jesus, my Helper and my Redeemer? How lovely I suddenly found it to be free from the loveliness of those vanities, so that now it was a joy

to renounce what I had been so afraid to lose. For You cast them out of me, O true and supreme Loveliness, You cast them out of me and took their place in me, You who are sweeter than all pleasure, yet not to flesh and blood; brighter than all light, yet deeper within than any secrets; loftier than all honour, but not to those who are lofty to themselves. Now my mind was free from the cares that had gnawed it, from aspiring and getting and weltering in filth and rubbing the scab of lust. And I talked with you as friends talk, my glory and my riches and my salvation, my Lord God.[4]

Prayer changes and certainly becomes easier. Previously meditation had been largely an inner soliloquy, that is, a measuring of self against the teachings of the Gospel; this now gives way to a gentle dialogue with Christ, characterized more by substance than by words.

The person is aware that prayer has slowed down, from a busy hymn (like "We Gather Together" or "Faith of Our Fathers") to a soft gentle melody ("Panis Angelicus" or the eight-fold Alleluia). Often the prayer consists of a few lines of Scripture repeated in the praise of the Lord.

The presence of God, and for most Christians the presence of Christ, becomes increasingly clear in the soul during the illuminative way. This presence is not a response to a theological conviction; it is an awareness that is independent of the individual's effort and volition. As it increases, the experience focuses on the person's emotional forces. St. Bonaventure suggests that we enter an inner temple where the divine icon blazes on the wall of our own being.[5] The powerful mechanism of sublimation channels into the mind a river of psychic energy which flows like lava during the years of illumination. The powerful unleashing of such energy provides the background of the Dark Night of the Soul, which would be impossible without the experience of illuminative prayer.

The person experiencing affective prayer should not hold on to old prayer forms. Vocal prayer, noisy encounter meetings, enthusiastic hymns, and popular devotions were all helpful and necessary in the purgative way, especially at the beginning. Now they can be laid aside. Liturgical prayer which we perform as a duty as members of a community or parish can unobtrusively be transformed. There are many appropriate ways to participate in the liturgy and only the uninformed expect everyone to participate in the same way. The liturgical reform fortunately provided for the different styles of celebration: One may participate in very engaged liturgies for teenagers or sedate ones for pre-Vatican II types, or quiet contemporary liturgy for people on retreat. (Teenagers sometimes prefer the latter type, too.) Popular devotions may be preserved and used in different ways. The Rosary or Stations of the Cross can be adapted to new and more effective prayer styles; the former especially has been a school of contemplative meditation for many.

The affective prayer of the Christian will be very much focused on the person of Christ. The Christological dogmas become an endless source of strength and growth. The mind should be fed by the New Testament. Prayer should be informed by intelligent teaching and commentaries, but will go far beyond mere exigetical examination. As the Russian Orthodox teacher on prayer, Bishop Ignatius Brianchaninov, suggests, the most powerful prayer unites mind and heart so that the mind produces the fuel for the fire burning on the altar of the heart.[6]

We have already mentioned several contemporary authors who are good guides to affective prayer, especially prayer centering on Christ. The third book of *The Imitation of Christ* or Clarence Enzler's popular *My Other Self* are examples of affective prayer put into written words.[7] Despite his prodigious intellectual powers, St. Augustine's *Confessions* seem to me the finest affective prayers ever written. Pure affective prayer breaks constantly through his intellectual discussions.

There is always the danger that the person at the level of affective prayer will become unfortunately a spiritual snob. The illuminative way can be dimmed by all the vices, including vanity and a touch of pride. To forestall such a development, participation in the liturgy within a parish or community is a necessary spiritual discipline. It is a salutary reminder that Jesus Christ was often in the Temple, which was not known for the mystical quality of its services or the spirituality of its priests. He was frequently surrounded by people who prayed at the most childish and cultic levels, yet these were the people he loved and listened to.

The term "contemplative meditation," which I came across first in the writings of F. C. Happold,[8] offers fascinating insights into the prayer of the illuminative way. Contemplation, as we shall see, is, in its highest form, an infused gift; it is related to the powers of the individual only in a secondary way. Meditation, on the other hand, is a very human endeavor with steps and techniques; it requires much human energy and initiative. The affective prayer of the illuminative way seems to combine the two forces. The infused virtues, especially faith and hope, open the person's inner ears to the voice of God. They are not fully prepared, however, to hear His Voice, which speaks in silence; thus the need for human effort and energy. Since we are not at all ready to listen to the Lord's simple and pure speech, we must filter His words through our thoughts. Many things of religion which intervene between us and the infinite God and His Holy Word are intended not to bring Him to us, but rather allow us to gradually approach Him as we become more purified and better prepared. This, I believe, is the purpose of affective prayer or contemplative meditation.

The Sacraments

THE EUCHARIST

No description of illuminative prayer would be complete without reference to the awareness of Christ in the Eucharist—as liturgical sacrifice, sacrament, and static Presence. The Eucharist has always been the focus of the illuminative prayer for Catholic saints. Depending on personal disposition, the theological climate of the time, or the level of the development of dogma, Christians have approached the Eucharistic Presence of Christ in different ways. At the risk of appearing novel, I would suggest that the illuminated see Christ everywhere and especially in the Eucharist because they have perceived Him first in the depth of their own being. Christ's universal presence is concentrated in the most significant and mysterious way in the Eucharistic celebration of salvation wrought through His loving sacrifice, in the intimate relationship epitomized by Holy Communion, and in the interpersonal intimacy clearly symbolized by the Real Presence. To attempt to assess the intuitive devotion of saints like Francis, Thomas Aquinas, Thérèse, and Maximilian Kolbe to the Eucharistic Presence in purely abstract terms of theology is to miss the point. Such profound religious experience does not depend upon abstract theological justification. Rather it is the task of liturgical theology to account intellectually for what is observable consistently in lives of great holiness.

The intuition of Christ's presence in the Eucharist then extends to other aspects of life for those in the illuminative way. Devotion to the Virgin Mother as a spiritual symbol, both of sanctified humanity and of the mystery of womanhood in general and motherhood and virginity in particular, as well as reverence for Mary as one's own spiritual mother, are characteristics of the illuminative experience. This has been true not only in Catholic and Orthodox spirituality, but also at times in Protestant Christianity. It goes beyond the scope of this book to examine the profound mystical experience of the Mother of Christ; we might recommend a meditative reading of the exposition of this theme at the end of the first and second encyclicals of Pope John Paul II.[9]

THE SACRAMENTAL WORLD

One of the most attractive qualities of the saints is their intuitive perception of God's presence in the material world. For primitive people the world was sacred often because it was dangerous. At times the world was seen as a dwelling place for demons, a cradle of life and a well of death. Civilized people have tended to see the world as a garden, a source of material goods. Yet they have frequently despoiled and polluted it through wantonness and greed. In the saint, however, and to some degree in the enlightened person, the world regains its original character as the first great book and revelation of God; Buddhist, Hindu, Moslem, Jew, and Christian come together at this book to praise the Lord. The sacramental world that speaks of the transcendent is the great ecumenical temple in which every seeker finds what he believes he is looking for. How deeply moved I was to find the presence of Jesus Christ in the beautiful gardens and Buddhist shrines of Kama Kura. Christ was really present there for me, although I am sure that no Buddhist would entirely have understood my experience. Yet I have been told that Buddhists who have gone to Assisi have felt spiritually very much at home.

The experience of the sacramental world comes easier to some than to others; an individual's perception of it, therefore, is not necessarily a sign that they have moved into the illuminative way. Those in the illuminative way are intuitive environmentalists, but not all environmentalists are enlightened. There may be some relationship between the two. One can hardly imagine a spiritual person consciously despoiling the environment or lacking in sensitivity to beauty, which is one of the voices of God.

For the Christian the sacramental world literally reflects Christ. This intuition is found among the early Christian writers like Clement of Alexandria. Appreciation of the sacramental world reached a high point in the Middle Ages, perhaps finding its purest expression in St. Francis's "Canticle of Brother Sun."[10] In the late medieval period the material world was even seen as a means by which God would attract people to love Him. The following poem by Jacopone da Todi suggests the purest sacramental sentiments:

How the Soul Through the Senses
Finds God in All Creatures

O Love, divine Love, why do You lay siege to me?
In a frenzy of love for me, You find no rest.

From five sides You move against me,
Hearing, sight, taste, touch, and scent
To come out is to be caught; I cannot hide from You.

If I come out through sight I see Love
Painted in every form and color,
Inviting me to come to You, to dwell in You.

If I leave through the door of hearing,
What I hear points only to You, Lord;
I cannot escape Love through this gate.

If I come out through taste, every flavor proclaims:
"Love, divine Love, hungering Love!
You have caught me on Your hook, for You want to reign in me."

If I leave through the door of scent
I sense You in all creation; You have caught me
And wounded me through that fragrance.

If I come out through the sense of touch
I find Your lineaments in every creature;
To try to flee from You is madness.

Love, I flee from You, afraid to give You my heart:
I see that You make me one with You,
I cease to be me and can no longer find myself.

If I see evil in a man or defect or temptation,
You fuse me with him, and make me suffer;
O Love without limits, who is it You love?

It is You, O Crucified Christ,
Who take possession of me,
Drawing me out of the sea to the shore;

There I suffer to see Your wounded heart.
Why did You endure the pain?
So that I might be healed.[11]

In summary, the illuminative way represents psychologically the effect of the lowering of defenses, the initial relinquishment of anger, and the gradual cessation of pathological need. Because it is transitional, this state is marked by very little in the way of a final accomplishment. Anxious fear is reduced, but still present. One perceives reality, particularly its transcendent aspects, more clearly, but by no means perfectly. We should keep this fact in mind as we turn now to the virtues and pitfalls of the illuminative way.

The Gifts of Virtue

According to many classic writers, the illuminative way is character-ized by the operation of infused virtue. Such a concept is quite at odds with much contemporary writing on the psychology of adjustment or on popular spirituality.

Modern people like to think of themselves as self-sufficient even in regard to the things of God. The notion of infused virtues is an affront to the modern mind. According to St. Thomas Aquinas the infused virtues are given by God and direct us toward God, although many pertain to activities of everyday life, for example, the control of appetites and the energetic performance of duties.[12] The moral virtues—pru-dence, justice, fortitude, and temperance—can exist as natural qualities or as infused virtues. When operative in the spiritual life of someone in the illuminative way, we say that these virtues have been ingrafted into us by God, even though they may have been present previously as natu-ral dispositions.[13] Good mental qualities and infused virtues differ in a number of ways. There is a difference in the psychological experience. A person may not actually delight in temperance and at times may be driven toward intemperance like an alcoholic; yet the infused virtue may well provide a strength beyond himself or herself. A person who prac-tices temperance because it is reasonable to do so is motivated differently than the one who is temperate in order to fulfill God's law. Matt Talbot, the well-known mystic and reformed alcoholic, found strength and moti-vation outside himself; others, too, have come to sobriety for the love of God.

Infused moral virtues are touched by the greatest of all virtues: char-ity. Faith and hope, as we have noted, are theological virtues which, unlike the moral virtues, have no real natural predispositions. The same is true of the love of God and love of neighbor. While there is an attrac-tion to the transcendent and while compassion is certainly found in many persons, the ability to love God purely for Himself and our neigh-bor with no expectation of return is purely a gift from God. This is particularly true in the case of love of enemies. (For a more thorough theological explanation of the virtues, I suggest *The Three Ages of the Interior Life* by Garrigou-Lagrange.)

Does the notion of infused virtues have any practical applications for our world vision as spiritually motivated people? It will also make a good deal of practical difference in the psychological and moral direction of our lives.

INFUSED VIRTUE AND WORLD VISION

The concept of infused virtues affects our world vision of human psychology. The spiritual person cannot conduct his or her life completely on the level of popular or scientific psychology. At best psychology can offer a philosophical ideal of the virtuous life. (It rarely does this.) It cannot know of infused virtues that assist people to go beyond their predictable limits. Since many people experience the effect of infused virtues often without knowing it, modern psychology has consistently underestimated the true potentials of human beings. In defense of the psychologists it should be said that observing what were supposed to be virtues of the devout, they frequently found only defense mechanisms such as sublimation and repression. One must forgive the psychologists, uninformed on the spiritual life, for being confused by the virtues and vices of the pious. It is my impression from my conversations with thoughtful psychologists that they really do not believe that the virtues of St. Francis or Ghandi are entirely explainable as sublimation of libido or even of any forces entirely subject to scientific examination.

Infused virtues also affect our view of morality. In reality we draw our practical share of morality not so much from our beliefs based on the teachings of Christ and the Church as from our surroundings. If we are inclined to be influenced by others, we usually accept a large portion of contemporary social mores. Many good Christians have lived in societies supported by slavery and dedicated to war and plundering and experienced only an occasional twinge of conscience, even if they personally were kind to slaves and tried to be peacemakers. A smaller proportion are psychologically inclined to be "no-sayers." Rightly or wrongly, they like to swim against the tide of public opinion and tend to base their moral judgments on what is critical of the social reality. Sometimes they make great contributions to the world, like the hermit who stopped the gladiatorial games; sometimes they look a bit silly, like those who sponsored the constitutional amendment against alcoholic beverages in the United States.

When those who have been helped by the power of infused virtues face the issues of contemporary morality, they must do so courageously but also with care and understanding. They may find it easy to practice some virtues which others find difficult. The significance of some moral teaching or eternal truth may be obvious to them and be lost on the vast majority who take their ethical norms from the actions of others.

I am not referring here to the ideal or the evangelical counsels, but simply to applying basic principles of morality related to peace, justice, and compassion.

An honest reading of Christ's teaching in the New Testament will show that He distinguished between precepts and counsels of spiritual refinement and that He treated people in different ways. There is no instance of Christ being severe to those addicted to sins of the flesh, although His teaching against harboring sinful sexual desires is very strong. On the other hand, there is no case of His being lenient with those guilty of religious hypocrisy.

A vibrant realization of the effect of infused virtues prepares the Christian to deal compassionately with those who fall short of one's own perception or performance. Experience should have taught us that without the power of infused virtues, moral and theological, we would be literally in the worst position, namely, that of someone who knows what is right and does what is wrong. It may well be that the experience of infused virtues and an understanding of their spiritual-psychological impact has caused the recurring phenomenon in Church history of the saints getting on so well with sinners. It is a truism that the saints, like Christ, have been the most unjudgmental of Christians.

INFUSED VIRTUE AND SELF-IMAGE

The journey through the purgative way usually leaves an individual with a badly battered self-image. Often a spiritual traveller has a poor self-image to begin with, and although it is not worsened by purgation, at the end of purgation one appears like an infected person who has been shaved and deloused. The result is an antiseptic but not attractive image. In my experience, most people in the first darknesses prefer not to discuss self-image at all.

The illuminative way, with the growing awareness of the effect of infused virtues, gives a person confidence based on God's gift. Self-righteousness can creep in, but it is a slow process because of the lasting memory of the darkness and the frightening realization of what one could really be. Consequently, someone in the illuminative way can be courageous without being brash, open to disturbing experiences without being endangered. Those who have yet to experience the illuminative way are often thrown off guard by this fact. Without the inner strength of the illuminative way they may attempt the same things as the enlightened, only to crumble in weakness. They will then feel cheated and misled.

RESOLUTION OF OPPOSITES

The illuminative way is usually an experience of late middle life which is also the period during which an individual normally encounters the psychological resolution of opposites. Spiritual writers have tended to identify the resolution of opposites as part of the illuminative way.[14]

There are polarities in the human personality representing extremes of attitudinal stages or behavior. We can be both destructive and constructive; restrained and self-denying on the one hand, and assertive and aggressive on the other. The same person can be at one time introverted and at another extroverted. We can be parsimonious or generous; we can be makers of peace or of war. We can be chaste and ascetic, or self-indulgent and self-gratifying. An ability to be dependent and independent is essential if one is to grow as defense mechanisms decline. Most people are in conflict about their aggressiveness and compliance and even self-depreciation. Guilt, the need to win others over, the fear of reprisal or the concern not to hurt others, all conspire to make a thoroughly conflicted person. The illuminative way with its clarification of goals, decline of defenses, reduction of basic anxiety through trust in God, provides an effective opportunity for the resolution of polarities.

LOVE OF GOD

From the earliest moments of our spiritual awakening we have been drawn by the love of God—a desire to possess and be possessed by the divine that has cost us dearly. Now as a result of the infused virtue of charity, the individual experiences a force within that includes gratitude, reverence, zeal, and inner exaltation which propels our actions and prayers. This force is gradually recognized as the dynamism behind affective prayer. At times it is so strong as to be frightening. "What will be left when the divine fire has consumed me entirely?" *Deus Ignis Consumens!* God is a consuming fire! The words of the first commandment at times glow in the mind and heart, and we long for God even when He is present. We may think that this is the end of the journey, but that is an old and common mistake.

The action of the infused virtues blends with the energy of sublimation. A fervent prayer life grows into the prayer of quiet, an almost silent adoration, beginning the second phase of the illuminative way. Even though this experience is very much the middle ground in the spiritual life, most human beings would surrender all they have to attain it. It often transforms their outer demeanor so they are taken for people in the unitive way. A stillness and gentleness mark them and make them both attractive to others and yet a bit awe-inspiring. Because of the power of the prayer of quiet, they may become less suited for practical tasks. The usual round of religious, pastoral, or familial duties is truly a burden to them, but because of the infused virtues they gladly fulfill them. Fortunately, the prayer of quiet often occurs in late middle age or old age and others are prepared or even anxious to assume their responsibilities. Those enjoying the prayer of quiet may seek solitude and a less disturbing way of life. They may erroneously interpret this as a call to the cloistered life and may be well advised to continue in their present state, neither seeking nor rejecting the special graces of prayer that come.

LOVE OF NEIGHBOR

Both stages of the illuminative way are characterized by increased generosity. The love of possessions gives way to the love that imitates God in desiring to give oneself away. The word "altruism" is often used, but it is inadequate, generally referring to the energetic forms of natural generosity. The virtue of love of neighbor has a fire and passion that the merely altruistic seldom demonstrate.

Gradually people are loved because they are the children of God and reflect the presence of Christ in so many ways. The glimpse of Christ's presence in the needy, which is granted during the purgative way, is replaced by a caring for all those whom we meet. Even enemies may be loved, and this is a sure sign of the operation of an infused virtue. Psychology can make no sense of this at all. In fact, to love one's enemies seems to be pathological.

The virtue of charity in the illuminative way does not overlook justice and its demands, because all infused virtues are correlated. One can hunger and thirst for justice and at the same time pray for the oppressors. An example of this is given by St. Maximilian Kolbe, who wrote "Do not be distressed by the troubles of our time, but offer your lives that all souls will be saved by divine love." The special charity called "apostolic zeal," i.e., the genuine desire to fulfill Christ's mission in bringing salvation to the world, is of singular importance in the illuminative way. Although theoretically all Christians are called to spread the Gospel in a way appropriate to their vocation, it is in fact likely that an apostolate, a work for the spiritual welfare of others, will be the opportunity only of the sort of people who may read this kind of book. If you are reading this book, you are probably called to be an apostle, a witness to the Gospel. Even if your vocation is one of prayer, in an enclosed life, either in community or alone, you are likely to have been chosen in God's Providence to do something consciously for His Kingdom. The effect of the illuminative way should be important to you.

A person in the purgative way may do the work of the apostolate with enthusiasm and professional interest. Fatigue, failure, and lack of opportunity, however, will be troublesome. Even when we are sure of doing God's will, we look for an earthly reward, or at least some reinforcement, as the apostles did. "What shall we have, who have given up everything?"

There is always a limit to what we will give because there is a genuine limit to what we can give. We are operating on our own strength and we use it up sending off the impulses of the infused virtues. It is a sad fact that religious life and the clerical state can produce such institutionalizations of mediocrity that any response to the zeal of infused charity is perceived as threatening to others. As individuals we are sometimes deaf to the call of infused charity; we compound this when we join others in criticizing those who feel inspired to do a bit more.

But once the momentum of the illuminative way has been achieved, the apostle cares little for the opinion of others. Indifference to criticism, detachment, and zeal are difficult for others to cope with. The apostle may be hurt as he or she looks for support and finds none. He or she may feel isolated and misunderstood, but will find support in the infused virtue of charity.

Modern psychologists who have examined the advanced stages of the interior life have noticed the effect of infused virtue without being able to identify what they see. Fritz Kunkel, an American psychiatrist interested in spirituality, has written perceptively of the operation of the infused virtues:

> The nearer we come to the center, the more we leave the images behind, the more are our fears turned into anxiety. And anxiety, if we face it, is turned into awe. What seemed to be the power of darkness now manifests itself as the power of light. After the great and strong wind comes the earthquake, then the fire, and then the still small voice (I Kings 19:11–13).
>
> The terrible and destructive aspect of the godhead—the "tremendum" in a theological language—originates as a subjective human experience, though an unavoidable one if our religious convictions and our rigid theology are smashed by the Grace of God. We live in a jail which we call our castle; a foreign soldier breaks through the doors, come to free us by blasting the walls of our castle—and we fight him with the last might of our broken Ego, calling him scoundrel, knave and devil, until we are exhausted, overwhelmed and disarmed. Then looking at the victor with disinterested objectivity we recognize him: St. Michael smilingly sheathes his sword.[15]

The Imitation of Christ contains a succinct description of the illuminative way that is perceptive, and omits no element of its positive side. Those wishing to understand this way and hoping to arrive there one day, might do well to ponder the following:

> Father of mercies, God of all consolation, Who with Your comfort sometimes refresh me, who am not worthy of it, I bless you always and glorify You with Your only begotten Son and the Holy Spirit, the Paraclete, forever and ever.

Lord God, my holy Lover, when You come into my heart, all that is within me will rejoice. You are my glory and the exultation of my heart. You are my hope and refuge in the day of my tribulation. But because my love is as yet weak, and my virtue imperfect, I must be strengthened and comforted by You. Visit me often, therefore, and teach me Your holy discipline. Free me from evil passions and cleanse my heart of all disorderly affection so that, healed and purified within, I may be fit to love, strong to suffer, and firm to persevere.

Love is an excellent thing, a very great blessing, indeed. It makes every difficulty easy, and bears all wrongs with equanimity. For it bears a burden without being weighted and renders sweet all that is bitter. The noble love of Jesus spurs to great deeds and excites longing for that which is more perfect. Love tends upwards: it will not be held down by anything low. Love wishes to be free and estranged from all worldly affections, lest its inward sight be obstructed, lest it be entangled in any temporal interest and overcome by adversity.

Nothing is sweeter than love, nothing stronger or higher or wider; nothing is more pleasant, nothing fuller, and nothing better in heaven or on earth, for love is born of God and cannot rest except in God, Who is above all created things.

One who is in love flies, runs, and rejoices; he is free, not bound. He gives all for all and possesses all in all, because he rests in the one sovereign Good, Who is above all things, and from Whom every good flows and proceeds. He does not look to the gift but turns himself above all gifts to the Giver.

Love often knows no limits, but overflows all bounds. Love feels no burden, thinks nothing of troubles, attempts more than he is able, and does not plead impossibility, because it believes that it may and can do all things. For this reason, it is able to do all, performing and effecting much where he who does not love fails and falls.

Love is watchful. Sleeping, it does not slumber. Wearied, it is not tired. Pressed, it is not straightened. Alarmed, it is not confused, but like a living flame, a burning torch, it forces its way upward and passes unharmed through every obstacle.

If a man loves, he will know the sound of this voice. For this warm affection of soul is a loud voice crying in the ears of God, and it says: "My God, my love, You are all mine and I am all Yours. Give me an increase of love, that I may learn to taste with the inward lips of my heart how sweet it is to love, how sweet to be dissolved in love and bathe in it. Let me be rapt in love. Let me rise above self in great fervor and wonder.[16]

Dangers and Trials of the Illuminative Way

It is difficult for the beginner to believe that such a peaceful description could pertain to a phase of life that also contains dangers. This fact makes the hazards of the illuminative way seem more insidious. We must carefully look at these perils, almost all of which are rooted in the purgative way. Mistakes made early on can bear bitter fruit later.

Before we consider dangers arising from previous mistakes, however, we should note that one risk inherent in the illuminative way has nothing to do with previous errors but is common to any form of progress. To grow is to expose oneself to unforeseen challenges. In the illuminative way we expose more and more of our real being, our inner psyche with its height, depth, power, and potential for good or ill. Personal dishonesty and inconsistency have eventually brought some spiritual travelers to self-destruction. Have you ever wondered what might have been Judas's fate if he had never heard the call, "Follow Me"?

The infused virtues are apparently necessary as a guide and to insure our balance as we look into our own soul. Not only the shadow, the dark side of the mind with its beasts and demons, but also the hidden unconscious may contain very disturbing elements. As the light shines on our vices and pseudovirtues, we can become disheartened and cynical about our own virtues or those of others.

The sensitive spiritual writer, Archbishop Fénelon, gives the following description of the dark side of the illuminative way:

> As light increases, we see ourselves to be worse than we thought. We are amazed at our former blindness as we see issuing forth from the depths of our heart a whole swarm of shameful feelings, like filthy reptiles crawling from a hidden cave. We never could have believed that we had harbored such things, and we stand aghast as we watch them gradually appear. But we must neither be amazed nor disheartened. We are not worse than we were; on the contrary, we are better. But while our faults diminish, the light by which we see them waxes brighter, and we are filled with horror. Bear in mind, for your comfort, that we only perceive our malady when the cure begins. So long as there is no sign of cure, we are unconscious of the depth of our disease; we are in a state of blind presumption and hardness; the prey of self-delusion. While we go with the stream, we are unconscious of its rapid course; but when we begin to stem it ever so little, it makes itself felt.[17]

Spiritual direction becomes a *sine qua non* if we are to avoid dangers while attempting to advance spiritually. A good director is a treasure, but even those without one may still get direction, as Father Van Kaam has pointed out so well in *The Dynamics of Spiritual Self-Direction.* However, when the dark recesses of our spirit become manifest, we especially need at least a friend to share our fears, and assure us that ours is not an uncommon experience. A person acting as a spiritual guide who is not open to the dark side of others is worse than no friend at all.

DANGERS FROM WITHIN

The greatest dangers of the illuminative way are spiritual "greed," a driven self-righteousness, and a conviction that one has been elected to carry out a special mission. Spiritual greed is a problem when we become so intrigued by the spiritual journey that we forget or minimize other responsibilities. Such an unhealthy sublimation indicates radical dissatisfaction with self for which one compensates by an ultraspiritual sense. Many saints, however, have noted that God is found in the fulfillment of life's ordinary duties.

The tendency toward spiritual self-righteousness is very common at this stage. We wish to share our recently acquired spiritual insights, but often others who have yet to arrive at our understanding are uninterested, embarrassed, or threatened by them. We may become angry at this point by a rebuff which can result in a bitter zeal, which is a thinly disguised form of aggression. Calm, experienced friends who have passed through the illuminative way are important at such a time to be supportive and understanding of the newly illuminated who are basically right but in the wrong way.

The most dangerous illusion is the idea of a special call. Many persons in the first flush of the illuminative way are troubled by a "Messianic complex." If we are inexperienced and unread, we may think we are unique, not realizing that our experience is common enough and a long way from the higher realms of spirituality. Again, patience and understanding will help when Providence allows this special person to fall into not so very special vices and problems.

St. John of the Cross lists three other dangers for those on the threshold of contemplative prayer: pride, sensuality, and spiritual avarice.[18] Old enemies, they now reappear in new form as a result, I suspect, of relinquishing many defense mechanisms, especially denial, repression, and reaction formation. Persons advanced this far are actually much less constricted in their functioning and must face sinful, self-centered inclinations they once thought had been overcome. In fact, these inclinations had only been denied and repressed; this may sometimes surprise even spiritual directors who may assume that they had ceased to be a problem in the illuminative way.

Pride may be a strong temptation for those in the illuminative way. They have a contribution to make to the spiritual well-being of others and possess a degree of confidence in matters which mystify and perhaps impress the less informed. Those in the illuminative way are likely to be chosen as teachers or guides. It is an easy escape to preach to others and have no message for oneself. It is also a great temptation to become angry with those who do not listen or who have a different approach to the spiritual life.

A kind of spiritual competitiveness springs up when a number of people are interested in these matters. Spiritual directors and writers often dislike one another; they compete and sometimes snipe at each other, indicating that pride is not yet dead.

There is still the possibility of a serious moral fall because of sensuality. It can be anger, detraction, or a sexual sin. In each instance, the person is grappling with elements of life repressed until now. Such a fall may be devastating and result in depression or desperation. What is worse, the individual may rationalize and deny the real moral significance of his or her behavior.

The most complex, elegant rationalizations are possible for those who have made some spiritual progress. They may "fall in love" for the first time or in a new way, since they are no longer repressed. There is often a fine line between exploring new and more loving ways of relating to others in Christ, and using one's new-found freedom for indulgence and delusion of self and others.

Thus, pride and its children, self-righteousness and self-deception, come back into life. St. John of the Cross does not hesitate to call these the attacks of the enemy and surely he referred to the Prince of Darkness. But it is possible that he might now attribute some of these attitudes to unconscious forces within.

St. John of the Cross mentions two others dangers on which modern psychology may be able to shed some light: spiritual sloth and spiritual tepidity.

Spiritual Sloth and Tepidity

The Spanish mystic notes that certain persons who have made some progress in the spiritual life (those he calls "beginners") may suddenly grow lax and tepid. They gradually lose interest, sometimes giving up completely the spiritual life, which then recedes into the past like a dream or an old love affair. If their career or profession obliges them to be "religious," such persons continue on but with no zest at all. The light of the illuminative way goes out and slowly they return to their previously well-defended state.

Often they become very defensive about their previous spiritual interest; they may try to distance themselves from it by cynicism and mockery, or they may grow depressed when recalling it. One of two things is taking place here. First, a good deal of their past strength had been the sublimation of repressed energy, especially self-assertion or sexual drive. Once the repression and sublimation are no longer as necessary because they have cognitively and voluntarily resolved some of their conflicts, much of their repressed energy is depleted. They have matured and in the process disconnected their adolescent power sources. One often observes this among young clergy or those who have recently outgrown emotionally charged encounter movements.

The remedy for tepidity is obvious. In his classic guide, Tanquerey suggests that one frequently consult a good confessor, be fervent in acts of prayer, and, earnestly if not enthusiastically, fulfill one's duties.[19]

Such a decision is the very foundation of existential psychotherapy and may, in fact, be the essence of any therapeutic process. Acts of the will undo spiritual sloth which is caused by a combination of circumstances: loss of sublimated energy, a certain boredom resulting from a lack of spiritual fireworks, and an unwillingness to give up one's own self-satisfaction.

Spiritual Paranoia

St. Ignatius Loyola, a master of discernment and eminent spiritual psychologist, cast his critical eye on the many people he knew in the illuminative way and formulated some very good rules for diagnosing what in modern terms might be called "spiritual paranoia," which he called an "evil spirit." St. Ignatius noticed in some fairly fervent people a tendency to get involved in projects which troubled them or interfered with others' spiritual growth. He maintained that if a project were really good, it would contain nothing contrary to God's will or to the soul's welfare. He noted that it is an evil spirit who suggests projects in harmony with the highest spiritual aspirations but also dependent on self-will or self-aggrandizement. Gradually through complacency, presumption, or disguised ambition in the form of excessive rigor or austerity, the project becomes an expression of self-love. Little by little a person's hard-won progress is lost and defenses are rebuilt. If called abruptly to account, the person trapped by the evil spirit can make an excellent defense: The person might explain, for example, that he or she is now an advanced person, having passed successfully through periods of trial and temptation, and is quite beyond the childish vice of self-love and self-will. And the person did indeed once advance beyond these obstacles, but has now unknowingly recreated them all.

St. Ignatius does not suggest that the answer is to take a holiday from making any effort; that is hardly what he was about. However, the great reformer does insist that we ask whether a project is integrated (my word) with our spiritual good and that of others, in its inception, formation, and final outcome. He indicates that if we find bitterness or things that lead to laxity and mediocrity, we should review the whole thought process to see where evil entered in. Ignatius especially emphasizes that a good spirit works gently, whereas an evil one is violent.

To this Tanquerey adds a few insights worth repeating. He suggests the following as signs of a bad spirit: ostentatious acts of virtue, contempt for little things, a desire to be sanctified in the grand manner, false humility, constant complaining and dissatisfaction that mask a refusal to suffer anything patiently.

Often a person struggling in the spiritual life does not know what to do when a good project presents itself. Most of us have enough self-knowledge to realize that even our best intentions are never pure, but we cannot wait until we are angels before we do anything. It is a good idea, however, to wait a week or so to see whether an idea survives the lapse of a little time. Most great ideas are simply that—ideas—and like most seeds that are planted, they do not take root. If an idea persists in spite of our benign neglect (for instance, if some human need keeps intruding itself), we should, after a period of prayer, work out a plan for a pilot program. If doors continue to open, we should remain with the project. If permission is needed, and given even reluctantly, it is a good sign. A good spirit bids us make our proposals carefully and with a degree of detachment. A sudden note of egotism or bitter zeal in our voice may not be the signal to abandon the project; it is, however, as St. Ignatius suggests, an indication to review the whole procedure and see where evil has come in.

At this point, the best thing that can happen is that we experience a strong inclination to quit, to let it all go; Providence will suddenly place in our path someone who will make it imperative that we try. There is a Yiddish saying, "Who needs it?" that may well sum up our feelings. If we persevere in spite of that, the chances are good that Providence is, in fact, calling us to that work.

It is commonly thought that if we begin a project for the Lord, the pieces will fall into place. It doesn't work out that way. One has only to consider God's greatest project, described in the four Gospels. The road of the Messiah was hardly strewn with flowers. It is good to recall the scene in St. John's Gospel (chap. 6) when many of Christ's disciples left Him after He spoke of the necessity to eat His flesh and drink His blood. How poignant is the question put to the few apostles who remained: "Will you also go away?"

Disasters befall projects of the good spirit, as well as those of the bad. Success has never been a sign of God's will. As Mother Teresa of Calcutta has observed, "God calls us to fidelity and not to success." It seems to me a sure sign that a certain project is the work of God if we have the grace to struggle on without bitterness in the face of difficulties and frustrations.

While searching for an example of this experience, I came to realize it would be dangerous to use someone else's troubles. Today, when so many lose their way on the spiritual road, it could be unseemly to trade on another person's turmoil to illustrate this problem. So I decided to use a personal experience, even though it is far from the illuminative way.

I spent my first fourteen years as a priest in a fascinating and engaging apostolate as chaplain to Children's Village in Dobbs Ferry, New York, a treatment center for 300 boys with emotional problems. I became deeply concerned for the welfare of boys eighteen and over who were no longer eligible for public assistance. One boy in particular—we will call him Jimmy—was "going down the drain." I saw him literally living in a bar, working for what he could eat and drink, and sleeping behind the bar at night. Another boy got thrown out into the street; when I brought him to a hotel suggested by the police, it turned out to be a brothel. Seeing a friar arrive with the police, everyone in the "hotel" fled, thinking the place was being raided.

It was clear I needed a residence for homeless boys. I thought it over, obtained the necessary permission, and looked a long time for an appropriate house. In Greenpoint, Brooklyn, I literally stumbled over an old club house which the generous people of the Polish parish gave me. Everything fell into place and the boy from the bar moved in. There were problems galore, but there were always answers. It took six months, but with the help of God and many friends the house was opened. It was fortunate I could not foresee the struggles ahead; otherwise I might have abandoned the project before it was underway. I remember struggling in prayer with vanity and pride; yet the struggle was not great for I knew very well that Providence had done it all. That was clear. I thought I was at peace, although I continued to be unduly anxious over the house.

The Lord needed to purify it all. I had asked that it be His work; now He would take it to Himself.

A young man whose looks I did not like, was brought to me. Allegedly he had recently arrived from Central America, but actually had just escaped from jail. He upset everyone and I told him he would have to get a job and leave within a week. He cursed at me and left immediately. The next day he broke into the house and did immense damage. He wrote obscenities on the newly paneled walls, wrecked the furnishings, and even enlisted another resident as his accomplice. In the police station I broke down and cried; fortunately, I did not return to that police station for ten years. The officers were not sympathetic and told me it was my own fault for trying to help this kind of person. For twenty-four hours straight, my assistant, Brother Timothy, a seminarian, Joe, and I worked to restore order. My vanity and pride were burned up in the one day of my life when I didn't even stop to pray. When I finally took a moment for prayer, God was there, amid the ruins of my egotism, clearer and brighter than ever.

Even when our works proceed from a good spirit, they may be all tangled up with self. Our motives will never be completely pure and we must allow God to purify us with His fire. His ways are not our ways. At times good things can be accomplished only with great difficulty and at other times He sends his angels to bear us up lest we be dashed upon the stones. In this case I still had to contend with the angry criminal who called up every day threatening to burn the house down. The police were much more helpful this time: They suggested I put a scare into him. I was pitted against Goliath—and without a slingshot. However, the Lord sent me a friend who does impersonations, including a superb imitation of a gangster. A psychodrama in which little was said but much implied was played out one day on a dangerous corner in Hell's Kitchen. That night my antagonist left for the Caribbean where he remained for three years, terrified of a group of hoodlums who had never heard of him. Our next encounter, which was very friendly, took place in jail. If God laughs and helps us to laugh when such a crisis has passed, it may be an indication that a good spirit is prompting us.

If we fail to discern the spirit motivating us, we run the risk of spiritual paranoia. We get on our high horse; we are "puffed up," as the old translation of Corinthians describes an uncharitable state. We inflict pain unnecessarily; we start looking at things to justify our worth and we rejoice at iniquity—especially that of others. Most of us are clever enough to attack some real vice, such as injustice, stupidity, tobacco, war, or promiscuity. We are on the rampage. Others have the audacity to fight back—Philistines that they are—and bitter zeal takes over our cause. Our wrath may be more harmful than the evil we attack. While Savonarola (who is really admirable for telling the truth) was storming up and down Italy predicting the scourges God had revealed to him, St. Catherine of Genoa was home looking after the sick and the poor. She never left Genoa or did anything more dramatic than organize prayer groups which cared for the sick poor. Yet history has judged that she, and not the fiery preacher, "began the effective reform of the Catholic Church in those troubled times."[20]

When we feel on the verge of spiritual paranoia, we should draw back a little and spend more time discussing the issue. After a period of fervent prayer, we should lay the whole matter before the Lord. Self-examination is in order here: Are we accidentally hurting others while taking disguised revenge? Are we judging others, thereby violating an explicit counsel of the Gospel? If we decide we have been a bit paranoid, grandiose, or operating with a persecution complex, we should humbly ask for the light to return to the right road and the grace to persevere on it. At this point, we often demur, fearing we lack the strength to do it all. Infused virtue now comes to the rescue, and we learn again the often-repeated lesson that we can do all things in Him who strengthens us.

LOVE OF JUSTICE

A final point must be made about the love of justice in the illuminative way. One of the infused moral virtues, justice is often overlooked by the devout. Spiritually oriented people often suffer a bit of injustice because of the envy of others. Since they themselves try to be fair and giving, they lose sight of the fact that we live in a wicked world. Frequently, they cannot cope with injustice so they do not see it; when they do see it, they remain silent. A tendency to silence is hardly an expression of the infused virtue of justice. We have a sad example of this in the two members of the Sanhedrin, Joseph of Arimathea and Nicodemus, who had the courage to ask for Christ's body but not to defend Him against an unjust sentence. I do not condemn them; they would have accomplished little or nothing by protest. I do, however, find a warning to myself in their actions, since they had to live with their silence for the rest of their lives.

Sometimes silence is the best, or only, course, but sometimes it is not. A person interested in spiritual growth must overcome the tendency to remain aloof from things of material concern. He or she should nourish a constant, dedicated interest in those who suffer from injustice. The more one can directly associate with the victims of injustice, share their lot, plead their cause and defend them, the more one will grow spiritually.

One of the revelations of the illuminative way is one's own absolute poverty and dependence. A quiet, loving, respectful sharing of the lot of the poor and identification with them will bring that message home to us and at the same time control the tidal wave of sorrow that begins to well up in our being as the illuminative way draws to a close. The joy of God has a sharp counterpoint: the tragedy that we do not love Him. The realization that God is the greatest victim of injustice, that "Love is not loved," begins to grow in the soul. We must, therefore, recognize the oppressed, the poor, the defrauded and trapped as our only hope of finding God in this world.

Chapter 8

The Third Stage of the Spiritual Life: The Unitive Way

This book is written for those who seek, that is, for those interested in the spiritual life who have made some progress toward its ultimate term: contemplation. Something should be said to those who seek after the experience of those who find—those who have arrived at the higher levels of the spiritual life. The following chapter is such an attempt. It should not be construed as a guide for those chosen souls who have arrived even at the beginning of the unitive way or even for those who are honored to be their spiritual guides. This chapter might be of some practical help in identifying periods of darkness, especially the Dark Night of the Senses.

This chapter is rather a summary based totally on the writings of great mystics, especially St. Bonaventure, St. Teresa of Avila, and St. John of the Cross. While these pages may help us identify a person who is in union with God or a person going through one of the initial trial periods of this union, their principal purpose is to give some idea to those on the spiritual journey of what may lie ahead. As we have observed in any developmental sequence, we are in some way at all stages of the journey at any particular time. It is not presumptuous then to take note when we experience a moment of contemplation even in its infused form. This is the graciousness of God, nothing else. It can give the traveller hope.

Only the reader who is unfamiliar with the writings of the mystics will be astonished by the steps and great heights described in this chapter. We realize now that what we have thought were high mountains are in fact foothills and that, when the mystics speak of real mountains, we are overawed because we had no previous conception of these things. It is like hearing of the Himalayas if you have always lived in the prairies. I suggest you allow yourself to be overawed by what you hear; it is good for humility.

I must note also that there is a sadness about this chapter, especially when one reads of the ordinary people who manage to scale great heights and comprehend hidden mysteries. Why have we tarried along the way and burdened ourselves with useless baggage? Why have we wasted the one earthly life we will ever have on something less than the pursuit of the Kingdom of God? This is followed by the most painful question of all, why have we not called those whom we love to a greater love of God? These questions must be faced if we are ever to know the depth of God's mercy. We are indeed unprofitable servants.

General Pattern of the Unitive Way

As described by St. John of the Cross and St. Teresa, our most accurate and scientific guides on this journey, the unitive way includes two distinct contemplative experiences, one of simple quiet contemplation and then the later phase of total contemplative absorption. The first or acquired contemplation is really the introduction to union and develops gradually in the later phases of the illuminative way especially as a heightening of the prayer of profound recollection. This transition appears to be a gradual one for the most part.

It goes beyond our purposes to dwell on the distinction between acquired and infused contemplation. Earlier writers usually do not allude to such a distinction, but in recent centuries the lines have been sharpened. Acquired contemplation according to Tanquerey "is, at bottom, nothing more than a simplified affective prayer" and may be defined as contemplation in which the simplification of our intellectual and affective acts is the result of our own activity aided by grace.[1]

Gradually, infused contemplation is given as an absolutely free gift. It is a very different experience in which the acts of the intellect and will have become simplified under the influence of a special grace which takes hold of us and causes us to receive lights and affections which God produces in us—but always with our consent.[2]

One accepts it, but in no way does one cause it. Infused contemplation begins with a prayer of great quietness. Usually this quietness is initially dry and arid, an experience properly called the Dark Night of the Senses. Then this is followed by a time of sweet quietness leading to a period of prayer which goes by the name of "full union with God." This leads to an almost complete overwhelming of the normal psychological processes of the person and is called "ecstatic union." Then comes the most awesome of all trials known to human beings, the Dark Night of the Spirit (properly so called). Finally, there is a transforming union, also called "Spiritual Marriage." If you are beginning to feel a bit dizzy reading these terms, be consoled. Figuratively, we are in outer space. We are like students of astronomy looking at the dim light of galaxies millions of light years off. Perhaps it gives us some glimpse of the reality of the mystery contained in the words "Eye has not seen, ear has not heard."

PSYCHOLOGY AND THE UNITIVE WAY

Contemporary psychology has done almost nothing to understand these higher regions of human accomplishment. Very few students of contemporary psychology are aware of the existence of states related to contemplation or to writings about them.[3] Consequently, I have to be a bit original, especially in the application of the theory of declining anxiety and defenses. Any observations of mine on what the unitive way may mean in terms of psychology, are obviously tentative and open to suggestion, criticism, or outright rejection. It is my hope that these observations may give rise to better speculations by more spiritually experienced people, who are also versed in that limited science called "modern psychology." At this point, using psychological concepts to understand contemplation, is like using Newton's telescope to measure the distance of galaxies.

The lack of contemporary theoretical studies particularly suggests the use of anecdotes as part of our discussion. The use of anecdotes is a very legitimate tool in the beginning of any psychological exploration. I have limited myself to accounts of people whom I have known personally and from whose lives I am able to make some inferences. It seemed better to draw illustrations from the lives of people who are now deceased since it would not be possible to conceal the identity of some of them whose lives were so unusual. Two of these people are fellow Capuchins; I should therefore disclaim any attempt to use this book for public relations. I am simply limited to cases of people whom I have known well and whom I have been able to observe carefully.

TRANSITION TO INFUSED CONTEMPLATION

A certain intuitive awareness of the beauty of some object or event, when it is perceived as a unity, has been traditionally called "contemplation." In recent years this kind of experience has been associated with the alpha state of consciousness. This is very much a voluntarily induced state, a very meaningful and engaging form of perception, but it is not what we mean by contemplation, although it may not be totally unrelated as a *psychophysiological* component.

Tanquerey defines infused contemplation clearly and succinctly in the following way: "A simple, loving, protracted gaze on God and things divine, under the influence of the gifts of the Holy Ghost and of a special actual grace which takes possession of us and causes us to act in a passive rather than active way."[4]

The difference between acquired and infused contemplation is perhaps best understood by analogy with activity/passivity, a favorite theme of St. John of the Cross. The analogy helps us to understand this great man's total dedication to and reliance on God. "If . . . this loving knowledge is received passively in the soul according to the supernatural mode of God, and not according to the natural mode of the soul, a person, if he wants to receive it, should be very annihilated in his natural operations, unhampered, idle, quiet, peaceful, and serene, according to the mode of God. The more the air is cleansed of vapors, and the quieter and more simple it is, the more the sun illumines and warms it. A person should not bear attachment to anything. . . . He should be very free and annihilated regarding all things."[5]

Rather than engage in a lengthy analysis of this definition, we will allow the concept of contemplation to grow as we study the following description.

First Phase of Contemplation—Simple Union with God

The transition from the illuminative way to union with God is accomplished by a change of emphasis, an increase of one phenomenon and a concurrent decrease of another, as so many developmental changes take place. During the experience of contemplative meditation, or prayer of simplicity, those at the end of illumination experience more and more episodes of contemplation quite beyond their own powers. Like the sparks or flashes of awareness of God they experienced long ago at the beginning of the journey, these experiences of awareness are not so much overpowering as they are mentally captivating. Acts of quiet recollection may precede and follow them. But these acts are obviously much more voluntary than the moment of quiet contemplation. The questions which suddenly confront the person are: Am I willing to surrender to and cherish these moments of intense awareness of the presence of God and am I willing to reinforce them by a life of habitual virtue and generous self-giving? This is not a new problem, but there is a special urgency about it. It is important to note that subjectively these states are very different from pathological states of self-alienation. There is no psychological conflict that one is escaping from. There is no real interference with duty, no lack of understanding of others. Quite the opposite: There is an openness to a presence quite beyond oneself—a presence of God which brings with it a new openness to the presence of other people and of other things. Von Hügel has used the word "panentheism," meaning all things in God. Although a philosophical term, it fits the subjective quality of the experience which must be carefully differentiated from that of a person on the threshold of a breakdown. The experienced director can usually see the difference quickly by the observation of different visual clues which will tell if a person is approaching the unity of love or the splintering of the psyche. As the experience of this new and simple acquired contemplation takes over and the affective prayer of the illuminative way decreases, there emerges a time of simple union with God.

One can observe the following behavioral characteristics of those at the transition to the unitive way. They have a great purity of heart, and do not fall into any deliberate sin even though frailty may cause them to regress in their behavior at times. They have a great control and mastery over their behavior, with little or no effort. They no longer rely upon repression, reaction formation, and other defenses which are always inadequate and always cause conflict. Watching a person in the unitive way is like watching a great musician playing an instrument over which he or she has complete mastery and control. A particular exception to this may be a person who is deeply scarred, the person with profound psychological wounds who has actually surrendered to God. It requires much more experience on the part of a director to perceive growth in this kind of person because of the presence of pathologies which coexist with the unitive way when there are still deep scars. An example of this kind of person is Francis Thompson, who was very obviously one of these damaged people and whose poetry reflects a high level of insight into the spiritual life:

> 'By this, O Singer, know we if thou see.
> When men shall say to thee: Lo! Christ is here,
> When men shall say to thee: Lo! Christ is there,
> Believe them: yea, and this—then art thou seer,
> When all thy crying clear
> Is but: Lo here! lo there!—ah me, lo everywhere!'

SOURCE OF THIS SIMPLE AWARENESS

If we ask what is the psychological foundation of this simple awareness of the presence of God, it seems to me that it is a purified desire or a simplified will. Naturally the actual source of this awareness of God's presence is in fact God's active presence in all things. The presence of Christ, of whom Thompson speaks so beautifully, is the presence of the

Logos, the Word in, through, and with whom all things were made. The individual Christian enlightened by faith will in the simple unitive way come to discover the presence of Christ—everywhere.

But the psychological question remains. How does this awareness occur? It is my impression that the awareness of God's presence grows because of a simple desire to accept the divine will and live according to it. Silence then reigns in the psyche of the person and the presence of God always there in reality now appears psychologically. A very perceptive analysis of this process is given by one of the great spiritual psychologists of the Middle Ages, Meister Eckhart, in his short sermon on detachment and the presence of God.[7] He is of the opinion that the essence of the psychological process of union with God is not the awareness of God, but rather the openness of the mind and will to God—undisturbed by contradictory desires, hidden goals, and unresolved conflicts, and open to reality on all levels because of the relinquishment of defense mechanisms and other unrealistic behavior.

THE GIFTS OF THE HOLY SPIRIT AND CONTEMPLATION

A number of spiritual writers see the time of the entrance into the unitive way as the appropriate moment to consider the influence of the gifts of the Holy Spirit. These are marvelous and intriguing elements of the spiritual life which are seldom given adequate attention.

We have already considered the difference between moral virtues (prudence, justice, courage, and temperance) and the theological virtues (faith, hope, and love). All Christian virtues, moral and theological, are infused gifts of God, although the moral virtues are built upon acquired good qualities, and the theological virtues are received only with sanctifying grace. The moral virtues, as distinct from good qualities, also call us to loftier goals, to live and labor for the salvation of others in imitation of Christ. Frequently Christians do not perceive the loftiness of their vocations because they do not consciously allude to the virtues. The gifts of the Holy Spirit are even more astonishing because they bring to the practice of all the virtues, including faith, hope, and love, a greater perfection. "The spirit of the Lord shall rest upon him: a spirit of wisdom and of understanding, a spirit of counsel and of strength, a spirit of knowledge and of fear of the Lord, and his delight shall be the fear of the Lord" (Isa. 11:2–3, New American Bible).[8] The Septuagint and the Vulgate read "piety" for "fear of the Lord" in its first occurrence, as is noted in the New American Bible. This text became the source of the traditional names of the gifts of the Holy Spirit, which would later be developed in Christian spirituality. When early in the spiritual life we have prayed beyond our level of spiritual maturity, we probably experienced the gifts of understanding and knowledge. The greatest of the gifts is wisdom, which makes us prefer the love of God over things of this passing world. Without the spirit of wisdom and the subtle operation of this gift even early in life, we would not be saved.[9]

If you have never given these gifts much thought, it is probably because their effectiveness becomes an obvious and vibrant part of an individual's life only when a good deal of purity of intention is achieved. One must appreciate these gifts in order to understand a person in the unitive way. They were given radically at Baptism and have been operating quietly in the life of the person all through this long journey. The flashes of the divine presence may indeed be seen as a result of the gifts which, according to St. Thomas and other theologians, are less active than infused virtues. The gifts do not cause us to do things as virtues do, but rather open us to a new docility to grace.[10] As a result of the gifts, in the whole living of our lives we become more open to the influences of grace. Perhaps a simple example will help. It is a virtue (courage) that causes us to be willing to face a difficult situation when we may be criticized, misunderstood, and unjustly treated. It is the gifts of the Holy Spirit—in this case wisdom, counsel, and courage—which operate within us in the midst of the trial and give us words and wisdom at that time. To use a very popular term, virtue gives us the power to do good, the gifts give us the ability to do it with "class." As someone said of natural talent (also a gift), you can't put it into a person when God has left it out.

The gifts of the Holy Spirit prompt us to do virtuous things and to accomplish them in appropriate ways. Such virtues as courage and faith gave St. Edmund Campion the strength to stand before his unjust judges and not capitulate even though he was half-dead from torture. He received the gifts as he made his great defense boldly and bravely with the result that one of his accusers converted and eventually became St. Philip Howard.

So important is the operation of the gifts of the Holy Spirit that St. Thomas Aquinas teaches that they are necessary for salvation, basing his argument on Romans 8:14–17: "Everyone moved by the spirit is a son of God. The spirit you receive is not the spirit of slaves bringing fear into your lives; it is the spirit of sons which makes us cry out, 'Abba, father!' The Spirit himself and our spirit bear united witness that we are the children of God. And if we are children we are heirs as well; heirs of God and co-heirs with Christ, sharing his suffering so as to share his glory." This contention of St. Thomas may appear to be startling, but it should cause us to consider how often in the past we have done good and followed God's law, or been led to repentance by some special inspiration. St. Thomas, citing Psalm 143:10, "May your good Spirit guide me on to level ground," notes that none can receive the inheritance of that land of the blessed, except that he be moved and led there by the Holy Spirit.[11] The operation of the gifts of the Holy Spirit is the very thing that makes all the works of religion interesting and vital. Even the truths of faith, when presented in a way that is not touched by the gifts, can seem very dreary.

Perhaps you have attended a sermon which was theologically very accurate and totally boring. The operation of the gifts was lacking. Or perhaps, on the other hand, you have wondered why a contemplative person was so fascinated by some spiritual theme which did not touch you at all. The gifts were not at work in you. The spiritually advanced can be very moved by a word of Scripture or a flower. This is not new-found religious enthusiasm which soon grows cold, but a profound, almost encompassing interest comparable to the absorption of a musical genius in some composition. (According to Garrigou-Lagrange, St. Thomas did not hesitate to draw an analogy between the natural inspiration to do some work extraordinarily well without deliberation, as in the case of creative genius, and the operation of the gifts of the Holy Spirit at a supernatural level.)[12] Garrigou-Lagrange calls the operation of the gifts an increasingly perfect docility to the "interior Master." He gives the following explanation and examples:

> The third mode of the divine motion in the order of grace is that by which God especially moves the free will of a spiritual man, who is disposed to the divine inspiration by the gifts of the Holy Ghost. Here the just soul is immediately directed, not by reason enlightened by faith, but by the Holy Ghost Himself in a superhuman manner . . . it is an eminent mode of operating grace which thus leads to the highest acts of the virtues and of the gifts: faith, illumined by the gift of understanding, becomes much more penetrating and contemplative; hope, enlightened by the gift of knowledge as to the vanity of all that is transitory, becomes perfect confidence and filial abandonment to Providence; and the illuminations of the gift of wisdom invite charity to the intimacy of divine union. As the bee or the carrier pigeon, directed by instinct, acts with a wonderful certainty revealing the Intelligence which directs them, just so, says St. Thomas, "the spiritual man is inclined to act, not principally through the movement of his own will, but by the instinct of the Holy Ghost, according to the words of Isaiah (59:19): 'when he shall come as a violent stream, which the spirit of the Lord driveth on.' "[13]

It goes beyond the scope of this book to examine each of the gifts and its operation, although it is worthwhile to point out that specific gifts are generally related to the practice of particular virtues. Together the gifts lead to the more perfect practice of the eight beatitudes and finally fill the soul with the fruits or spiritual rewards of the virtuous Christian life. The following schema is given by Garrigou-Lagrange and provides an excellent guide for meditative study of the gifts.[14]

	Virtues	Gifts	Beatitudes	Fruits of the Holy Ghost (Gal. 5:22–23)
theological virtues bearing directly on the end	charity	wisdom	peacemakers	
	faith	under-standing	pure of heart	charity peace joy patience benignity
	hope	knowl-edge	those who weep	
moral virtues bearing directly on the means	prudence justice	counsel	the merciful	
	(religion)	piety	the meek	goodness longanimity faith
	fortitude	fortitude	those who hunger after justice	modesty continency chastity
	temper-ance	fear	the poor in spirit	

(Left-side brace label: The grace of the virtues and of the gifts)

THE PRAYER OF SIMPLE CONTEMPLATION

The person entering the unitive way is summoned by God into a simple supernatural awareness beyond self, an awareness of God's presence, of Christ within. There are numerous magnificent descriptions of the initial experience of acquired contemplation, which is also referred to as simple contemplation because it is characterized by a prayer of great simplicity. For readers unfamiliar with contemplative literature, I have carefully selected three descriptions: one ancient, St. Gregory of Nyssa; one from the Catholic Reformation, St. Teresa of Avila; and one modern, Thomas Merton. A meditative reading of the three quotations should give some notion of simple contemplation. The excerpt from St. Gregory is highly platonic in terminology and outlook. It does express, however, the general impression of those who arrive at contemplation that they must pass through a period of the Dark Night of the Senses and find the divine nature within.

> The contemplation of God is not effected by sight and hearing, nor is it comprehended by any of the customary perceptions of the mind. For no eye has seen, and no ear has heard, nor does it belong to those things which usually enter into the heart of man. He who would approach the knowledge of things sublime must first purify his manner of life from all sensual and irrational emotion. He must wash from his understanding every opinion derived from some preconception and withdraw himself from his customary intercourse with his own companion, that is, with his sense perceptions, which are, as it were, wedded to our nature as its companion. When he is so purified, then he assaults the mountain. . . . For leaving behind everything that is observed, not only what sense comprehends but also what the intelligence thinks it sees, it keeps on penetrating deeper until by the intelligence's yearning for understanding it gains access to the invisible and the incomprehensible, and there it sees God. This is the true knowledge of what is sought; this is the seeing that consists in not seeing, because that which is sought transcends all knowledge, being separated on all sides by incomprehensibility as by a kind of darkness. Wherefore John the sublime, who penetrated into the luminous darkness, says, *No one has ever seen God,* thus asserting that knowledge of the divine essence is unattainable not only by men but also by every intelligent creature.[15]

St. Gregory's description of the divine darkness should not mislead us: It does not mean that a person moves totally outside himself, drawn, as it were, into some region that is separated from his own being. While such a notion may have been popular in ancient times, it is not what St. Gregory is speaking about. He makes the following observation in his sixth sermon on the beatitudes:

> The Lord does not say that it is blessed to know something about God, but rather to possess God in oneself: *Blessed are the clean of heart, for they shall see God* (Matt. 5:8). By this I do not think he means that the man who purifies the eye of his soul will enjoy an immediate vision of God; rather that this marvellous saying teaches us the same lesson which the Word expressed more clearly to others when he said: "The Kingdom of God is within you" (Luke 17:21). And this teaches us that the man who purifies his heart of every creature and of every passionate impulse will see the image of the divine nature in his own beauty. So too in this short sentence the Word, I think, is giving us the following advice: All you mortals, who have within yourselves a desire to behold the supreme good, when you are told that the majesty of God is exalted above the heavens, that the divine glory is inexpressible, its beauty indescribable, its nature inaccessible, do not despair at never being able to behold what you desire. For you do have within your

grasp the degree of knowledge of God which you can attain. For, when God made you, he at once endowed your nature with this perfection; upon the structure of your nature he imprinted an imitation of the perfections of his own nature, just as one would impress upon wax the outline of an emblem. But the wickedness that has been poured all over this divine engraving has made your perfection useless and hidden it with a vicious coating. You must then wash away, by a life of virtue, the dirt that has come to cling to your heart like plaster, and then your divine beauty will once again shine forth.[16]

The first lesson to be learned is that contemplation is a kind of darkness for all our powers, even the intellect; thus this simple relation to God, unlike the contemplative meditation of the illuminative way, goes beyond our conscious awareness of the truths of faith. It is a gift given in a Dark Night.

We turn next to St. Teresa of Avila, perhaps the easiest mystic to understand because of her lucid illustrations and nonacademic approach; she will be our guide for much of what follows concerning the unitive way. St. Teresa gives a charming example of simple contemplation, illustrating that it is a very personal gift. She uses the word "grace," which, I think, is best understood as the gifts of the Holy Spirit.

I spent a good many years doing a great deal of reading and understanding nothing of what I read; for a long time, though God was teaching me, I could not utter a word to explain His teaching to others, and this was no light trial to me. When His Majesty so wills, He can teach everything in a moment, in a way that amazes me. I can truthfully say this: though I used to talk with many spiritual persons, who would try to explain what the Lord was teaching me so that I might be able to speak about it, I was so stupid that I could not get the slightest profit from their instructions. Possibly, as His Majesty has always been my teacher—may He be blessed for everything, for I am thoroughly ashamed of being able to say that this is the truth—it may have been His will that I should be indebted to no one else for my knowledge. In any case, without my wishing it or asking for it, . . . God suddenly gave me a completely clear understanding of the whole thing, so that I was able to speak about it in such a way that people were astounded. And I myself was more astounded even than my own confessors, for I was more conscious than they of my own stupidity. This happened only a short time ago. So I do not now attempt to learn what the Lord has not taught me, unless it be something affecting my conscience.[17]

After seeing the importance St. Teresa places on the passivity of the unitive state, we can better appreciate an example of unitive prayer given in the preceding chapter of her autobiography. Speaking of the soul as an interior garden to be cultivated, she offers this example of contemplation:

> Let us not consider how this garden can be watered, so that we may know what we have to do, what labor it will cost us, if the gain will outweigh the labor and for how long this labor must be borne. It seems to me that the garden can be watered in four ways: by taking the water from a well, which costs us great labor; or by a water-wheel and buckets, when the water is drawn by a windlass; or by a stream or a brook, which waters the ground much better, for it saturates it more thoroughly and there is less need to water it often, so that the gardener's labor is much less; or by heavy rain, when the Lord waters it with no labor of ours, a way incomparably better than any of those which have been described.[18]

Finally we come to a description of contemplation from Thomas Merton which should be extremely helpful because it is written in contemporary terms. While it may lack the clarity of St. Teresa's homely examples, it emphasizes that contemplation is indeed a response to an interior Master or Teacher calling us beyond our natural powers by the work of the gifts of the Holy Spirit:

> Contemplation is the highest expression of man's intellectual and spiritual life. It is that life itself, fully awake, fully active, fully aware that it is alive. It is spiritual wonder. It is spontaneous awe at the sacredness of life, of being. It is a vivid realization of the fact that life and being in us proceed from an invisible, transcendent and infinitely abundant Source. Contemplation is, above all, awareness of the reality of that Source. It *knows* the Source, obscurely, inexplicably, but with a certitude that goes both beyond reason and beyond simple faith. For contemplation is a kind of spiritual vision to which both reason and faith aspire, by their very nature, because without it they must always remain incomplete. Yet contemplation is not vision because it sees "without seeing" and knows "without knowing." It is a more profound depth of faith, a knowledge too deep to be grasped in images, in words or even in clear concepts. It can be suggested by words, symbols, but in the very moment of trying to indicate what it knows the contemplative mind takes back what it has said, and denies what it has affirmed. . . . The contemplation of which I speak here is not philosophical. It is not the static awareness of metaphysical essences apprehended as spiritual objects, unchanging and eternal. It is not the contemplation of abstract ideas. It is the religious apprehension of God, through my life in God, or through "sonship" as the New Testament says. "For whoever are led by the Spirit of God, they are the sons of God. . . . The Spirit Himself gives testimony to our own spirit that we are the sons of God." "To as many as received Him He gave the power to become the sons of God. . . ." And so the contemplation of which I speak is a religious and transcendent gift. It is not something

to which we can attain alone, by intellectual effort, by perfecting our natural powers. It is not a kind of self-hypnosis, resulting from concentration on our own inner spiritual being. It is not the fruit of our own efforts. It is the gift of God who, in His mercy, completes the hidden and mysterious work of creation in us by enlightening our minds and hearts, by awakening in us the awareness that we are words spoken in His One Word, and that Creating Spirit (*Creator Spiritus*) dwells in us, and we in Him. That we are "in Christ" and that Christ lives in us. That the natural life in us has been completed, elevated, transformed and fulfilled in Christ by the Holy Spirit. Contemplation is the awareness and realization, even in some sense *experience,* of what each Christian obscurely believes: It is no longer I that live but Christ lives in me.[19]

These three powerful quotations stress that contemplation is absolutely a gift. However, as I have indicated already, it would be a mistake to assume that contemplation is ordinarily given without any preparation on the part of the individual. It is possible for God, in His Providence, to give extraordinary gifts far beyond any preparation, as He gave the gift of a mystical vision to St. Bernadette. However, it is not what one might call the normal course of events in spirituality. The lives of the mystics give evidence of a long and tedious personal preparation for the gift of contemplation. Contemplation does not flow from the personality or ego; rather, personality has been prepared, as St. Gregory of Nyssa suggests, by a cleansing so as to come to the discovery of that which was already there.

In his remarkable book *Studies and the Psychology of the Mystics,* Joseph Maréchal eloquently describes the individual's relationship with the contemplative gifts he receives:

> The contemplative . . . fixes his inner gaze on an idea which is the purest expression of God, Absolute Unity. He thus supports his efforts on the most central line of the natural development of the mind. Moreover, thanks to the convergent and often prolonged exercise of vocal and mental prayer, of moral activity, asceticism, humility, he has connected, and connects more closely each day, with his idea of God all that is dearest and most intimate to him: God has become the keystone of the arch of his Ego, the point from which he views all his proceedings, the pregnant symbol, the assimilative force of all his experiences, the ideal of all his dreams, the center of all his affections, the dominating principle of all his actions—in short, the center of equilibrium and the vital impulse of his whole psychological being. And when the contemplative, set free from the diversity of time and space, enters into prayer, the powerful coordination which he has prepared in himself by the whole course of his life awakes and is locked in the bosom of a growing recollection. Let us hear what is said on this point, not by the mystic alone, but even by a simple man of prayer: "Lord, thou art wholly hidden in the heart of each thing. . . .

I beseech thee, turn my heart toward thee, into the interior of myself, into the depths of my soul, so that there, in the silence of creatures and the quieting of inordinate thoughts, I may remain with thee, unceasingly behold thy presence, love and worship thee, hear thy voice, discover to thee the wretchedness of my exile and find comfort in thee."

THE DARK NIGHT OF THE SENSES

Shortly after the beginning of the prayer of simple union the individual is plunged into the first Dark Night properly so called, or the Night of the Senses. We have discussed the contemplative prayer of simple union prior to the Dark Night so that we might be able to examine the relationship between the two, which, psychologically, may be one of cause and effect. No one has described the two Dark Nights, this one and the later one, called the Dark Night of the Spirit, better than St. John of the Cross, who should be read while keeping in mind that what he writes is specifically related to experiences of the unitive way. The writings of St. John of the Cross are applicable only in an analogous way to the experiences of suffering and darkness described earlier at the end of the purgative way.

St. John of the Cross makes use of several analogies to clarify the purpose of the darkness. The best, I think, is that of the fire and the log. The whole process is well described:

> For the sake of further clarity in this matter, we ought to note that this purgative and loving knowledge or divine light we are speaking of, has the same effect on the soul that fire has on a log of wood. The soul is purged and prepared for union with the divine light just as the wood is prepared for transformation into the fire. Fire, when applied to wood, first dehumidifies it, dispelling all moisture and making it give off any water it contains. Then it gradually turns the wood black, makes it dark and ugly, and even causes it to emit a bad odor. By drying out the wood, the fire brings to light and expells all those ugly and dark accidents which are contrary to fire. Finally, by heating and enkindling it from without, the fire transforms the wood into itself and makes it as beautiful as it is itself. Once transformed, the wood no longer has any activity or passivity of its own, except for its weight and its quantity, which is denser than the fire.[21]

The analogy here, it seems to me, is that the darkness, called "aridity," is simply a psychological consequence of the new level of functioning.[22] However, it also includes *the frightening experience* of being in the grip of forces like fire beyond one's control. This experience can be distinguished from ordinary boredom and ennui because in the darkness the person finds no comfort in anything—God or creatures. The individual wants to please God desperately, but feels that he or she is going backward and has done nothing. And finally the person is unable to meditate and reflect. It seems that psychologically the individual is being forced to silence within by reason of the collapse of the most powerful of the defense mechanisms, which is sublimation. Not only does infused contemplation not require sublimation; it is impeded by it. Before the concept of defense mechanisms was known explicitly two generations ago, almost all spiritual writers saw this Dark Night of the Senses as a providential forcing of the individual into inner silence and self-surrender. While their view is certainly true, the added factor of the relinquishing of sublimation amplifies our understanding of the Dark Night. Other defenses, such as denial, rationalization, and intellectualization, which have survived the illuminative way in a very moderated form are now all but obliterated, leaving the person defenseless and psychologically naked. As a result of the gradual relinquishing of defense mechanisms the forces of the id or libido make a last assault. Tanquerey mentions that terrible temptations against faith, hope, chastity, and patience are predictable. Scruples, worries, and conflicts may rage in the mind causing the symptoms of a kind of neurasthenia or what may be called a nervous breakdown.[23]

Lastly, the person entering the unitive way is likely to encounter many interpersonal difficulties and misunderstandings, which spiritual writers suggest are the result of the ill will of others. However, I am not so sure. Perhaps the person going from illumination to union feels alienated and this feeling may beget further alienation. Friends become estranged because they do not receive accustomed support. Critics and enemies (never lacking to the mature person who is reasonably honest) are likely to be hypercritical (even though they may be fairly spiritual). Since our image of the virtuous Christian is more often based on religious art calendars than on the Gospel, we may find ourselves put off by the person whose priorities have been radically altered by the experience of the unitive way.

Finally, the world steps in. Those possessed of worldly values are always annoyed (a weak word) by the person of upright life. They "bend their bow" and may do personal damage to the life and reputation of the individual. John of the Cross himself underwent this suffering. Cardinal Newman, who had reason to know, observed that the more a man is drawn to God, the less the world will understand him. In Tanquerey's view a person going through the Dark Night is also likely to suffer "evils from without," such as illness, helplessness in vocational duties, and the feeling that one is considered stupid.[24] These sufferings could reflect a passive aggression that may overtake a person in time of crisis, but I have invariably observed that a mysterious collection of misfortunes overtakes people at this time. The spiritual director begins to sense a struggle with an uncanny set of calamities that may seem like Providence in reverse.

The final deliverance from this aridity has been described by St. Teresa in a passage that is very profitable and revealing. She recognizes that grace has saved her without her own consent. "There is no remedy in this tempest but to wait for the mercy of God."[25] She did not resist it, it simply came. St. Augustine has taught the same about his own conversion. "You shouted out and broke through my deafness, you burned brightly and chased away my blindness."[26] Garrigou-Lagrange indicates that many people before they have this experience feel that grace becomes efficacious by our own consent; after the experience they can only agree with Augustine, Thomas, and Teresa that the opposite is true.[27]

Two further observations on this time of trial seem in order at this point. Considering the personal difficulties from without that are often described, it is possible that they are part of a "midlife crisis." Very strong people like John and Teresa may not have been aware that age and stages of life were affecting them; nor perhaps did they realize that extraordinarily gifted people make others uncomfortable and resentful. Those in the public eye who are moving into the unitive way are especially vulnerable, both to the hostility of others and to the vicissitudes of age. They may not be prepared to surrender the management of works they were given to establish, as Teresa was, or to bear abuse from those they had once befriended, as John did. Perhaps these trials should be looked upon as similar to those of parents who suffer because of rejecting children, or of teachers who see their students go off in directions quite contrary to what they had taught. Both experiences are likely to occur with intensity at the end of midlife.

Suggestions for Helpers

For someone going through the Dark Night of the Senses, a friend in need is indeed a tremendous blessing. If you are called upon to befriend and support a person during this crisis, the following suggestions may be helpful:

1. Be sensitive to the depth of suffering which a mature person may disguise.
2. Be encouraging but strong, and insist that the individual keep busy at normal duties.
3. Identify the problem as clearly a spiritual darkness and use short, selected passages from the mystics, especially St. Teresa and St. John of the Cross, to convince the person that this experience is in fact a Dark Night.

4. It can be beneficial for the person to have two spiritual friends, one who is insistent and tough and the other who is kind and supportive. It is difficult for one person to fulfill both tasks and usually one chooses to be only kind and supportive. This may prolong the crisis.
5. The person in darkness may find great relief in working with the poor and afflicted.
6. Watch for the signs of the end of the Dark Night, namely, a painful and persistent desire for a more intimate union with God. This feeling can bring the greatest discomfort of all, but it should be pointed out that such longing will open the person to divine deliverance.
7. Finally, the image of the arid desert is useful. If you stand in the desert on a still day, nothing moves. It is very much like being inside a painting. There appears to be no life or beauty. Slowly you notice a certain beauty, powerful and beyond emotion or thought. Then you have become accustomed to the beauty of the desert where God is found.

THE UNITIVE PRAYER OF QUIET

Much of what we have said about the prayer of simple contemplation also applies to the next phase of the unitive way, which is called the "prayer of quiet." Since this work is not meant to be a guide for persons in the unitive way, let us simply state that this phase includes three successive steps:

1. A profound passive recollection leading to great quietness in which all the person's faculties are held in joyful fascination at the awareness of God's presence.
2. The overpowering awareness of the presence of God.
3. A kind of wakeful sleep in which one is conscious, but in which all psychological powers have come to rest in God.

A very beautiful description of these steps is given in the fourth mansion of *The Interior Castle* by St. Teresa. Perhaps for the reader it is best to give a contemporary example and description of what a person in this state might look like to his or her friends.

THE LAST YEARS OF FRANK SHEED

The name of Frank Sheed and his wife Maisie Ward are known to millions of readers of religious books. For half a century Sheed and Ward dedicated themselves completely to an apostolate of writing and publishing. Although I had known Frank when I was a teenager, I was privileged to know him well only after he had retired (as a result of a mutual friendship we shared with the Killilea family). During the last seven years of his life I had the opportunity a few times a year to observe this remarkable Christian, especially as he cared for his beloved wife in her last illness and as he prepared for his own final journey. It was and is my impression that Frank Sheed's last years demonstrated very well the unitive way as it might be lived not so much by a monk or nun but rather by a layperson who still feels much at home and at peace in the everyday world. Frank loved humble and plain things. He lived in furnished rooms in Jersey City and particularly appreciated the sturdy faith and direct manners for which the city is known. Frank travelled and lectured and bore witness to Christ around the English-speaking world from Australia to Britain up until the last months of his life. He never complained, although he was in really miserable health. A few events illustrate the very powerful experiences that a great Christian may come to. A short time after his wife's death I mentioned that he must miss Maisie very much. He immediately looked into my eyes and said, "Oh, on the contrary, I feel closer to her than ever before." This was not a conventional observation and it was clear he very literally meant it. Frank never minced words.

Often I would see Frank drawn into a gentle recollection. He often appeared to be listening to something that others could not hear. At the liturgy he was very devout, but seemed abstracted from the particular point of the Mass that we were at. He seemed to attend the liturgy *in globo* rather than in parts.

One day I came upon him sitting in very quiet recollection in his room for a long time. Foolishly I said to this man who had published a thousand books, "Frank, can I get you something to read?" He looked up and said, "Oh my goodness, I have read it all. I just like to listen."

Frank Sheed was not one to make a show of his devotion. He was a very modest man when it came to such things. You could learn the most by what he did not say, as is often the case with wise people. He didn't complain, he didn't argue, he didn't make judgments or at least he tried to make as few as he could about some theologians who he felt had gone too far. Even these would be couched rather carefully and gently. He might become a bit more expressive if it was about a whole situation he disagreed with rather than any particular person.

There is no question for those who knew him well that God was extremely present to Frank Sheed. Christ was everywhere he went. He found great joy in finding His presence in all sorts of things, great and small, but especially in human relationships. Those who knew him well would remark that it was quite impossible to know him and not feel that he was your friend, that he knew you in some special way.

These illustrations from the life of Frank Sheed may give the reader clues as to what to watch for in the life of simple union of someone whose vocation and modesty does not permit them to be expressive about the inner life.

Second Phase of Contemplation—Full Union and Ecstasy

The next two phases of the high spiritual life are usually considered separately. Since we are not attempting a thorough description of these states and since the latter seems to be a logical consequence of the former, we will consider the two of them together. Full union with God means simply that between the movement of the human mind and will and the loving designs of God there is complete harmony. Various analogies abound. St. Teresa's homely one on the silkworm and the butterfly demonstrates the totally transforming power of this gift. She first gives a description of the silkworm:

> You must have already heard about His marvels manifested in the way the silk originates, for only He could have invented something like that. The silkworms come from seeds about the size of little grains of pepper. . . . When the warm weather comes and the leaves begin to appear on the mulberry tree, the seeds start to live but they are dead until then. With their little mouths they themselves go about spinning silk and making some very thick little cocoons in which they enclose themselves. The silkworm, which is ugly and fat, then dies, and a little white butterfly, which is very pretty, comes from the cocoon."[28]

The burning zeal, the total detachment from self, and the perfect obedience of the individual all conspire to produce the image of a totally new being (St. Teresa's little white butterfly). The person is perfectly at peace, unafraid of any harm that anyone might do and filled with an inconspicuous and loving generosity. Persons in this state have great power to win people over, to read and touch hearts, and often to be a powerful healing presence.

Frequently the image of a magnet and its attraction to metal is used by authors, including Eckhart and St. Francis de Sales.[29] Often images of human love are invoked especially by St. Bernard, St. Bonaventure, and St. John of the Cross.[30] St. Catherine of Genoa gives the following description which reflects fully the total union with God that the individual feels at the end of spiritual purification:

> The soul, no matter how intense its sufferings, values the ordinance of God above all things, for He is above and beyond whatever may be felt or conceived. Such knowledge does not come from intellect or will, as I have said. It comes from God, with a rush. God busies the soul with Himself, in no matter how slight a way, and the soul, wrapped up in God, cannot but be oblivious to all else.[31]

Perhaps the most powerful psychological awareness is the absolute certitude of God's presence in the soul. Psychologically one may speculate that all defenses have now been reduced to practically nothing and that one is dealing with a human being who appears to have been healed of the wounds of original sin. Because persons at this level no longer experience the need for human reinforcement and approval, they are quiet and gentle and very unobtrusive. For the most part they are older people and the world is happy to pass them by or give them a patronizing pat on the head. If they are younger and involved in the lives of others like St. John of the Cross, they are likely to be in for trouble. Certainly the reaction of the SS guards to St. Maximilian Kolbe may suggest that toward the end of this life he was at least in this high state of contemplation. The same would be true of Sister Teresa Benedicta of the Cross, O.C.D. (Edith Stein), who found grace, great peace, and prayerfulness working in the terrible confusion of the death camp.

The effects of this union on one's interpersonal relationships can be seen in the following quotation from a letter describing Sister Benedicta a few days before her death at Auschwitz. Julius Markan, a Jewish businessman from Cologne, left the following description of her in the Westerbork Camp:

> Among the prisoners who were brought in on the fifth of August, Sister Benedicta stood out on account of her calmness and composure. The distress in the barracks, the stir caused by the new arrivals, was indescribable. Sister Benedicta was just like an angel, going around among the women, comforting them, helping them and calming them. Many of the mothers were near to distraction. . . . Sister Benedicta took care of the little children, washed them and combed them, looked after their feeding and other needs. During the whole of her stay there, she washed and cleaned for people, following one act of charity with another until everyone wondered at her goodness.[32]

According to the most advanced mystics, this great composure and union with God are sometimes accompanied by an experience called "ecstasy." It is important to look more carefully and see what ecstasy is and what it is not. Most human beings aware of different psychological states are conscious of certain pre-ecstatic experiences. These experiences are characterized by the interruption of common perception and absorption in some delightful stimulus. Natural ecstasy can be aesthetic, sexual, or even athletic. Aldous Huxley in *The Doors of Perception* has done extensive studies of total recollection where the individual becomes so centered in the particular perception that all external faculties are suspended and one neither hears nor sees anything. In the Charismatic Renewal people often have the experience known as "slaying in the spirit" (When in certain circumstances they fall to the floor in what feels like a comfortable and pleasant sleep for a few seconds). It is not clear whether this should be called ecstasy, but certainly it has some of the qualities and has been known to happen to people who have made a definite resolution not to succumb. Although these experiences may be related, they are not what we speak of here. St. Teresa gives us a good description of what has been recognized as a geniune interior ecstasy. She appears to describe two stages: first, a powerful sense of wonder which comes upon the individual for just a short period of time, a moment; second, a unique experience which the saint calls a wound.

> Let us begin, then, to discuss the manner in which the Spouse deals with the soul and how before He belongs to it completely He makes it desire Him vehemently by certain delicate means the soul itself does not understand. . . . These are impulses so delicate and refined, for they proceed from very deep within the interior part of the soul, that I don't know any comparison that will fit it. They are far different from all that we can acquire of ourselves here below and even from the spiritual delights that were mentioned. For often when a person is distracted and forgetful of God, His Majesty will awaken it. His action is as quick as a falling comet. And as clearly as it hears a thunderclap, even though no sound is heard, the soul understands that it was called by God. . . . It feels that it is wounded in the most exquisite way, but it doesn't learn how or by whom it was wounded. It knows clearly that the wound is something precious, and it would never want to be cured. It knows that He is present, but He doesn't want to reveal the manner in which He allows Himself to be enjoyed. And the pain is great although delightful and sweet.[33]

The second experience of ecstasy the saint calls "rapture." It is often described as being borne on eagles' wings or being in flight. The following description of St. Teresa makes one suspect that it is the same psychological experience as St. Francis felt at the time of his stigmatization. It is important to note that St. Teresa believes strongly that the individual in rapture understands the secrets of God. Otherwise she considers these experiences simply to be emotional episodes.

> One kind of rapture is that in which the soul even though not in prayer is touched by some word it remembers or hears about God. It

seems that His Majesty from the interior of the soul makes the spark we mentioned increase, for He is moved with compassion and seeing the soul suffer so long a time in its desire. All burnt up, the soul is renewed like the phoenix, and one can devoutly believe that its faults are pardoned. Now that it is so pure, the Lord joins it with Himself, without any understanding of what is happening except these two; nor does the soul itself understand in a way that can afterward be explained. Yet, it does have interior understanding, for this experience is not like that of fainting or convulsion; in these latter nothing is understood inwardly and outwardly. [34]

It might be said that St. Teresa makes it clear that in this rapture the person is conscious of the inner world and certainly is conscious of the forgiveness of sins. This is really a beautiful experience of deliverance. After this the secrets of God are revealed. St. Teresa uses the homely example of visiting the treasure room of the Duchess of Alba and being overwhelmed by all the precious objects, but drawing little inspiration from this array of earthly splendor. But now she suggests that the Lord let her visit the treasure room so that she could make an analogy between it and the awareness of the secrets of God. She states that a person in this state of suspension is shown secrets about heavenly things which remain impressed on the memory. If it happens that these visions are what she calls "intellectual," the person does not know how to speak about them. There must be visions during these moments that are so sublime, she asserts, that no one on earth has the necessary understanding to explain them to someone else.

St. Bonaventure in the following quotation about contemplation seems to parallel the experience of St. Teresa:

> Filled with all of these intellectual illuminations, our mind like the house of God is inhabited by divine Wisdom; it is made a daughter of God, His spouse and friend; it is made a member of Christ the head, His sister and co-heir; it is made a temple of the Holy Spirit, grounded in faith, built up by hope and dedicated to God by holiness of mind and body. All this is accomplished by a most sincere love of Christ which is brought forth in our hearts by the Holy Spirit who has been given to us and without whom we cannot know the secret things of God. [35]

St. Bonaventure's description of the stigmatization of St. Francis is one of the most fascinating accounts of a spiritual ecstasy which was accompanied by a physical miracle. In the *Life of St. Francis* we read:

> By the Seraphic ardor of his desires, he was being borne aloft into God; and by his sweet compassion he was being transformed into Him who chose to be crucified because of the excess of His love. On a

certain morning about the feast of the Exaltation of the Cross, while Francis was praying in the mountainside, he saw a Seraph with six fiery and shining wings descend from the height of heaven. And when in swift flight the Seraph reached a spot in the figure of a man crucified, with his hands and feet extended in the form of a cross and fastened to a cross. Two of the wings were lifted above the head, two were extended for flight, and two covered his whole body. When Francis saw this, he was overwhelmed and his heart was flooded with a mixture of joy and sorrow. He rejoiced because of the gracious way Christ looked upon him under the appearance of the Seraph, but the fact that he was fastened to a cross, pierced his soul with a sort of compassionate sorrow. He wondered exceedingly at the sight of so unfathomable a vision, realizing that the weakness of Christ's passion was in no way compatible with the immortality of the Seraph's spiritual nature. Eventually he understood by a revelation from the Lord that divine providence had shown him this vision so that, as Christ's lover, he might learn in advance that he was to be totally transformed into the likeness of Christ crucified.[36]

It must be mentioned that these experiences described autobiographically by St. Teresa and by St. Bonaventure of St. Francis bear a literary parallel with 2 Corinthians 12:1–4, where St. Paul describes his rapture into paradise. Biblical scholars have written a great deal about this unique report of St. Paul and seem to agree that it was something very personal for him and that it was an experience quite different in its quality and interpretation from what the pagan Greek devotees of mysticism would have referred to as "a journey to heaven." It is not to our purpose to go into the question of the exegesis of this text. It is, however, logical to point out that both St. Teresa and St. Bonaventure may have been influenced in their description by the words of St. Paul, namely, that he was "caught up into paradise and heard things which must not and cannot be put into human language."[37]

St. Teresa speaks of seeing other worlds. She is always practical and makes the point that all of this experience is intended to leave the soul filled with longing to enjoy completely the One who draws it to Himself. She clearly speaks of a death wish very different from the pathological preoccupation with self-destruction recognized in psychology.[38] The person drawn to this level of rapture must practice a special detachment in order to stay in this valley of tears. The rest of the world, even the ecclesiastical world, failed very badly in its attempts to comprehend those who are borne on eagles' wings. If you are curious about these states, I suggest that you read carefully the *Interior Castle* and also St. Bonaventure's *The Soul's Journey into God*.

Tanquerey takes a much more specific approach to the phenomenon of ecstasy than does St. Teresa. He sums up the psychological observations of people in this state by saying that ecstasy is characterized by physical insensitivity and the slowing down of life processes, a kind of immobility in which the eyes remain fixed on some invisible "objects," a sense of fatigue at the end of the ecstasy, followed by the full return of vigor. He points out that inner faculties are suspended on various levels; sometimes a person may be able to recall the experience, sometimes not.

A few contemporary experimental psychologists have looked at these phenomena which are related to periods of intense recollection and prayer. They have generally concluded that such states do not necessarily represent pathological forms of dissociation and withdrawal because of the absence of other symptoms associated with personality disorganization. Rather than being pathological states, these profound religious experiences may represent the individual's highest integration of functions. Kenneth Wapnick makes the most practical suggestion for determining whether a genuine mystical experience has taken place or whether psychotic phenomena are being reported. He suggests that we simply evaluate the psychological effects of these states and determine whether they are related to unification of the functions of the individual or to disintegration.[39] Unfortunately the very sophisticated studies of Arthur J. Deikman require a fairly high level of familiarity with the concepts of experimental psychology. His work, however, is quite creative and anyone interested in the subject may find it profitable to read his studies. Deikman's experiments point out that in mystical states a certain deautomatization takes place, leaving the individual with the experience of intense realness, unity, and ineffability. From a pragmatic point of view this manner of functioning is less efficient. However, as Deikman points out, it leaves the individual's mind free to experience aspects of the real world formerly excluded or ignored. From a psychological point of view he would see the individual focusing consciousness on things that we are not likely to focus on in our ordinary management of psychological functions.[40]

Kenneth Wapnick also did a careful comparison of the effects of religious ecstasy and of psychotic withdrawal comparing St. Teresa's accounts with the narration of a particularly literate psychiatric patient. Wapnick seems to generalize the conclusion of most research in this area, namely, the necessity of evaluating the effects of the ecstatic experience on the total life adjustment and psychological functioning of the individual. The following account of an unusual opportunity I had to observe ecstasy in the life of a man well known and venerated for his personal holiness is worth recording. It should dispel doubts of those who wonder if this experience really occurs and it should also illustrate a number of the observations made by St. Teresa and others.

THE ECSTASY OF FATHER SOLANUS

Father Solanus Casey was a priest who lived and worked most of his life in Detroit and who died there at the age of eighty-six in 1957. At the time of his death he was venerated by thousands of people as a person of great spiritual depth and humility and also as a healer. He was possessed of many remarkable parapsychological and paramystical gifts such as an ability to foretell future events. This very humble man had worked for years as the porter or doorkeeper of various Capuchin monasteries in New York and for thirty years in Detroit where he also was the moving spirit behind a large soup kitchen for the poor.

When I arrived at the Capuchin novitiate in Huntington, Indiana, in 1950, Father Solanus was there and obviously was a person of very profound spiritual dimensions. He spent his days in prayer receiving an endless procession of people who came to ask for his counsel and prayers and even for healing. Although he had never preached a sermon or heard confessions (because early in life he had failed theology), he did celebrate the Eucharist in a very recollected, yet unostentatious way. In fact the only example of exceptional behavior I observed in the year I lived with him is as follows:

It was a very hot night and I was unable to sleep. About three o'clock in the morning I decided to walk around the cloister a few times and came to the side door leading into the sanctuary of the friars' chapel. After a few moments kneeling in the dark I became aware that someone else was in the chapel quite close to me. Slightly startled, I reached over and put on the spotlight which flooded the sanctuary with bright lights. About ten feet in front of me, kneeling on the top step of the altar with his arms extended in an attitude of profound prayer was Father Solanus. He appeared to be totally unaware that the lights had gone on although his eyes were partly opened and he was gazing in the most intense way at the tabernacle on the altar. I am sure that he did not know that I was there because it would have been totally uncharacteristic of him to remain in this extraordinary posture if he knew he was being observed. I watched this scene for three to four minutes. He never moved at all and seemed to be scarcely breathing. After thirty years, I recall the profound sense of presence I observed in his fixed stare at the tabernacle. I do not recall ever seeing anyone in such fixed attention, although I had observed something remotely similar at a great moment in a musical presentation or as an effective preacher reached the high point of a sermon. I have never seen a human being more absorbed in anything in my life. After a few minutes I felt that I was intruding on an event so private and intimate that I should not have been there. I put out the light and left. I later learned that it was not uncommon for the first brothers down in the morning to find Father Solanus already in the chapel either praying or sometimes asleep curled up at the foot of the altar.

Although Father Solanus' life was filled with the unusual, and with people coming for help who often were healed or assisted, he was a very sane man. He was quiet and self-effacing. He had a good sense of humor and interest in other people and was always courteous and deferential. Although extremely ascetic, he took care of his health and in his late seventies was the first jogger I had ever known. Despite his reputation for holiness he loved to entertain the novices with his fiddle and was fond of playing "Pop Goes the Weasel" and "Mother McCree." The cause of Father Solanus has been presented to the Holy See by the bishops of the United States for consideration for beatification.[41]

THE DARK NIGHT OF THE SPIRIT

The best of all guides when considering the ultimate night, that of the spirit, is St. John of the Cross who not only describes its different aspects, but emphatically states that its purpose is purification. He paints a picture of extremely advanced souls undergoing purification by periods of darkness and aridity, or plunged into utter darkness convinced that God has abandoned them forever.[42] He lists certain imperfections of persons at this level suggesting that the "stains of the old man still linger in the spirit." The desire for absolute purity may be a difficult concept to grasp, but in *The Living Flame of Love* he clarifies the problem when he speaks of memory, intellect, and will as vast caverns of the soul, as deep and empty as what they are destined to possess. He points out that at this level "any little thing which adheres in them will burden and bewitch them" and yet when the caverns are empty and pure, the thirst and hunger for God is overwhelming and fills the soul with pain. When the purification we have described has taken place and the divine has not yet communicated itself in perfect union, there is experienced an impatient love so that the person must be filled or die. Thus we find here a darkness that is a reaction to imperfection and absolute desire.

· It is possible that the ego is coming apart. Such an idea should, in my opinion, at least be explored. The person and not the ego is called by a beauty and goodness totally beyond all previous experience and all psychological capacity.

St. Bonaventure illustrates this experience of the absolute by his use of superlatives to show the inadequacy of language at this level. He maintains that the creative essence, God the Trinity, "superessential, superdivine and supereminent overseer of divine wisdom of Christians, directs us into superunknown, superluminous and most sublime summit of mystical communication." But this experience is "hidden in the superluminous darkness of the silence teaching secretly in the utmost obscurity."[43]

It may be that both purification and the destruction of ego mechanisms are taking place here. Be that as it may, the ultimate result of the trial, epitomized by the words of the Crucified, "My God, my God, why have you forsaken me?" is total peace and rest for all faculties of the psyche, both sensory and spiritual. All is now stilled.[44]

The way has been prepared for the ultimate experience possible for a human being in this earthly existence: a state of being so beautiful that those who have experienced it say it is the beginning of the vision of God.

TRANSFORMING UNION OR SPIRITUAL MARRIAGE

Even our spiritual guides find it difficult to describe this highest level of the spiritual mountain. We had analogies to work with in our understanding of ecstasy and rapture, but as St. Teresa points out in the Seventh Mansion, this is something completely different. She states that the advanced person was previously called to the most sublime part of the soul (in rapture), but now is called to its *center,* to experience the vision of God. "Our God now desires to remove the scales from the soul's eyes and let it see and understand, although in a strange way, something of the favor He gives it."[45]

The experience of Transforming Union is usually described in terms of a vision of the Trinity and the union of all desire and decision, a complete harmony of the individual with the divine being. St. Teresa gives the example of the rain of heaven and ground water so mingled that they are inseparable. To have some concept of this lofty state we will consider both elements, the vision and the union of the will.
St. Teresa writes of the vision:

> When the soul is brought into that dwelling place, the most blessed Trinity, all three persons, through an intellectual vision, is revealed to it through a certain representation of the truth. First there comes an enkindling of the spirit in the manner of a cloud of magnificent splendor; and these persons are distinct and through an admirable knowledge the soul understands as a most profound truth that all three persons are one substance and one power and one knowledge and one God alone. It knows in such a way that what we hold by faith it understands, we can say, through sight although the sight is not with bodily eyes nor the eyes of the soul, because we are not dealing with an imaginative vision. Here all three persons communicate to it, speak to it, and explain those words of the Lord in the Gospel; that He and the Father and the Holy Spirit will come to dwell with the soul that loves Him and keeps His commandments.[46]

St. Bonaventure uses the symbol of the cherubims placed on top of the Ark of the Covenant. In it their faces are turned toward the Mercy Seat which he takes to be the focus of the Divine Presence. He says that our soul is like one cherub "contemplating God's essential attributes . . . and then the other cherub contemplating the properties of the Persons . . . you are amazed that communicability exists with individuality, consubstantiality with plurality . . . coequality with order, coeternity with production, mutual intimacy with sending forth."

He continues, "this consideration is the perfection of the mind's illumination when, as if on the sixth day of creation, it sees man made to the image of God." St. Bonaventure gives us some notion of the psychological effects of this experience: "For transcending yourself and all things, by the immeasurable and absolute ecstasy of a pure mind, leaving behind all things and freed from all things, you will ascend to the superessential ray of the divine darkness."[47]

It is almost impossible to comprehend the intellectual experience the mystic finds at this level. Their words give us simply an impression of light within light. The other aspect of this transforming union is perhaps easier to deal with, the union of the wills. At times in our lives our personal preferences and the will of God have seemed to intersect and we were filled with joy and a sense of well-being. Similar, but immensely superior, is the experience of bringing our desire totally into conformity with God's will. This is the supreme homeostasis—that is, the perfect and permanent balance between psychological need and fulfillment, a balance founded not on passing reality but in absolute and changeless being. It is the essence of peace. To illustrate this level of spiritual development I could easily cite examples in the life of St. Teresa or some other great mystic. I have chosen instead to describe someone I have experienced myself, an utterly unknown and unrecognized man who I think brought together in the simplest way the two great elements of transforming union: the vision of God and the peace of His will.

THE EXPERIENCE OF FATHER ISIDORE

When I arrived at the Capuchin novitiate in Santa Inez, California, I was met by the novice master, my classmate, Father Marian, with the words, "We have a saint with us." He referred to Father Isidore Kennedy, who had been born in Drombane, County Tipperary, Ireland, in 1897, and who was about seventy-three years old at that time. Being a saint-watcher, I immediately went to work and arranged to sit next to this man who looked every bit a saint, slender with a white beard and a charming smile. I learned that he had just been released from the hospital after a stay of several weeks "to get his lungs dried out." Hospitals had greatly improved over the years, he assured me, and he had a "grand" visit; "they were so lovely to me." I learned that this had been his sixty-sixth hospitalization since he had contracted tuberculosis as a very young friar in his teens. I learned, by asking several of the questions of a saint-watcher, that he felt that each of his assignments had been an improvement over the one before. He had indeed usually been stationed alone in little desert towns where he said he had never been lonely because of the Blessed Sacrament.

Amid pleasant conversation peppered with riddles and jokes and the etymology of Irish names, I learned that he had accepted the certainty of death at the age of eighteen and that, when he had not died, he had decided to live the rest of his life as a gift from God in conformity to the divine will as it was shown to him. I learned that in all those years he had never complained; indeed he had experienced great joy. His minister provincial, Father Enda, revealed to me the odd fact that "he had always been perfectly obedient, but that he had also always done his own thing," which was praying and caring for the poor. The little cabins which he had for rectories became shelters for the tumbleweeds of the west. I learned that now that he was retired, he spent several hours every day sitting quietly in the chapel in profound recollection. I was bold enough to take a seat behind him one day and discovered that his back did not touch the bench and that he was breathing at a very slow rate. He seemed to be oblivious of all sights and sounds, although if he were assigned to answer the phone or door, he would immediately respond. The novices referred to this profound recollection as "Izzy's trip."

On my last day at Santa Inez the core of this hidden life was to be laid bare and I was to hear what I believe is the best description of the unitive way I have ever heard. When Father Isidore came to my room to receive the Sacrament of Reconciliation (or as was said then, "to confess"), I was literally awestruck by the humility and innocence of this man and begged him to sit down. I asked him for the secret of his life. He at first denied that he had a secret, but after some coaxing I got him to understand that I was interested in how people prayed. His answer, which I did not reveal until after his death on October 1, 1973, contains, I think, the experience of transforming union. "Well, my secret, if you want to call it that, is not much. It is just sort of . . . an imagination that comes to me when things aren't just up to the mark. It's come to me since I got sick as a lad, and it comes now often in the day. Whenever I stop to think about it, it seems to me that I have spent my entire life sitting in the place of St. John at the Last Supper."

Chapter 9

The Next Good Step

As we complete our survey of the spiritual journey and recall the steps of personal development and maturation as described in contemporary psychological studies, we must be struck by the complexity of the individual and the difficulty of understanding any one person's position in the spiritual life. The dangers of ignoring either the spiritual or the psychological factors have already been pointed out. It is only when we bring these two components together in the rich individuality of each person's life that the real dimensions of a living response to the call of God emerge.

An analogy here may be useful. To plot the location of a ship at sea it is necessary to calculate its latitude and longitude; the point of intersection is the precise location of the vessel. Even then you know little about the ship, its size, destination, energy source, cargo, and the ability of its crew. To learn these facts, which are not simply details but the heart of the matter, you have to examine the ship in its individual reality. This is an apt analogy for the person on the journey through life toward God. One must consider the person in terms of the two lines: spiritual growth and psychological maturity; next one must evaluate the individual forces that have shaped the person and his or her goals, as well as the different energy sources actuating his or her life. We have seen that in terms of spiritual development these sources, like grace and the gifts of the Holy Spirit, are similar to the powers outside the ship itself; they may be compared to winds and tides which are essential if one is to reach port. In this chapter we shall attempt a useful summary of all these factors.

There follows a series of questions addressed to the reader. I suggest you read the meditation after the question and apply it to yourself. If and when you consider someone else's spiritual journey, these questions and meditations may be helpful because you have first addressed them to the person you know best. Finally, as you apply them to yourself with candor and honesty, you deepen your own knowledge of God. St. Augustine recognized the relationship between knowledge of self and of God in his prayer, "O God, that I may know myself and know you, and do all things for the sake of you." The meditations are written as prayers in the manner of Augustine's *Confessions*.

1. By what voice do I hear God call me?

Is it Your unity that calls to me in the inner turmoil of my soul, O Lord, giving me some stability in the confusion that I see within and without, and which causes me so much fear? Is it that oneness of Your life and purpose so apparent in the laws of nature and so distorted in the confusion of human history that calls to my inmost being?

Or is it Your truth, unchanging and unchangeable, calling from Your unity and Your boundless knowledge of all things that summons me? Do I find my peace in the perception of some aspect of that truth by which the dark conflicts of human existence are brought to order and made comprehensible?

Is it Your goodness, O Lord, that I seek in my disappointment and grief when I see good persons and good things made ugly or destroyed? I have rejoiced always in Your goodness like a child playing in a meadow; it has filled me with delight and now I know that I am drawn beyond all good things to seek You who are goodness itself.

Or am I one drawn mostly by beauty, which I have often experienced: things delightful to see or hear, to taste or touch, pleasing every sense and especially my mind and imagination? Have I heard You calling me in the beautiful, even when I was a child, in sunsets, in songs; am I constantly saddened because the very possession of beauty makes it fade away, reminding me to seek You who are beauty that never fades?

Or do You speak to me now with one voice, now with another? Do You not call me with two voices at once? Do You call with all voices which to You are one? Is not the difference of Your voices to be found in me and not in You who are absolutely One, and yet the source of all multiplicity and variety? Do You, who are all truth and goodness and beauty, use all things which are passing in their variety and multiplicity to call me? Do You not even call me in evil circumstances: when conflict rages because we have allowed freedom to cause disharmony and have forgotten that we are Your children whom You love? Give me, O God, who are father and mother to my spirit, the grace to respond to Your call with all my being, that in time I may come to You and be ready to know and love

You. Remind me that to love You I must escape from the prison of my own self-love and love those who are loved by You.

2. Who am I psychologically?

In the Gospel, Lord Jesus Christ, You revealed both our weakness and our strength. You, who knew with human thoughts and loved with a human heart, let Your apostles learn the depth of their dreadful weakness only after You had revealed the glory of Your love for them, especially on Mt. Tabor and at Your Last Supper. O Lord, each day You show me my needs, my wounds, my little insanities, the scars of my life. You reveal how You seek me in these things and in these very weaknesses You show me Your loving care. When I flee from You and betray You, You call me, ready to reveal Your mercy if only I will not close my ears to You.

Show me, my Lord and Savior, my guilt and fear in the light of Your gentle teaching, and reveal my cupidity in Your Sermon on the Mount. Overcome my anxiety by Your prayer in Gethsemane, break open my selfishness and worldly spirit by Your example carrying the Cross on the Way of Sorrows. And by the words on the Cross, make me strong in the conflicts and darkness of life. But most of all by Your death and Resurrection, bring me to peace and to a knowledge of Your love; take away from me the worst of all terrors, the fear of oblivion and of falling into nothingness. Help me to see that life is a journey and death a door which You open to a more abundant life.

Let me not be afraid to love others because death appears to sever all bonds. Let me not fear to open my heart to them and receive their hearts in return. Let me believe that in You all human love can, if it will, find a hope lasting beyond the grave. In the sorrows of this life let me not withdraw into depression or hide in desperation; help me instead to know that the true joys of love and friendship point to a reality of greater love shared and mysteriously transformed, so that we shall love each other as You have loved us. Be my healing and courage when human love wounds me. You have been wounded and Your wounds are a sign to Your children of that love that never fades and is able to forgive all and sanctify even those who have wounded.

3. Where am I spiritually?

Grant, O Holy Spirit, that I may not shrink from this question and hide in false humility, saying, "I am nowhere," for that would be to deny

Your work in my soul. I heard Your call and responded at first with joy and gladness; later I realized the price of going on and my heart grew faint. Have I paid the great price yet or do I still quibble and cling to ugliness because I am afraid of Your beauty and power to draw me on? Have I believed with all my power and surrendered to Your mysteries so that You may teach me even more? Have I trusted and accepted Your gift of hope even when all I cherished was snatched away? Have I believed that You do not send calamities, but out of them You are able to bring what is better? Have I believed, O God, that Your will is not the good or the better, but the best?

Have I seen Your light shining within and all around me, and rejoiced with all my heart as it streamed into the inner resources of my being? Has Your light given me peace and quiet rest in prayer unlike anything I could have imagined? Have I let Your grace and virtue draw me from evil deeds and desires to do what is good? Have I let Your creating gifts flow through me to those for whom they were destined, or have I bargained with them in the marketplace of life hoping for some passing reward? Have I traded Your light for the shadow of human acceptance? Have I failed to be Your vessel of blessing because I insisted on carrying along cloak and staff and traveling bag when I should have gone with nothing but Your power? Have I let You draw me into the silent desert of the soul where I might hear Your voice? Have I been attentive as You bestowed Your gifts and have I opened my mind to You, my best teacher, and received Your gifts of wisdom and reverence which never fade? Have I shared those precious gifts with those whom I love; have I offered them to those who despise me so that we might be friends again? Have I permitted You alone to save me in the Dark Night or have I cringed and run back, not trusting in Your love that has no bounds? When I learned that Your friends have heard secret words and have everywhere seen Your holy signs, have I desired to follow them or have I shrugged my shoulders and laughed? Have I played the fool and measured eternity with the yardstick of time?

O Holy Spirit, when I met those who were truly blessed, the pure of heart and humble of mind, the real peacemakers who loved in the face of hate, have I recognized and acknowledged in them the greatest of all Your works? Have I listened attentively as the unseen and unknown martyrs and confessors praise You even in this world? Have I joined them, however weakly, in their chorus of praise which alone keeps this world from self-destruction, or have I listened more clearly to sounding brass and clanging cymbals?

When, O Lord, when shall I love You and all others in You? When shall I desire You as the deer pants for running streams? When shall I let my soul be raised on eagle's wings? No, O Lord, this is not the real question; this is not the best prayer. Teach me that wherever I am, I shall take the next good step on the journey to You. Let me be willing to do what is most real: to hear You as You stand and knock in the reality of NOW, and of HERE, where I stand ready to take the next good step toward You; and with Your continued help, to take the next, and the next. . . . Amen.

Appendix

Historical Note on the Doctrine of the Three Ways

Since we have defined the spiritual life as the response to faith, it is interesting to note that the theoretical outline of the spiritual life which is deeply imbedded in the traditions of the Church is not primarily based on theological considerations or restricted to Christianity at all. It is fundamentally a psychological theory, based on the observation of a variety of spiritually sophisticated directors and guides among the world religions down the centuries. True, it has been accommodated to the Christian experience by Augustine, Gregory of Nyssa, and other Fathers and Doctors of the Church, and by mystics and spiritual writers. In Catholicism, it is called the doctrine of the three ways, although it is not doctrinal in the sense that its ideas are revealed; rather, it is simply a teaching based on observation. Nevertheless, the three ways or stages of development can be considered theologically and such modern authors as Tanquerey, Garrigou-Lagrange, and Bouyer have done so with great theological insight.[1] Even then the theology must be laced with psychological observation based on practical experience. These modern authors follow a mystical tradition, clearly articulated in the Middle Ages by several writers including Bonaventure whose work *The Souls's Journey into God* ought to be read by anyone interested in the subject.[2] St. John of the Cross and the Counter-Reformation mystical psychologists used this doctrine and enhanced it with further observation.

There are any number of expressions of this teaching in other existing world religions and unquestionably there are many examples of it in the Graeco-Roman philosophical religion. Perhaps the following quotation from Abi'l-Khayr, a tenth-century Moslem mystic, can best illustrate the acceptance of this teaching by non-Christian writers. Abi'l-Khayr lists six stages, each successive two of them representing one step of the spiritual life. The "gates" represent periods of darkness or transition which long ago were associated with the passage from one stage to another.

> He was asked, "When shall a man be freed from his wants?" "When God shall free him," he replied. This is not affected by a man's exertion, but by the grace and help of God. First of all, He brings forth in him the desire to attain this goal. Then He opens to him the gate of repentance. Then He throws him into self-mortification, so that he continues to strive and, for a while, to pride himself upon his efforts, thinking that he is advancing or achieving something; but afterwards he falls into despair and feels no joy. Then he knows that his work is not pure, but tainted; he repents of the acts of devotion which he had thought to be his own, but perceives that they were done by God's grace and help, and that he was guilty of polytheism in attributing them to his own exertion. When this becomes manifest, a feeling of joy enters his heart. Then God opens to him the gate of certainty, so that for a time he takes anything from one and accepts contumely and endures abasement, and knows for certain by Whom it is brought to pass, and doubt concerning this is removed from his heart. Then God opens to him the gate of love, and here too egoism shows itself for a time and he is exposed to blame, which means that in his love of God he meets fearlessly whatsoever may befall him and recks not of reproach; but still he thinks "I love," and finds no rest until he perceives that it is God who loves him and keeps him in the state of loving, and that this is the result of divine love and grace, not of his own endeavor. Then God opens to him the gate of unity and causes him to know that all actions depend on God Almighty. Hereupon he perceives that all is He, and all is by Him, and all is His; that He has laid this self-conceit upon His creatures in order to prove them, and that He, in His omnipotence, ordains that they shall hold this false belief, because omnipotence is His attribute, so that when they regard His attributes they shall know that He is the Lord. What formerly was hearsay now becomes known to him intuitively, as he contemplates the works of God. Then he entirely recognizes that he has not the right to say "I" or "mine." At this stage he beholds his helplessness: desires fall away from him and he becomes free and calm. He wishes that which God wishes; his own wishes are gone, he is emancipated from his wants, and has gained peace and joy in both worlds![3]

DOCTRINE OF THE THREE WAYS—ALIVE AND WELL

In modern times many writers have illustrated the three ways using a psychologically oriented approach. This trend reflects a growing interest in introspective psychology which can be noted as early as St. John of the Cross and St. Teresa. One of the most interesting modern authors in this tradition was the Anglican laywoman Evelyn Underhill whose work, inspired in many ways by her spiritual guide, von Hügel, contributed substantially to the understanding of the three ways by adding a prelude, namely, the "awakening."[4] The contemporary writer Father Adrian van Kaam has also brought a great deal of insight to the discussion of the three ways, although he has not added so literally to the formula as did Evelyn Underhill. His *Dynamics of Spiritual Self-Direction* and *The Transcendent Self* provide illuminating insights of contemporary psychological theory to the understanding of the doctrine of the three ways and to mystical theology in general.[5] Father William Johnston, S.J., has taken up specific questions related especially to the experience of prayer, meditation, and contemplation in the more advanced stages of the three ways.[6] In a most attractive way, Father Henri Nouwen has discussed psychological insights into the experience of beginners and those moving toward the illuminative way.[7] Father George Maloney, S.J., with his unique background in Eastern and Western mystical traditions, has been able to build bridges between these two different approaches and shed a new light on the understanding of the illuminative way and illuminative and unitive prayer.[8]

Several pragmatic books have focused on a particular concept of the journey without directly alluding to the doctrine of the three ways, to which, however, the authors clearly relate their works. Other present-day works give evidence that the experience of the three ways is very much part of the contemporary scene: Father William McNamara's fresh and vibrant approach to the Carmelite tradition; Father Basil Pennington's discussion of techniques related to contemplative meditation; and Father Edward Farrell's effective introduction of meditative prayer on a popular level.[9] Professor Morton Kelsey's works reflect a deep understanding of spirituality as a journey of purgation and demonstrate a growing awareness of the spiritual quality of all levels of human experience.[10] Sister Ruth Burrows, an English Carmelite, has given us several very helpful books on more advanced forms of prayer,[11] while a busy Jesuit missionary, Father Thomas H. Green, has sent back to America some very illuminating short works which can be read with profit in good times and bad.[12]

Many contemporary spiritual writers, almost all of whom have been influenced by modern psychological theory, have contributed to our knowledge of spiritual experience as a result of taking up one of the phases of the spiritual journey. While certain authors may not employ the term "the three ways," the reader will have no trouble discerning their insights within the structure of this ancient teaching. Among authors who have applied clinical psychology in a serious way to spiritual development, one must mention particularly the work of Father Luigi Rulla, S. J., and his associates.[13] Another creative approach has been taken by Dr. John McDonagh who has attempted a synthesis of clinical theory and personal religious experience.[14]

Notes

PART I: The Psychology of Spirituality

Chapter 1: The Call of God

1. G. W. Allport, *Waiting for the Lord,* ed. P. Bertocci (New York: Macmillan, 1978), pp. 56–58.

2. E. O'Brien, *The Varieties of Mystical Experience* (New York: Holt, Rinehart & Winston, 1964), pp. 3–6.

3. W. James, *The Varieties of Religious Experience* (New York: Modern Library, 1902).

4. F. von Hügel, *The Mystical Element in Religion,* 4th ed. (London: James Clark, 1961), p. 65.

5. To learn from this book, it is extremely important to understand this distinction. Almost all distinctions applied to persons are similar to this one. When we say a person is young or old, friendly or unfriendly, even good or bad, we place a person in one category which denotes a relationship to another. To be young is to be growing old. To be very good implies the possibility of a change to being unvirtuous or bad.

6. Von Hügel, *The Mystical Element in Religion,* pp. 220–25.

7. *The Life of St. Thomas Aquinas,* ed. Kenelm Foster (London: Longmans, Green, 1959), p. 46.

8. B. Russell, *Mysticism and Logic* (London: Allen & Unwin, n.d.), pp. 1–32.

9. Bonaventure, *The Soul's Journey into God, The Tree of Life, The Life of St. Francis,* trans. E. Cousins, Classics of Western Spirituality (New York: Paulist Press, 1979), pp. 185–90.

10. Plato, *Symposium,* 211, in *The Dialogues,* trans. B. Jowett, 4th ed. (Oxford: Clarendon Press, 1953).

11. Augustine, *Confessions,* trans. F. Sheed (New York: Sheed & Ward, 1965), X, vi and xxvii.

Chapter 2: How Christian Is My Spirituality?

1. The interested reader is advised to study L. Bouyer's *Introduction to Spirituality* (Collegeville, Minn.: Liturgical Press, 1961), chaps. 1, 10, 12. An excellent comparison of Eastern and Western spirituality is to be found in W. Johnston's *The Still Point* (New York: Harper & Row, Perennial Library, 1971), chaps. 2, 3, and 4.

2. See, for example, Plato *The Republic,* book X, in *The Dialogues,* trans. B. Jowett, 4th ed. (Oxford: Clarendon Press, 1953).

3. Cited in A. Wikenhauser, *Pauline Mysticism* (New York: Herder & Herder, 1960), p. 232. The entire chap. 4 can be read with profit as a study of the differences and similarity between Neoplatonism and Christianity.

4. Cited in A. Fremantle, *Woman's Way to God* (New York: St. Martin's Press, 1977), pp. 53–54.

5. Cited in H. Weiner, *9½ Mystics: The Kabbala Today* (New York: Collier, 1969), p. 4. Also cf. Abraham Isaac Kook, *The Lights of Penitence, The Moral Principles, Lights of Holiness,*

Essays, Letters, and Poems, trans. Ben Zion Bokser, Classics of Western Spirituality (New York: Paulist Press, 1978).

6. For further study, cf. D. R. Blumenthal, *Understanding Jewish Mysticism,* 2 vols. (New York: KTAV Publishing, 1978, 1982).

7. D. Yankelovich, *New Rules* (New York: Random House, 1981), pp. 241 ff.

8. *Fundamentals of Catholic Dogma,* ed. L. Ott (Dublin: Mercier Press, 1954, pp. 96 ff.

9. H. U. von Balthasar, *Prayer* (New York: Paulist Press, 1967), pp. 44–45.

10. Pope John Paul II, *Redemptor Hominis* (Boston: St. Paul Editions, 1979).

11. G. W. Allport, *The Individual and His Religion* (New York: Macmillan, 1950), pp. 61 ff.

12. Augustine, *Soliloquies,* trans. R. E. Cleveland (1910), as given in *An Augustine Reader,* ed. J. O'Meara (Garden City, New York: Doubleday, 1973), p. 38.

13. For an excellent summary of the controversy between Pelagius and Augustine, see T. J. Van Bavel, O.S.A. *Christians in the World* (New York: Catholic Book Publishing Co., 1980), pp. 38–41.

14. From Epistle 232:5, 6 as translated in E. Przywara, *The Augustine Synthesis* (New York: Sheed & Ward, 1945), p. 170.

15. K. E. Kirk, *The Vision of God* (New York: Harper Torchbooks, n.d.) pp. 174 ff.

16. H. U. von Balthasar, *Prayer,* pp. 8–9.

17. John of the Cross, *The Ascent of Mount Carmel,* bk. II, chap. XXII, 5; cited in *Come South Wind,* ed. M. L. Shrady (New York: Pantheon Books, 1957), p. 41.

18. K. Rahner, *Foundations of Christian Faith* (New York: Crossroad, 1978), pp. 106–8.

Chapter 3: Understanding Human Development

1. E. Erikson, *Childhood and Society* (New York: W. W. Norton Co., 1950).

2. There are many books by and about Jung. One that might easily be read and relates in a general way to this subject is: C. G. Jung, *The Undiscovered Self,* trans. R. Hull (New York: New American Library, 1957).

3. G. W. Allport, *Becoming* (New Haven: Yale University Press, 1955).

4. D. Levinson, *Seasons of a Man's Life* (New York: Knopf, 1978).

5. E. Whitehead and J. Whitehead, *Christian Life Patterns* (Garden City, N.Y.: Doubleday, 1979).

6. The implications of this dynamic evolutionary view have been carefully examined by Bernard J. Boelen in a study of psychological maturity which is an interesting combination of philosophical and psychological insights: *Personal Maturity* (New York: Continuum/Seabury, 1978).

7. Catherine of Siena, *The Dialogue,* trans. Suzanne Noffke, O.P., Classics of Western Spirituality (New York: Paulist, 1980), chap. 63. Cf. R. Garrigou-Lagrange, *The Three Ages of the Interior Life* (St. Louis: B. Herder, 1948), vol. 2, chap. 3; this is a classic study of the three ways.

8. The first stage of the task or challenge is moral integration and the development of faith and trust. In the second stage, the individual is filled with a growing spontaneous sense of the indwelling of the Triune God and of zeal and energy in doing good works. In the last stage, having passed through an intense darkness, the individual lives in union with God, and, as much as possible, the life of the saints begins.

9. In a very interesting account of a contemporary "conversion," Emilie Griffin has dealt very well with the question of psychological interpretation of conversion. It is her rather startling answer to accept the possibility of some psychological components in any conversion event, but still to maintain their personal and theological significance. This is a very challenging view for those who are all too anxious to analyze any religious experience, or even all meaningful human experience. Cf. E. Griffin, *Turning,* (New York: Doubleday, 1980).

10. K. Hulme, *The Nun's Story* (Toronto: Little, Brown, 1956).

11. B. Neugarten, *Middle Age and Aging* (Chicago: University of Chicago Press, 1968).

12. G. Vaillant, *Adaptation to Life* (Boston: Little, Brown, 1977).

13. O. Lewis, *La Vida* (New York: Random House, 1965).

14. E. F. Frazer, *The Negro Family in the United States* (Chicago: University of Chicago Press, 1966).

15. J. Fowler and S. Keen, *Life Maps* (Waco, Tex.: Word Books, 1978).

16. E. Whitehead and J. Whitehead, *Christian Life Patterns.*

17. Cf. T. Tyrrell, *Urgent Longings* (Whitinsville, Mass.: Affirmation Books, 1980).

18. E. Whitehead and J. Whitehead, *Christian Life Patterns,* p. 73.

19. D. Yankelovich, *New Rules,* (New York: Random House, 1981), chap. 3.

20. Cf. T. J. Van Bavel, *Christians in the World* (New York: Catholic Book Publishing Co., 1980), pp. 80–95.

21. See especially H. S. Sullivan, *The Interpersonal Theory of Psychiatry* (New York: Norton, 1953).

22. E. Erikson, *Childhood and Society,* p. 267.

23. V. Frankl, *Man's Search for Meaning* (Boston: Beacon Press, 1962).

24. E. Whitehead and J. Whitehead, *Christian Life Patterns,* p. 114.

25. E. Becker, *The Denial of Death* (New York: The Free Press, 1973).

26. S. Kierkegaard, *Christian Discourses,* trans. W. Lowrie (London: Oxford University Press, 1939), pp. 112–13.

27. F. J. Sheed, *Death into Life* (New York: Arena Lettres, 1977), p. 133.

28. A. Speer, *Inside the Third Reich: Memoirs,* trans. R. and C. Winston (New York: Macmillan, 1970), p. 101.

Chapter 4: Development: Religious and Spiritual

1. F. von Hügel, *The Mystical Element in Religion,* 4th ed. (London: James Clark, 1961), pp. 50–53.

2. G. W. Allport, *The Individual and His Religion* (New York: Macmillan, 1950); also, W. H. Clarke, *Psychology of Religion* (New York: Macmillan, 1958), and P. Babin, *Faith and the Adolescent* (New York: Herder, 1965).

3. F. C. Happold, *The Journey Inwards* (London: Darton, Longman and Todd, 1968), p. 34.

4. von Hügel, *The Mystical Element in Religion,* Preface to the 2d edition (1923), p. vii.

5. J. H. Newman, *Essays Critical and Historical* (London: Longmans, Green, 1901), pp. 31–33.

6. F. Thompson, "The Mistress of Vision," in *Poetical Works* (London: Oxford University Press, 1969), p. 186.

7. R. Schnackenburg, *Belief in the New Testament* (New York: Paulist Press, 1974).

8. H. U. von Balthasar, *Prayer* (New York: Paulist Press), chap. 2.

9. K. Rahner, *Ignatius of Loyla,* trans. Rosaleen Ockenden (London: Collins, 1978), p. 12.

10. Augustine, *Confessions,* trans. F. Sheed (New York: Sheed & Ward, 1965), XI, ix.

11. T. Celano, *Legenda Secunda: Lives of St Francis of Assisi,* trans. A. G. Ferrers Howell (London, 1908); as cited in E. Underhill, p. 180.

12. D. Hammarskjold, *Markings* (New York: Knopf, 1970).

13. A. Huxley, *The Perennial Philosophy* (New York: Harper & Bros, 1944), pp. 96, 101 ff.

14. Catherine of Genoa, *Purgation and Purgatory, The Spiritual Dialogue,* trans. S. Hughes, Classics of Western Spirituality (New York: Paulist Press, 1979), pp. 105 ff.

15. J. B. Chautard O.C.S.O., *The Soul of the Apostolate* (Trappist, Ky.: Abbey of Gethsemani, 1946), pt. 4, pp. 103–45.

16. A. van Kaam, *Spirituality and the Gentle Life* (Denville, N.J.: Dimension Books, 1976, 1980).

17. E. Whitehead and J. Whitehead, *Christian Life Patterns* (Garden City, N.Y.: Doubleday, 1979), p. 128.

18. Cf. E. Cousins, *Bonaventure and the Coincidence of Opposites* (Chicago: Franciscan Herald Press, 1977), pp. 73–78, 247–49; and the Bonaventure volume, edited by Cousins, in the Classics of Western Spirituality, pp. 24–27.

19. John of the Cross, *The Dark Night,* in *The Collected Works of St. John of the Cross,* trans. K. Kavanaugh, O.C.D., and O. Rodriguez, O.C.D. (Washington, D.C.: ICS, 1973), pp. 295 ff.

20. Cited in E. Underhill, *Mysticism* (New York: Dutton, 1961), p. 412.

Chapter 5: Psychology and Spirituality

1. *Altered States of Consciousness,* ed. C. Tart (New York: John Wiley, 1969), especially articles of Deikman.

2. F. Braceland and M. Stock O. P., *Modern Psychiatry: A Handbook for Believers* (New York: Doubleday, 1963); G. Zilboorg, *Psychoanalysis and Religion* (New York: Farrar, Straus and Giroux, 1962); A. Joyce and M. Stern, eds., *Holiness and Mental Health* (New York: Paulist Press, 1972).

3. Cited in P. C. Vitz, *Psychology as Religion: The Cult of Self-Worship* (Grand Rapids, Mich.: Eerdmans, 1977), p. 49.

4. C. Lasch, *The Culture of Narcissism* (New York: W. W. Norton, 1975); W. Kilpatrick, *Identity and Intimacy* (New York: Dell, 1975).

5. D. Yankelovich, *New Rules* (New York: Random House, 1981), pp. 234 ff.

6. Vitz, *Psychology as Religion: The Cult of Self-Worship,* p. 49.

7. V. Frankl, *The Doctor and the Soul* (New York: Knopf, 1966), p. xxi.

8. Yankelovich, *New Rules,* p. 250.

PART II: A PSYCHOLOGICAL UNDERSTANDING OF THE THREE WAYS

Chapter 6: The First Stage of the Spiritual Life: The Purgation

1. *To Live in Christ Jesus* (Washington, D.C.: USCC, 1976).

2. *Pope John Paul II in America* (Boston: St. Paul Editions, 1980), pp. 173–92.

3. K. Meninger, *Whatever Happened to Sin?* (New York: Hawthorne Books, 1973).

4. *Fundamentals of Catholic Dogma,* ed. L. Ott (Cork: Mercier Press, 1954), pp. 479 ff.

5. Pope John Paul II, *Letter to All Bishops and Priests of Holy Thursday, 1979* (Boston: St. Paul Editions, 1979), sec. 10.

6. Augustine, *Confessions,* VIII, xii.

7. *Rule of St. Francis,* chap. 9. Cf. also *The Writings of Francis and Clare,* ed. R. Armstrong, O.F.M. Cap., and I. Brady, O.F.M. (Ramsey, N.J.: Paulist Press, 1982).

8. *The Ascent of Mount Carmel,* bk. II, chap. 3, in *The Collected Works of St. John of the Cross,* trans. K. Kavanaugh, O.C.D. and O. Rodriguez, O.C.D., (Washington, D.C.: ICS Publications, 1973), pp. 110–11.

9. Blaise Pascal, cited in *The Soul Afire,* ed. H. A. Reinhold (New York: Doubleday Image Books, 1973), pp. 356–57.

10. E. Przywara, S.J., *An Augustine Synthesis* (New York: Sheed & Ward, 1945), p. 59.

11. It is important here to note that in Catholic theology there are other understandings of the dark knowledge of mature faith. The interpretation given here is essentially Augustinian. From the Thomistic point of view, the essential obscurity of the truths of faith is, of course, recognized. However, the emphasis is on the purification of the intellect from an aesthetic of intellectual curiosity. The following quotation from *Spiritual Theology* by the distinguished Dominican theologian, Father Jordan Aumann, casts a Thomistic light on the question we have discussed from an Augustinian viewpoint.

It does not matter that faith is essentially about things that are not seen clearly and is therefore necessarily obscure. In fact, it is precisely because of this that faith can provide the only knowledge possible concerning the intimate life of God, who cannot be adequately represented by any created intelligible species. The clear vision and knowledge of God are reserved for us in the beatific vision in glory, but even in this life, faith enables us to attain in some measure to the unfathomable mystery of God, though the knowledge be dark and obscure. By reason of its object, the knowledge of faith is superior to all sensible and intellectual evidence that we could have of God in this life. It is necessary that the soul inform all its life and actions with the light of faith, and cling ever more firmly to the truth proposed for faith on the authority of God. Gradually one can reach the point of judging all things through the light of faith and, indeed, to see all things as God sees them (*Spiritual Theology* [Huntingdon, Ind.: Our Sunday Visitor Press, 1979], pp. 189–90).

12. Pope John Paul II, *Redemptor Hominis* 8, trans. Vatican Polyglot Press (Boston: St. Paul Editions).

13. *Gaudium et Spes*, 22; cited in *Redemptor Hominis*, 8.

14. R. Guardini, *Faith and Modern Man* (London: Catholic Book Club, 1952), chap. 7.

15. S. Kierkegaard, *Christian Discourses*, trans. W. Lowrie (London: Oxford University Press, 1939), pp. 113–14.

16. Gerald Heard, in *The Choice is Always Ours*, ed. D. B. Phillips (Wheaton, Ill.: Re-Quest Books, 1975), pp. 153–4.

17. J. H. Newman, *Meditations and Devotions* (Wheathampstead, Hertfordshire: Anthony Clarke Books), pp. 6–7.

Chapter 7: The Second Stage of the Spiritual Life:
The Illuminative Way

1. C. Butler, *Western Mysticism*, 2nd ed. (New York: Harper & Row, 1966), p. 28.

2. Augustine, *Confessions*, XIII, xvi.

3. T. Merton, *Contemplation in a World of Action* (Garden City, N.Y.: Doubleday Image Book, 1973), p. 175–6.

4. Augustine, *Confessions*, IX, i.

5. Bonaventure, *The Soul's Journey into God . . .*, trans. E. Cousins, Classics of Western Spirituality (New York: Paulist, 1979), pp. 87 ff.

6. *The Art of Prayer*, ed. Igumen Chariton of Valermo and T. Ware (London: Faber & Faber, 1966).

7. C. Enzler, *My Other Self* (Denville, N.J.: Dimension Books, 1958).

8. F. C. Happold, *Prayer and Meditation* (London: Pelican Books, 1971).

9. Pope John Paul II, *Redemptor Hominis* and *Dives in Misericordia*.

10. Francis of Assisi, *The Writings of Francis and Clare* (see chap. 6, n. 7 above).

11. Jacopone da Todi, *Lauds*, trans. S. and E. Hughes, Classics of Western Spirituality (New York: Paulist Press, 1982), no. 82, p. 239.

12. Thomas Aquinas, *Summa Theologica*, IIa; IIae, q. 63. Cf. A. Tanquerey, *The Spiritual Life: Ascetical Mystical Theology* (Tournai, Belgium: Desclée, 1930), chap 2, pp. 472 ff.

13. St. Thomas, ibid.

14. Cf. E. Whitehead and J. Whitehead, *Christian Life Patterns* (Garden City, N.Y.: Doubleday, 1979), pp. 142 ff., for a good discussion of polarities in midlife.

15. F. Kunkel, *In Search of Maturity;* as cited in *The Choice is Always Ours*, ed. D. B. Phillips (Wheaton Ill.: Re-Quest Books, 1975), p. 157.

16. *Imitation of Christ* (Milwaukee: Bruce, 1949), bk. III, chap. 5.

17. *Spiritual Letters of Archbishop Fénelon*, trans. H. L. Lear (New York: Longmans, Green, 1909); as cited in *The Choice Is Always Ours*, ed. D. B. Phillips (Wheaton, Ill.: Re-Quest Books, 1975), p. 199.

18. John of the Cross, *The Dark Night*, I, 2–7.

19. Tanquerey, *The Spiritual Life*, p. 596.

20. J. Olin, *The Catholic Reformation from Savanarola to Loyola* (New York: Harper & Row, 1969), pp. 16–17.

Chapter 8: The Third Stage of the Spiritual Life:
The Unitive Way

1. Tanquerey, *The Spiritual Life: Ascetical Mystical Theology* (Tournai, Belgium: Desclée, 1930), pp. 605–6.

2. Ibid.

3. Among those rare students of spiritual psychology not already mentioned, one should be aware of Joseph Maréchal, S.J., of Louvain, *Studies in the Psychology of the Mystics*

London: Burns, Oates & Washbourne, 1927; available through Magi Books, 33 Buckingham Drive, Albany, N.Y. 12208), and of Hilda Graef, *Mystics of our Times* (Ramsey, N.J.: Paulist Press/Deus Books, 1962).

4. Tanquerey, p. 650, n. 8.

5. St. John of the Cross, *The Living Flame of Love,* stanza III, 34.

6. F. Thompson, "Orient Ode," in *Poetical Works* (London: Oxford University Press, 1969), p. 202.

7. Meister Eckhart, *The Essential Sermons, Commentaries, Treatises and Defenses,* trans. Edmund Colledge and Bernard McGinn, Classics of Western Spirituality (Ramsey, N.J.: Paulist Press, 1981), pp. 251–52.

8. These gifts are defined by St. Thomas as essentially supernatural permanent qualities whereby a person is perfected to obey readily the Holy Spirit: *Summa Theo.* IIa, IIae, q. 9, a. 3; and Ia, IIae, q. 68, a. 8.

9. R. Garrigou-Lagrange, O.P., *Christian Perfection and Contemplation* St. Louis: B. Herder Book Co., 1946), pp. 271 ff. Those interested in the theology and virtues and gifts are recommended to this excellent summary.

10. Tanquerey, p. 609. He summarizes the principal theological notes, especially St. Thomas. Those interested in the theology of the gifts should refer to Tanquerey or Garrigou-Lagrange.

11. Cited in Garrigou-Lagrange, p. 280.

12. Ibid. p. 288.

13. Ibid. p. 292–93.

14. Ibid. p. 296.

15. Gregory of Nyssa, *The Life of Moses,* trans. by A. J. Malherbe and E. Ferguson, Classics of Western Spirituality (New York: Paulist Press, 1978), pp. 93–95.

16. Gregory of Nyssa, *From Glory to Glory,* trans and ed. J. Danielou, S. J., and H. Musurillo, S. J. (New York: Charles Scribner's Sons, 1961), pp. 98–101.

17. Teresa of Avila, *The Life of Teresa of Jesus,* trans. E. A. Peers (New York: Doubleday Image Books, 1960), pp. 136–37.

18. Ibid., p. 128.

19. T. Merton, *New Seeds of Contemplation* (New York: New Directions, 1972), pp. 1–4.

20. Maréchal, *Psychology of the Mystics,* p. 176.

21. John of the Cross, *The Dark Night,* bk. II, chap. 10, in *The Collected Works,* p. 350.

22. This is not unlike the experience of darkness described in *The Cloud of Unknowing.* For a recent edition, cf. *The Cloud of Unknowing,* ed. W. Johnston, S. J. (Garden City, N.Y.: Doubleday Image, 1973).

23. Tanquerey, pp. 668–71.

24. Ibid.

25. Teresa of Avila, *Interior Castle,* VI, 1, 10, in *The Collected Works of St. Teresa of Avila,* trans. K. Kavanaugh, O.C.D., and O. Rodriguez, O.C.D. (Washington, D.C.: ICS, 1980), vol. 2, p. 364.

26. Augustine, *Confessions,* X, xxvii.

27. Garrigou-Lagrange, *Christian Perfection and Contemplation,* p. 254.

28. Teresa of Avila, *Interior Castle,* V, 2.

29. Meister Eckhart, "The Counsels," trans. Colledge and McGinn (see n. 7 above). Francis de Sales, *The Love of God,* trans. J. K. Ryan (Garden City, N. Y.: Doubleday, 1963), vol. 2, VI, chap. 7.

30. *Works of St. Bernard of Clairvaux,* vol. III, *On the Song of Songs* (Kalamazoo, Mich.: Cistercian Publications, 1976); Bonaventure, *The Soul's Journey into God,* especially chaps. 4–7; St. John of the Cross uses this imagery especially in his poetry.

31. Catherine of Genoa, *Purgation and Purgatory,* trans. S. Hughes, p. 87.

32. Teresa de Spiritu Sancto, O.D.C., *Edith Stein,* trans. C. Hastings and D. Nicholl (London and New York: Sheed & Ward, 1952), p. 217.

33. Teresa of Avila, *Interior Castle,* VI, 2, pp. 366–67.

34. Ibid. VI, 4, p. 379–80.

35. Bonaventure, *The Soul's Journey into God . . . The Life of St. Francis,* trans. E. Cousins, Classics of Western Spirituality (New York: Paulist, 1979), p. 93.

36. Ibid. p. 305–6.

37. For a discussion of the exegesis of this passage, confer A. Wikenhauser, *Pauline Mysticism* (New York: Herder & Herder, 1960).

38. Teresa of Avila, *Interior Castle,* VI, 6, p. 391.

39. Kenneth Wapunick, "Mysticism and Schizophrenia," in John White ed., *The Highest State of Consciousness* (Garden City, N.Y.: Doubleday, 1972), pp. 153 ff.

40. A. J. Deikman, "Deautomization and the Mystic Experience," in *Altered States of Consciousness,* ed. Charles Tart (Garden City, New York: Anchor Books, 1972), chap. II (reprinted from *Psychiatry* vol. 29, 1966).

41. J. Derum, *The Porter of St. Bonaventure* (The Father Solanus Guild, 1730 Mt. Elliott Ave., Detroit, Mich. 48207).

42. John of the Cross, *The Dark Night,* pp. 329 ff.

43. Bonaventure, op. cit., p. 114.

44. John of the Cross, *The Dark Night,* p. 387.

45. Teresa of Avila, *Interior Castle,* VII, 1.

46. Ibid., p. 430. The scripture quotation is John 14.

47. Bonaventure, op. cit., pp. 106–8.

Appendix: Historical Note on the Doctrine of the Three Ways

1. A. Tanquerey, *The Spiritual Life: Ascetical Mystical Theology* (Tournai, Belgium: Desclée, 1930; R. Garrigou-Lagrange, *The Three Ways of the Interior Life* (St. Louis: B. Herder, 1948); L. Bouyer, *Introduction to Spirituality* (New York: Desclèe, 1961).

2. Bonaventure, *The Soul's Journey into God. . . .,* trans. E Cousins, Classics of Western Spirituality (New York: Paulist Press, 1979).

3. Abu Said ibn Abi'l-Khayr, cited in *Treasury of Traditional Wisdom,* ed. W. Perry (New York: Simon and Schuster, 1971), p. 553.

4. Evelyn Underhill, *Mysticism* (New York: E. P. Dutton, 1961).

5. A. van Kaam, *The Dynamics of Spiritual Self-Direction* (Denville, N.J.: Dimension Books, 1976); *The Transcendent Self* (Denville, N.J.: Dimension Books, 1979).

6. W. Johnston, *The Inner Eye of Love* (New York: Harper & Row, 1978).

7. H. Nouwen, *Reaching Out* (Garden City, N.Y.: Doubleday, 1975).

8. G. Maloney, *Inward Stillness* (Denville, N.J.: Dimension Books, 1975).

9. W. McNamara, *Mystical Passion* (New York: Paulist Press, 1977); M. B. Pennington, *Daily We Touch Him* (Garden City, N.Y.: Doubleday, 1981); E. Farrell, *Prayer Is a Hunger* (Denville, N.J.: Dimension Books, 1972).

10. M. Kelsey, *The Other Side of Silence* (New York: Paulist Press, 1976).

11. R. Burrows, *Guidelines for Mystical Prayer; Interior Castle Explored* (Denville, N.J.: Dimension Books, 1980).

12. T. Green, *Opening to God* (Notre Dame, Ind.: Ave Maria Press, 1977), *When the Well Runs Dry* (Notre Dame, Ind.: Ave Maria Press, 1979).

13. L. Rulla, S. J., *Depth Psychology and Vocation* (Chicago: Loyola University Press, 1971).

14. J. McDonagh, *Christian Psychology: Toward a New Synthesis* (New York: Crossroad, 1982).

Index